T0314135

The Philadelphia Stock Exchange
and the City It Made

The Philadelphia Stock Exchange

and the City It Made

Domenic Vitiello

with

George E. Thomas

PENN

UNIVERSITY OF PENNSYLVANIA PRESS

PHILADELPHIA

Published by
University of Pennsylvania Press
Philadelphia, Pennsylvania 19104-4112

Printed in the United States of America
on acid-free paper
10 9 8 7 6 5 4 3 2 1

Library of Congress Cataloging-in-Publication Data
Vitiello, Domenic.
    The Philadelphia Stock Exchange and the city it made / Domenic Vitiello, with
George E. Thomas.
        p.   cm.
    Includes bibliographical references and index.
    ISBN 978-0-8122-4224-9 (hbk. : alk. paper)
    1. Philadelphia Stock Exchange—History.   2. Stock exchanges— Pennsylvania
—Philadelphia—History.   3. Finance—Pennsylvania—Philadelphia—History.
4. Philadelphia (Pa.)—History.   I. Thomas, George E.   II. Title.
HG5131.P5V58   2010
332.64′274—dc22
                                                                            2009043386

Contents

Preface

In 2002, the leaders of the Philadelphia Stock Exchange (PHLX) engaged my colleague George E. Thomas and me to write a book tracing the institution's history. We soon understood that we had been hired to draft its obituary. But we had to wait six years to get to the end of the story, a sale to the NASDAQ approved by the Securities and Exchange Commission (SEC) in 2008. In the meantime, the exchange went through major changes that added new chapters to its more than two centuries of making markets. For most of that history, it also profoundly shaped the city and world around it. This book is primarily a history of the institution's relationship with its city and the wider world.

This project was initiated by Meyer "Sandy" Frucher, the chairman and CEO of the Philadelphia Stock Exchange, and John F. Wallace, a longtime member and vice chairman of the exchange, both of whom supported the research in myriad ways. Stephen Sears and Ben Craig helped us refine the focus of the book at its beginning and end, respectively. Mary Ellen Heim and Joseph Keslar coordinated interviews with present and former members and employees of the exchange; and Joseph arranged for the exchange's records to be preserved at the Historical Society of Pennsylvania. Barbara Sorid shepherded the entire project, gracefully keeping its many moving parts in line.

The record of the exchange's history of more than two centuries is uneven and sometimes thin. Reconstructing this history therefore required triangulating a variety of sources. For the eighteenth and nineteenth centuries, the ledgers and letters of member brokerage houses offered a useful window into the market, as well as into brokers' activities outside of the exchange. Some of the exchange's own records survive from the late nineteenth century; and board meeting minutes, annual reports, and other printed materials are relatively abundant for the twentieth century. Newspapers, business publications, corporate records, and the work of many talented Philadelphia historians of various eras helped fill out the story of the institution and the economy around it. Many people kindly assisted this research, including the staffs of the Historical Society of Pennsylvania, the Free Library of Philadelphia, the Urban Archives at Temple University, the City of Philadelphia Archives, Van Pelt Library at the University of Pennsylvania, and especially William Howe, the custodian of the stock exchange.[1]

For the decades after World War II, interviews with past and present leaders, members, and staff of the exchange helped make that era come alive. Many people gave generously of their time, including formal interviews—in many cases, more than once—among them, Michael Belman, Al Brinkman, Tom Cameron, John Egan, Doris Elwell, Richard Feinberg, Sandy Frucher, Nick Giordano, Richard Hamilton, Karen Janney, Fred Martin, Thomas Martinelli, Malcolm Pryor, Arnold Staloff, Don Stanton, Norman Steisel, Bill Terrell, Barry Tague, William Uchimoto, Joseph Wagner, John F. Wallace, and Elkins Wetherill. Many people shared old documents and photographs; and Nick Giordano's video interviews with an earlier generation of exchange leaders afforded eyewitness accounts back to the 1920s. Informal interviews with Paul Cerecino and others at Bill O'Shea's party for retired staff helped fill out the history of technology and office culture. Staff and members of the exchange also permitted us to observe life on the trading floor, throughout the offices, and the all-important computers and wiring of the place.

Other scholars made important contributions to this project. Robert Wright shared data on early American corporate finance, offered feedback on an early draft, and helped orient me (an urban historian) to financial history. The economist John Caskey shared his research on the exchange's late twentieth-century history. Colleagues and mentors at the University of Pennsylvania including Leah Gordon, Andrew Heath, Walter Licht, Michael Katz, Jordan Ross, Tom Sugrue, and Laura Wolf-Powers gave thoughtful advice on various parts of the book. Finally, special thanks are due to Eugenie Birch and Gary Hack for their initial suggestion to Sandy Frucher to contact George about Philadelphia history, for their support of my research, and for Genie's mentorship of me as a planning historian.

Most of this account of the exchange's history is mine, and responsibility for any errors in detail or interpretation lies with me. My colleague George Thomas researched and drafted the architectural and cultural history narrative, which I then integrated with the economic, institutional, and urban development narrative. The editors Soumya Iyer and Susanna Margolis helped make rough drafts of this book read far better, and Susanna added some of the celebratory flair that reflects this project's origins in the marketing department of the exchange. At the exchange, Dennis Boylan, Ben Craig, Richard Hamilton, Barbara Sorid, Norman Steisel, Bill Terrell, and John Wallace helped with fact checking.

Susan Snyder and Christy Kwan produced new and adapted maps that help illustrate the exchange and its members' evolving place in the urban and world economy. Ashley Hahn and George Thomas selected and procured images, including some photographs of their own. Bill Whitaker, Erika Lindsey, and Bruce Hansen supplied some final scans. The staff of the Free Library of Philadelphia Print and Picture Department, R. A. Friedman at the Historical Society of Pennsylvania, and the staff of the Smithsonian Institution prepared many of these images. Richard Biddle connected me to Geoffrey Biddle, who kindly shared his portrait of Thomas Biddle.

Finally, Jo Joslyn, Erica Ginsburg, Yumeko Kawano, and the rest of the staff at the University of Pennsylvania Press deserve many thanks and high praise for their diligence, patience, and assistance in coordinating a project with many moving parts and a long history of its own.

Domenic Vitiello

Introduction

In 1973, Elkins Wetherill was waiting at the Paris airport when a perfect stranger walked across the lobby and said, "You're the son of a bitch who's destroying the New York Stock Exchange!"[1] Wetherill was taken aback. He was the president of the Philadelphia-Baltimore-Washington Stock Exchange (PBW), which accounted for barely 2 percent of all securities trading in America. Surely it could not compete with the world's dominant market on Wall Street. Why should he and his tiny institution elicit such vehement reactions—from someone he had never even met?

Presumably the stranger was a New York capitalist who understood the implications of Wetherill's mission in France. The president of the PBW was recruiting European banks to join his exchange, stealing lucrative trading business from members of the New York Stock Exchange (NYSE), which did not allow foreign members.

The PBW was a player on the global stage despite the sad state of the cities it represented. Philadelphia, where the exchange resided, had fallen off the nation's economic map, its once mighty factories and railroads in ruin. The same could be said of Baltimore, whose exchange had merged into Philadelphia's just to survive. And Washington had *never* had an economy to speak of.

By the 1970s, financial experts from Wall Street to the SEC saw little reason for the Philadelphia Stock Exchange (PHLX) to exist. Most Philadelphians in the late twentieth century had not even heard of the institution, or did not realize it remained open. But, ironically, in the darkest days of the city's economic history, the exchange and its members were busy remaking financial capitalism, experimenting and innovating with foreign membership and other new ways to trade. Although the metropolitan economy around them no longer mattered much in the national and world economies, Philadelphia capital created new markets and even forced New York and other exchanges to keep up.

The Philadelphia Stock Exchange in History:
The Plan of This Book

This was nothing new. At various points in its history, the NYSE had copied the trading practices of its counterpart in the Quaker City. What was new in the twentieth century was that the fortunes of Philadelphia's financiers diverged from those of their own city. Trading on the exchange became largely "derivative" of financial markets in New York. By contrast, in the eighteenth and nineteenth centuries, Philadelphia financial institutions had been central to the development of the city and its place in the world economy. Indeed, for most of the exchange's history, its markets and members helped build and maintain networks of information, transportation, and capital exchange that supported economic growth within the region as well as connections to other regions of North America and the globe.

This book explores the many ways in which the Philadelphia Stock Exchange and its members shaped the regional, national, and world economies across very different eras of economic history. It follows the exchange and its antecedents over more than two hundred and fifty years. As the first chapter recounts, in the eighteenth century merchants gathered in portside coffee houses to make the city the economic capital of colonial and revolutionary America. To trade in the massive federal debt resulting from the War of Independence, in 1790 a small group of traders founded the Philadelphia Board of Brokers, the first stock exchange in the Western Hemisphere. It was renamed the Philadelphia Stock Exchange in 1875, and again in 1975, when it became known by its acronym, the PHLX, pronounced "Phil-Ex."

Philadelphia remained the financial capital of the republic until the demise of the second Bank of the United States in 1836, ultimately losing that status to New York. The Board of Brokers' struggles to make a place for itself and its city in the early American economy are related in Chapters 2 and 3. Its competition and comparison with New York is a theme of nearly every chapter.

The Quaker City also owed its nineteenth-century designation as the "Workshop of the World," the nation's leading center of industry, at least partly to the Board of Brokers. Though manufacturers did not issue publicly traded stock until the end of the century, the coal and iron mines, oil wells, telegraphs, and railroads that powered the region's factories and linked them to national markets all raised their capital on the board. Its role in American industrialization is detailed in Chapter 4. Chapter 5 follows the exchange and its members in the Civil War and postwar decades, when they underwrote first the Union victory and then the streetcar networks, gas and electric utilities, and real estate trusts that built the modern metropolis.

Tragically, the late nineteenth-century stagnation of Philadelphia's stock market contributed to the loss of industrial wealth, undermining the city's ability to compete in the world economy of the twentieth century. This decline is explored in Chapter 6. The story of the region's industry—and most of its economy—ended around the time of Elkins Wetherill's incident in the Paris airport. But the story of the exchange would continue, as retold in Chapters 7 and 8. Even as Philadelphia's economy came crashing down around it, the institution revived in the era after World War II, once again becoming an innovator in methods and financial products to trade. The stock exchange's past half-century reveals how some Philadelphians—and their colleagues from New York—coped with the institution's (and the city's) diminished status in a changing world.

At its heart, this is a story about making and remaking metropolitan markets. Across the practically three centuries surveyed in this book, the Philadelphia Stock Exchange and its antecedents took diverse forms and directions, corresponding to very different eras of economic history. Like any long-term history, this narrative necessarily sacrifices a certain level of detail in any given age. What it gains is an understanding of the institution's role in urban economic development and economic restructuring over time.

Markets help make cities. And this book is as much an urban history as an economic history, tracing an institution and its members' ability to shape a city and its place in the world.[2] Today, economic development is a sub-specialty of city planning and policy, in great part concerned with attracting and retaining desirable firms and workers in the quest to achieve or maintain a city's place within regional and global economies. This field formally took shape in the mid-twentieth century, yet it has a prehistory in which a variety of public and private institutions—stock exchanges among them—assumed deliberate roles in shaping metropolitan growth. The PHLX, its members, and allied firms and institutions played an important, conscious part in guiding the growth of both the Philadelphia region and its connections to other parts of the globe—especially in the eighteenth and nineteenth centuries, but also in the twentieth and twenty-first.

Most histories of stock exchanges focus on markets, leadership, and trading practices. This book likewise recounts the PHLX's internal history and its place in national and world markets. But it also engages another, urban narrative, tracing the evolving relationship between the exchange and the city. For people concerned with cities and their development, this study offers a long-term history of the public-private partnerships and private sector-led urban development popular today.[3] More generally, it traces the networks of firms and institutions revealed by the securities market and its participants.[4]

The PHLX and its networks were simultaneously—and at turns—local, regional, national, and global in their outlook and impacts. Though it became just a "regional" exchange in the twentieth century, the Board of Brokers was established to be a national market, and Philadelphia financiers have always traded within a global context. Since the emergence of financial capitalism in the colonial era, brokers of commodities, currency, and securities have brought buyers and sellers together, mediating economic relationships of all sorts. Exchanges have served as the forums for their transactions, shaping the markets that underwrite cities, nations, and their economies.[5] The chapters that follow seek to understand the ways in which one community of brokers made and remade its place in the national and world economy.

The PHLX and Its City in the Long History of Globalization and Nation Building

The present is an era of globalization, of increasing interaction and integration of the world's economies and cultures. The notion—and the realities—of globalization often seem so massive, amorphous, and inexorable that we cannot grasp how our individual actions could affect the world around us. Yet it is people and institutions (which themselves are just organized groups of people) that make change happen on local and global scales.

Cities and their financial institutions play special roles in shaping globalization. Cities today strive to be "global cities," the command and control centers of the world economy. Not coincidentally, the most powerful global cities are the biggest financial centers—New York, London, Tokyo, and to a lesser extent Chicago, Singapore, and so on down the list of influential places. A few select financial institutions—securities and commodities exchanges and the banks and brokerage houses that cluster around them—

effectively determine these cities' status. They develop the networks of information, technology, and trade that link the world and its markets together. They thus regulate and facilitate the flow of capital into and out of private and public enterprise—and between different regions.[6]

Philadelphia aspires to make the list of global cities, and its boosters have cooked up elaborate plans to climb that hierarchy, including efforts to grow its financial sector. But it has a long way to go, it seems. Today, as in the 1970s, few people outside of the financial industry are aware that there ever was a Philadelphia Stock Exchange or that it survived into the twenty-first century. There are no longer even any major commercial banks head-quartered in the city. In that sector, Philadelphia is effectively an outpost of Pittsburgh, Charlotte, Providence, and Cherry Hill, New Jersey—none of which is itself remotely a global city.

However, as any elementary school student in the United States knows, Philadelphia was once the nation's capital, the most important urban center of the revolutionary era and the early republic. This was as much a result of finance as it was of politics. The city's merchants underwrote the War of Independence, as they would the War of 1812 and the Civil War. The Board of Brokers and its members played key roles in building the young nation's economy, and in regulating its financial markets in the absence of a national bank for most of the nineteenth century.

As the history of the PHLX illustrates, Philadelphia was also very much a global city in earlier eras of economic history. Indeed, the notion that globalization is a new phenomenon is utterly false. The Internet may be relatively new, but for some two hundred years the exchange and its members have traveled the "information superhighways" of different eras. They even helped build many of these systems, linking the markets of cities across North America and around the world.

This history of the PHLX is thus necessarily a history of economic glob-alization, intertwined with a history of city building and nation building. The exchange's successes and failures—and in turn many of Philadelphia's transformations—have derived from its members' ability or inability to stake out an advantageous place in the national and world economies. In general, when the PHLX, its leaders, and members have built effective social, technological, and trading networks to create and capture new mar-kets, they have succeeded in expanding their own—and their city's—power and influence in the United States and beyond. These strategies have taken numerous forms, from seemingly mundane rule changes, to the invention of new products to trade, to investments in superior technology. Some national and global forces have been beyond the exchange's power to affect. But when its members have remained attuned to those changes, they have usually found ways to turn them to their advantage. In contrast, in eras when the exchange has looked inward, adopting conservative tactics, its markets and its importance have contracted and declined.

At the writing of this book, the PHLX still operates, though it has merged into the NASDAQ, giving the world's largest electronic stock market the world's third most active options market. In an era of "virtual" transactions and securities exchanges that operate as exclusively electronic trading platforms, the question of *why* the institution still exists (not to mention why it exists in Philadelphia), albeit as a subsidiary of the NASDAQ, is perhaps more relevant than ever. Of course, the answer to this question has varied considerably across different eras of economic history. And presumably the markets created by the PHLX will take on new forms in the twenty-first century, whether in Philadelphia or in the place we call the virtual world. But that is getting ahead of the story. This tale of the Philadelphia Stock Exchange begins with its prehistory, as a group of merchants on the edge of the British Empire strove to institutionalize their place in the emerging world economy of the eighteenth century.

1

Revolutions in Capitalism:
The Origins of the Philadelphia Stock Exchange

As his term of office came to a close on October 7, 1746, Mayor James Hamilton of Philadelphia disappointed members of the City Council looking for a good time and a free drink. The mayor departed from the tradition of funding "an Entertainment" for the council to celebrate the end of his administration. Instead, he opted "to give a Sum of Money equal at least to the Sums usually expended on such occasions, to be laid out in something permanently Useful to the City." Signaling the dawn of a new era for Philadelphia's economy, Hamilton offered "the Sum of One Hundred & Fifty Pounds towards erecting an Exchange, or some other Publick Building . . . for the like uses with that of the Royal Exchange in London."[1]

What was at stake in Mayor Hamilton's choice? Put simply, Philadelphians wanted their city to be the London of the New World, the foremost center of trade and culture in the British colonies. The mayor recognized, as we do today, that financial institutions are vital to maintaining a city's economic place in the world. By the mid-eighteenth century, the imperial powers of Europe had created very much a world economy. Philadelphia's merchants, including James Hamilton (who was only a part-time politician), were full participants in the series of commercial, financial, and political revolutions that remade the economy and society of the early modern world. The origins of the Philadelphia Stock Exchange lay in these revolutions in capitalism.

In the 1740s and 1750s, Philadelphians set about institutionalizing their city's position as the foremost metropolis of the Western Hemisphere. The city's most famous adopted son, Benjamin Franklin, initiated the College of Philadelphia (today's University of Pennsylvania), the Library Company, the American Philosophical Society, Pennsylvania Hospital, and the Philadelphia Contributionship for the Insurance of Houses from Loss by Fire. These institutions fostered research that kept doctors, educators, and early manufacturers at the cutting edge of Enlightenment science. They created the civic infrastructure necessary to coordinate the education, health, and safety of a rapidly growing city. All of these institutions play similar roles two hundred and fifty years later, some as "anchor institutions" that employ and redevelop large parts of the city.

Yet it was Franklin's rival in the printing business, William Bradford, who in 1754 founded the city's most important early financial institution, the London Coffee House. This institution effectively preempted the initiative launched by Mayor Hamilton eight years earlier. The mayor's fund, which by then totaled £460, equivalent to as much as $1 million today, would pay for the erection of a new city hall, though not until after the American Revolution.[2]

A difficult personality, Bradford hailed from a family of contrarian newspapermen—his grandfather, uncle, and son were all prosecuted for defying the government. In 1742, at the age of twenty-three, he left his native New York and came to Philadelphia, where he began printing the *Pennsylvania Journal*. Its masthead was adorned with the image of a snake chopped into segments, with the motto "unite or die." A dozen years later, he launched the anti-British *Weekly Advertiser*, which squared off directly against Franklin's pro-British paper. In the 1770s, the London Coffee House would become a launching pad for the American Revolution, a cause to which Franklin, of course, would come around, as well.

Perhaps it was something in the printer's ink that led these two men to build institutions. More likely it was their appreciation for managing the flow of information in what we today term a "networked society." To twenty-first-century Americans, the coffee house again seems like a natural place to do business, even trade stock from wireless devices while sipping cappuccino. But the notion that this is something new is false (except for the wireless part). For eighteenth-century merchants in Europe and its colonies, coffee houses were *the* place to do business of all sorts.

In fact, events in Philadelphia mirrored conditions in the city its leaders sought to emulate. More than half a century earlier, facing a crackdown on their speculative activities in the Royal Exchange, London's stockbrokers decamped to the district of coffee houses clustered around the English capital's port. There, they were among the first to receive information about cargo arriving on inbound ships, news of wars, stock prices in Amsterdam and on the continent, and other developments of commercial import.

Bradford's London Coffee House was similarly positioned at the edge of Philadelphia's waterfront. On the periphery of the imperial Atlantic world, the coffee house provided a forum for merchants to integrate Pennsylvania into the emerging world economy. At the same time, they helped push back the frontiers of early capitalism, coordinating the expansion of the regional economy into the North American interior. These two overlapping scales—regional and global—would characterize the economic geography in which the Philadelphia Stock Exchange and its antecedents would operate for most of their history.

Philadelphia and the Birth of Financial Capitalism

From its very beginnings, the Quaker City was a financial venture. William Penn exchanged the debt the king owed his father for land in the New World, and he established his proprietary colony in 1681 as a limited offering. Penn controlled all markets for land. Select London merchants formed the Free Society of Traders, to which the proprietor granted a monopoly on economic activities such as fur trade with the Indians, fisheries in the Delaware Bay, and a variety of early industries.[3] This pattern of favoritism toward particular groups of insider merchants typified the political economy of European powers' imperial trading zones, a system historians call mercantilism. But in open colonies like Pennsylvania, where settlers were welcome regardless of their religion, a more open, diverse economy soon emerged.

Just as the London stockbrokers revolted against the tight controls of the Royal Exchange in the 1690s, Philadelphia merchants in the 1680s broke the monopoly of the ironically named Free Society of Traders. They, too, established the economic center of the colony at Front and Walnut Streets, overlooking the port. There, sailors, merchants, servants, and slaves climbed a set of stone public stairways up the bank of the Delaware from the merchant Samuel Carpenter's long wharf, while a crane at the top raised heavy cargo up the escarpment. Clustered at the top of the bank were several warehouses, a brewery, the Globe Inn, and Carpenter's Coffee House. This last establishment quickly became the city's "political and mercantile headquarters—the Exchange—of the day," where ship captains, merchants, craftsmen, and farmers gathered to trade news and commodities. Since their purpose was conversation rather than oblivion, Carpenter's coffee house suspended the sale of alcohol altogether in 1703. The establishment and its merchant patrons were immediately rewarded, as the City Council adopted the place as the seat of local government.[4]

Caffeine helped induce exchange. The fad of drinking steeped infusions of the ground roasted bean that had traveled from the Spanish possessions in the New World to Spain spread quickly along maritime routes through Europe and then back across the ocean to the Americas. The beverage was considered good for business, providing a modicum of exhilaration without the inebriation of the beer, wine, and ale that most city dwellers preferred in an era when urban water supplies were dangerously contaminated.[5] It most certainly fueled the exchange of information and commodities among ship captains, stockjobbers, and other merchants across the world of commerce, making capitalism itself an increasingly intertwined network.[6]

The merchants gathered at coffee houses in Philadelphia and ports around the world fostered the rise of financial capitalism itself. The widening variety of available commodities, larger and more dispersed markets, and longer waiting periods associated with transatlantic and East Indian trade required merchants to mobilize greater capital and manage more complex networks of investors, suppliers, sailors, wholesalers and retailers. To float what the modern world calls venture capital for such fixed capital assets as ships and to accumulate the stocks of inventory capital in their cargo holds and warehouses, imperial governments and their merchant subjects created financial capital in the form of transferable and negotiable claims on these physical stocks.[7] The great capital cities like Amsterdam, London, and Paris, where foreign merchants, consular agents, and newspaper publishers congregated, quickly developed markets for the exchange of these financial claims that were independent of the markets for commodities themselves.[8] These were the first stock markets.

In early Philadelphia, merchants exchanged relatively few stocks in such early public companies as the Dutch East India Company or the Hudson's Bay Company. More commonly, they traded shares in ships, underwriting the construction and the voyages of vessels that plied the Atlantic Ocean, the Mediterranean Sea, and occasionally even the Indian Ocean. Indeed "over 6,000 shares in some 3,200 vessels were traded at Philadelphia between 1726 and 1776," attracting investors from other colonies, as well as Europe and the Caribbean.[9] Shipping involved high risks but could reap high rewards, thus it was fitting that merchants spread both the risk and returns through partial ownership. Yet trading shares in ships was but a small part of the financial and commercial activities of early capitalists gathered at Carpenter's or later the London Coffee House.

Colonial era merchants were generalists in the economic development of Philadelphia. The majority pursued the coastal and West Indian provisioning trades, shipping grain, flour, bread, pork, beef, and shingles to Barbados, Kingston, and other island ports in return for sugar, molasses, and rum, which was typically brought back to Pennsylvania or exchanged in Boston or Newport for European manufactured goods. The colony's largest merchants traded with a variety of European ports. They bartered manufactured goods for furs and pelts from Native Americans in the interior, wresting a portion of the Iroquois trade away from New York and trading directly with London, Bristol, and Antwerp.[10]

The Quaker City's trading contacts throughout the Atlantic were inextricably linked to the rich soils of its large hinterland, which supported a growing agricultural economy. Integrating it all was capital. Merchants in the city helped finance the opening of roads to the interior, the establishment of inns and trading posts, and the construction of mills—in short, building the infrastructure that drew the territories of Pennsylvania, Delaware, New Jersey, and Maryland into their orbit. They also owned the ships that brought German, English, Irish, African, and other voluntary, indentured, and enslaved labor to the region.[11]

A metropolitan economy grew up around the activities of the farmers and merchants (Figures 1 and 2). Wagoners and flatboat operators carried foodstuffs to the city and returned with iron tools, textiles, shoes, and other manufactured goods to be sold at hinterland stores and trading posts. On the outskirts of the city, millers and butchers processed grain, lumber, and livestock from the countryside. In town, shopkeepers, grocers, tailors, and smiths provided city dwellers with their everyday necessities, while the keepers of taverns, inns, and boardinghouses accommodated visitors and recent arrivals. Along the riverfront, shipbuilders, riggers, sail makers, and coopers outfitted vessels and made barrels for shipping dry goods, and the port was crowded with stevedores, carters, and laborers carrying goods between ships and warehouses.[12] The merchants and their ships integrated Philadelphia into the world economy, building especially strong connections to the West Indies, Europe, and other parts of North America.

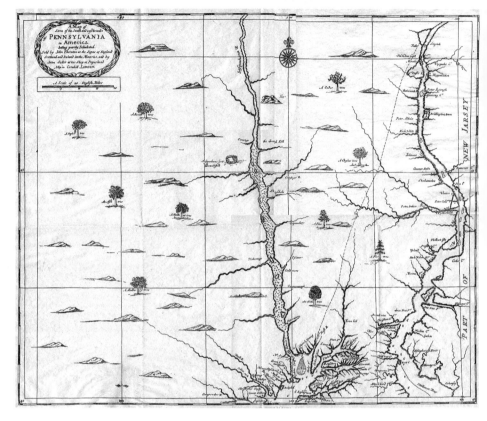

Figure 1. Thomas Holme, *A Map of Some of the South and East Bounds of Pennsylvania in America, Being Partly Inhabited*, 1681. Courtesy of Lower Merion Historical Society. Used to market the colony to settlers and investors, this map depicts the natural wealth of Pennsylvania, noting diverse species of hardwood trees and waterways enabling trade with the interior.

By the mid-eighteenth century, Philadelphia had become the "bread-basket of the Atlantic." Droughts in southern Europe made Marseille, Cadiz, and Lisbon regular ports of call for Quaker City ships. The city's leading merchant houses of this era—Willing and Morris, Clement Biddle, and the Wharton family, to name a few—leveraged this demand for the region's grain into larger trading networks and greater access to credit and capital than were previously enjoyed by the likes of Samuel Carpenter a

Figure 2. Thomas Holme, *A Map of the Improved Part of the Province of Pennsilvania in America*, 1695. Library of Congress, Geography and Map Division. By the middle of its second decade, Philadelphia had developed a regional economy in which farmers and craftspeople supplied merchants with exports from the city's hinterland.

generation earlier.[13] In addition to growing the flour trade and related processing, they encouraged fur traders to penetrate the Ohio Valley in search of deerskins and beaver pelts. They furnished a wide array of products, including Madeira wine from the islands off Africa, Muscovado sugar from the Caribbean, and spermaceti candles from Newfoundland to a booming consumer market at home.[14] The increasing scale and complexity of these markets spurred Mayor Hamilton and then William Bradford to initiate financial institutions.

The London Coffee House

One thing differentiated Bradford's London Coffee House from its antecedents—and from contemporary competitors, which quickly became obsolete. It was a private membership association in which merchant subscribers invested and enjoyed exclusive rights to organize their own market. Bradford advertised widely, even in Franklin's *Pennsylvania Gazette*: "The subscribers to opening a publick coffee-house in this city, are desired to meet at the Court-house on Friday, the nineteenth instant, at three a clock in the afternoon, to choose trustees agreeable to the plan subscribed."[15] When enough subscribers appeared, Bradford signed a lease on the property.[16] He promoted his London Coffee House as "a licensed place to which will come and be centered the news from all parts of the world, an exchange upon which our merchants may walk and a place of resort where our chief citizens in every department of life can meet each other and converse upon subjects which concerns the city and State."[17]

The London Coffee House was ideally positioned to dominate the city's trade. Situated between the High Street market and the port, in close proximity to the Quaker Meeting House, the courthouse, and Christ Church at Second Street, the coffee house received the city's mail. As the preferred gathering place for the governor and other officials, who adjourned from the recently constructed State House four blocks to the west, the coffee house was the site of considerable political debate, typically over economic policy.[18] Its location on High Street made it the obvious place for face-to-face commerce, for the street functioned as the media center for the expanding city, with newspaper offices and print shops publishing reports of auctions, exchanges, and other commercial activities taking place at the port and at such adjacent coffee houses and taverns as those of the Widow Roberts and the Widow James.[19]

Figure 3. Drawing of the London Coffee House. From John F. Watson, *Annals of Philadelphia and Pennsylvania* (Philadelphia: Stuart, 1877). The London Coffee House, with its outdoor slave market at the right.

Like many of the institutions founded in the same generation by Franklin, the exchange at Bradford's "publick coffee house" was in a sense both public and private. Though its downstairs room was open to all, subscribers paid annual fees to use the private second floor room and enjoyed influence over the house rules. Unlike most colonial coffee houses, the London Coffee House did not offer lodging, operating as less of an inn and more of a gathering place for trading and public conversation. In the second story great room, the building's thin walls afforded visual—if not always aural—privacy for members, distinguishing the exchange from an open street market at least. Both upstairs and downstairs, the London Coffee House's mercantile clientele bartered real estate, shares in ships, and all manner of commodities while sipping coffee, lemonade, wine, and liquor.

The building's front shed or awning linked what went on inside to the markets that extended west along High Street (Figures 3 and 4). Philadelphia's principal nineteenth-century antiquarian, John Watson, called this front shed "the most public place," to which merchants "brought all vendues of horses, carriages, and groceries, &c."[20] Bradford's *Pennsylvania*

Figure 4. William Birch, *High Street, with the First Presbyterian Church*. Steel engraving, 1799. Print and Picture Collection, The Free Library of Philadelphia. Birch depicted High Street as an urbane setting, with the public market at the left and shops, homes, and civic institutions at the right.

Gazette and Benjamin Franklin's *Pennsylvania Journal* were dotted with advertisements of public events, auctions, and sales at the site—everything from "the Ship BRITANNIA (Burthen 350 Tons, or thereabouts) with all her Tackle, Apparel, &c" in May of 1765 to the sale in July of "TWELVE or Fourteen valuable NEGROES, consisting of young Men, Women, Boys and Girls; they have all had the Small Pox, can talk English, and are seasoned to the Country." In addition to serving as the city's primary slave market, indentured servants were sometimes traded at this public post.

In April 1762, Bradford's *Pennsylvania Journal and Weekly Advertiser* gave notice that "an Insurance Office for Insuring Shipping and Merchandise, will be opened at the London Coffee House, where Risks in general will be under wrote, and all Persons may have their Insurance made with care and Expedition by John Kidd and William Bradford."[21] Financed by the London Coffee House's subscribers, this new office complemented the exchange of ships and commodities with a service vital to Philadelphia's maritime trade, and it further centralized the city's commercial and financial activity at the coffee house. Insurance, banking, and securities exchange would ultimately become the anchors of the city's financial district.

Of course, there was another kind of activity fomenting at the coffee house as well. From this de facto exchange of the Quaker City, Bradford and his clients helped lay the foundations of America's political and economic independence (Figure 5). For Pennsylvania merchants, the American Revolution was very much a financial revolution.

Roots of the American Financial Revolution

To understand that financial revolution, it is necessary to go back to the French and Indian War and to its economic and financial implications for Pennsylvania in general and Philadelphia merchants in particular. The war, North America's version of Europe's Seven Years' War, broke out between the English and French over the Indian trade in western Pennsylvania in 1754, the same year the London Coffee House was founded. It lasted nine years, until 1763, during which time it rendered the economy more liquid while expanding the scale and scope of investment opportunities and financial services. At war's end, when King George III and his Parliament decided to curtail those opportunities, they met disapproval, disgruntlement, and eventually defiance.

Right from the first shot of the war, commodity prices rose sharply, benefiting both farmers and merchants. Increased taxation during the 1750s and 1760s contributed to the boom by limiting demand for imported manufactures and aiding the Americans' balance of trade. More significantly, the British government flooded Philadelphia with bills of exchange—early forms of paper money—to provision its forces in western Pennsylvania. This prompted local merchants to move into military contracting and to leverage their new liquid assets into increased trade in European manufactures.[22]

The increased liquidity of the American economy encouraged Philadelphia merchants to experiment with investment and enter into increasingly flexible contracts.[23] One of the city's largest merchants, and a regular at the London Coffee House, Thomas Willing, established a line of credit with the London merchant banker David Barclay. Willing's colleague William Shippen contracted with an agent in Maryland to purchase bills of exchange

Figure 5. Portrait of William Bradford. From Thomas Scharf and Thompson Westcott, *History of Philadelphia, 1609–1884* (Philadelphia: Everts, 1884). While not as famous today as his rival Benjamin Franklin, William Bradford helped institutionalize the city's markets and its community of merchants.

on his account when exchange rates in Baltimore fell below those in Philadelphia. Sharp price fluctuations associated with the wartime economy led merchants to employ an early form of options: Willing, for example, took goods on commission with predetermined prices at which he could buy the goods himself, enhancing his ability to speculate. The war also "prompted him to engage in some very old trade techniques, like 'forestalling' (withholding goods from market in anticipation of higher prices) and 'networking' (establishing new business relationships and encouraging existing ones through correspondence and the exchange of information and even gifts)."[24]

As the British and French navies battled for nearly a decade, enforcing embargoes and unleashing privateers to capture enemy vessels, both the risks and the payoffs of shipping increased. At ports in desperate need of supplies, ship captains could charge exorbitant prices for their cargo, leading merchants to concentrate more on the speed of their operations and adopt more detailed cost accounting techniques to track their businesses. The greater liabilities of trade during wartime caused marine insurance premiums to soar. In response, Thomas Willing and five other merchants entered into a limited partnership in 1757 capitalized at £80,000, which enabled them to insure their vessels for larger sums than those offered by underwriters in London. Although the association was a temporary measure, some of its members continued to underwrite their own ventures throughout the 1760s.[25] It was this opportunity that inspired William Bradford to get into the insurance business.

Philadelphia merchants also influenced the development of public sector finance in this period. In 1757, Willing led a group of influential merchants that pushed "an Act for preventing Abuses in the Indian Trade" through the provincial Assembly, initiating deficit financing of public operations through negotiable bond issues. The law authorized the Commissioners for Indian Affairs, headed by Willing, to borrow up to £4,000 by issuing certificates at 6 percent interest for five years, and the Assembly raised the debt ceiling to £10,000 the following year. Under the protection of the British army, this group of Philadelphia merchants virtually monopolized trade with the Indians, sending gunpowder and other dry goods to the interior in exchange for deerskins, commissioning the construction of trunks, chests, and boxes for packing goods, and covering the costs of services ranging from portage to drying skins. Investors included a variety of city merchants and hinterland traders, though the majority of stockholders were wealthy women—some of them widows—for whom the Indian Commissioners' bond issue represented a new and welcome investment opportunity.[26]

But the British government threatened the colonists' abilities to prosper through its subsequent efforts to pay off the war debt by increasing taxes. As Philadelphia and New York merchants gained a greater proportion of transatlantic trade during and after the war, many merchants in England pressed Parliament for reforms that would restore their own competitive advantages in imperial shipping. In addition to the imposition of a monopoly in the tea trade, the London West India merchants used their ties to King George III to gain exclusive rights to import rum into Great Britain, Ireland, and Quebec. Through such attempts to restrict trade both outside and inside the empire, Parliament and the Crown effectively told the colonists that whatever markets they made were not theirs to keep and control.[27]

Brewing Independence

The Crown's restriction of colonial economic opportunity held a central place in the revolutionary ideologies of North American merchants. Parliamentary acts such as the Sugar, Stamp, and Townshend Acts, drove up the costs of doing business in the colonies. The Currency Act of 1764, representing a significant blow to North American finance, is a case in point. Initiated by London merchants who traded tobacco from Virginia and North Carolina, the act prohibited colonies from issuing bills of credit as legal tender. As specie drained out of North America, the continent's economy slumped, the ranks of its poor swelled, and its merchants were squeezed for capital and credit.

In a private attempt to mitigate this crisis, Thomas Willing, his partner Robert Morris, and other exporters concerned with the "Scarcity of Cash," the decline in exchange rates "for large Sums from 67 and a Half per Cent. to 50 per Cent.," and the prospect of "a still greater Fall of Exchange," established a short-lived, unincorporated bank. Primarily in return for commodities, these merchants issued "a number of their joint and several Promissory Notes, for Five Pounds each, amounting to Twenty Thousand Pounds, Pennsylvania Currency, payable to the Bearers within Nine Months, with Interest at the Rate of Five per Cent. per Annum."[28] The effect was temporary, at best, and did not redress the more fundamental restrictions on trade.

On the eve of the Revolution, the London Coffee House became the city's unofficial headquarters of rebellion. It hosted meetings of the city's Committee on Safety, as well as spontaneous riots and burnings of the Stamp Act. William Bradford emblazoned the masthead of the *Pennsylvania Journal* with skulls, crossbones, pickaxes, and coffins to denote his opposition to the British laws and announced his intention to stop publishing his paper rather than pay for the stamps.

Although the Boston Tea Party of 1773 is remembered as the seminal revolt against Parliament's new taxes, fewer students of the American Revolution learn that this uprising against the tax on tea was initiated at the coffee house in Philadelphia. In October, Bradford called prominent merchants to a town meeting, at which they drew up spirited declarations labeling the tea tax a "violent attack upon the liberties of America," with "a direct tendency to . . . introduce arbitrary government and slavery." They concluded that resistance "is a duty which every freeman in America owes to his country, to himself, and to his posterity."[29]

Three weeks later, in early November, a town meeting in Boston adopted these resolutions nearly word for word. On December 16, Bostonians followed through, dumping the East India Company's tea into their harbor. A separate tea ship heading for Philadelphia arrived at the mouth of the Delaware River a week later. Bradford organized a "Committee for Tarring and Feathering" that threatened arson upon the merchant house of James and Drinker, the agents for the East India Company. But violence proved unnecessary, as James and Drinker resigned their positions as sales agents and sent the ship back to England.

On December 31, 1773, Bradford's *Pennsylvania Journal* reported Paul Revere's arrival with news of the Boston Tea Party, which was "received here with general satisfaction. On its being read to a crowded audience at the Coffee-House, a loud shout of applause was given, and the bells immediately set to ringing. Several gusts of Indignation broke forth against" the Crown's colonial governors, "who had compelled the people to such a disagreeable step. And at the same time there was expressed a general approbation of the spirit and resolution of the Bostonians."[30] Demonstrations of revolutionary fervor continued the following May, when effigies of British statesmen, "after being exposed for several hours in a cart, were hung on a gallows erected near the Coffee House, set on fire by [Franklin's] electric fire, and consumed to ashes, about 6 o'clock in the evening."[31]

In the summer of 1774, representatives of the colonies convened the

Continental Congress in Philadelphia, and their more radical members were frequent visitors to Bradford's establishment. That year, the Congress named Bradford its official printer, giving him a formal position in the revolutionary government. On July 8, 1776, after the Declaration of Independence was read aloud in the State House grounds, the king's coat of arms was taken from the Supreme Court chambers in the State House and carried five blocks to the London Coffee House, where it was burned in the street.[32]

But William Bradford's revolutionary fervor was so great that his coffee house lost its position as the city's exchange. When the war broke out, he joined the Pennsylvania militia. Serving as a major and then a colonel, he saw action in the battles of Trenton and Princeton, and was wounded in the latter. He was at Fort Mifflin south of Philadelphia when the British bombarded it in November 1777. When the imperial troops withdrew, he returned to the city in ill health and financially ruined.

The City Tavern

In the fall of 1776, with Bradford away and the coffee house neglected, a group of prominent businessmen including George Clymer, Edward and Joseph Shippen, and John Cadwalader transferred the city's exchange to a new location. They chose as their base the newly constructed City Tavern, in the city's new central business artery on Second Street, just above Walnut. Second Street connected the old concentration of markets and counting houses along High Street to a growing area of elite homes (in what is today Society Hill) and the New Market at Pine Street. It was principally from this community of wealthy merchants that the subscribers to the City Tavern were drawn.

The building itself—a far more elaborate structure than the London Coffee House—reflected the class of its clientele. The project's budget, kept by John Cadwalader, one of the city's wealthiest citizens, suggests that few expenses were spared on its construction. Substantial sums were spent for carving and upholstery. The bill for "Wire-work" and "Hanging Bells" speaks to the pull bells that could call servants to various rooms. Considered stylish and "genteel," the City Tavern marked a new level of urbanity for Philadelphia.[33] It also continued the pattern of coffee houses serving as centers of information and economic development.

Yet it was a more regulated market, with higher barriers to entry. The

City Tavern usurped the role of Philadelphia's exchange from the London Coffee House when it "specially appropriated" its two front rooms for trading activities from noon to two o'clock and again from six to eight in the evening.[34] While it shared with the old coffee house the characteristic of semi-public, semi-private accommodation, City Tavern subscribers paid £25 in subscription fees, a much greater sum than the annual dues of 30 shillings at Bradford's place. Both its higher cost and its Declaration of Trust made it clear that access would be limited to more substantial merchants like the subscribers Robert Morris, John Nesbitt, Tench Francis, John Nixon, and Thomas Willing.[35] A significant number of the trustees and subscribers sat on the City Council, and several would sign the Declaration of Independence.[36] While George Washington directed troops on the battlefield, and Thomas Paine and Thomas Jefferson waged a war of words, it was this group of capitalists—most notably Robert Morris—who would help the thirteen colonies win the War of Independence in the counting house and on the trade routes of the Atlantic.

Financing Independence

Philadelphia capital won the American Revolution. At least that's how the city's merchants viewed the war. Cut off from British credit and capital in 1776, the Americans paid for much of the war by over-issuing paper currency, both centrally from Congress and in individual states, effectively monetizing the Continental economy. No longer able to depend upon London's markets and merchant houses for capital and credit, Robert Morris and his merchant colleagues were transformed from middlemen to creditors who assumed far greater risk and responsibility.[37] The economic historian John McCusker has argued that the American Revolution "might thus be seen as the ultimate employment of colonial risk capital."[38]

For the City Tavern, the presence of the revolutionary government during the Continental Congress helped to keep the establishment afloat. When John Adams and the Massachusetts delegates arrived in Philadelphia on August 29, 1774, they were feted there with "a Supper . . . as elegant as ever was laid upon a Table."[39] It became the hangout of delegates and deal makers.

As the Revolution heated up, the big financial players at the City Tavern devised strategies for both public and private profit. Military and civilian demand for provisions coupled with wartime inflation presented merchants with unprecedented opportunities to speculate in staple commodities—even as they advanced the revolutionary cause. In June 1776, for example, the Committee of Secret Correspondence, comprising Robert Morris, Benjamin Franklin, Benjamin Harrison, and John Dickinson—who met frequently at the City Tavern—sent ships including the *Retaliation* and *Independence* to Martinique to procure muskets in anticipation of the coming battles.[40]

Later, when the British occupied the city in 1777, the tavern's business was interrupted, together with the affairs of merchant houses and government. And while many patriot merchants fled Philadelphia for a time, a number of prominent Quakers—including Thomas Willing—remained in town, officially pacifist and publicly neutral. Despite his low profile, however, Willing secretly corresponded with Robert Morris and other colleagues outside the city, enabling Morris to use their firm's capital and connections to build a large and lucrative military provisioning business.

This provisioning kept the army moving. Morris and his colleagues paid for needed military supplies in promissory notes issued by Congress and produced by local printers. Philadelphia merchants then helped sustain the value of this paper money, making the rebel nation a financially viable enterprise. Morris recognized this when he wrote to Boston's John Hancock, the president of the Continental Congress, in early 1777, articulating his city's role as the central economic engine of the thirteen colonies' quest for independence: "You will consider Philadelphia from its centrical situation, the extent of its commerce, the number of its artificers, manufacturers and other circumstances, to be to the United States what the heart is to the human body in circulating the blood." Like a human heart, the city and its merchants and manufacturers kept the military supply lines—and indeed the broader economy—of the colonies pumping even as British ships blockaded American ports. "The continental currency is perpetually passing and repassing through [Philadelphia] for commercial and other purposes," Morris told Hancock, "and it carries with it from hence, wherever it goes some proportion [of the value] it bears here."[41] The economic activity of the city created value.

But the changing value of money in the wartime economy soon backfired on Robert Morris. The big commissions earned by the firm of Willing and Morris and allied firms and the enormous markups charged to the public caused outrage among consumers suffering from shortages and inflation, especially of staples like flour. In Philadelphia, crowds became particularly agitated in 1779, marching in the streets and likening Morris's commercial despotism to the royal taxation that had sparked the war in the first place. The popular Committee on Prices responded by launching an investigation of Morris and attempting to set prices on more than thirty commodities required by civilians and soldiers alike.[42]

Different sorts of injustice befell smaller merchants. The dry goods merchant Matthew McConnell was away fighting in the Battle of Brandywine when the same Continental Army in which he served seized his stores of rum. After the war, in 1780, he successfully petitioned Congress for repayment, though the loss represented a significant, if temporary, setback.[43] This experience apparently fed McConnell's interest in public and private finance in the new nation. A decade later, in 1790, he would become the founding president of the Philadelphia Board of Brokers, the first stock exchange in the Americas, established to trade federal debt (and later renamed the Philadelphia Stock Exchange).

Toward a Financial System

In the decade leading up to the establishment of the Board of Brokers, Philadelphia merchants helped shape the United States' nascent financial system. Morris and Willing responded to the challenges to their unregulated manipulation of the wartime economy by developing more formal, quasi-public institutions to support the American army and government. They used the City Tavern as their forum for cementing the ties between the mercantile and political interests of Philadelphia businessmen.

On June 17, 1780, Morris called a meeting at the tavern to found the Bank of Pennsylvania. The gathering netted pledges for £315,000 from ninety-two subscribers, including John Nesbitt, George Clymer, and Tench Francis. After conferring with a committee of Congress, the bank's directors were authorized to borrow on credit and issue interest-bearing notes for "the sole purposes of purchasing provisions and rum for the use of the Continental Army, of transporting them to camp . . . and of discharging their notes and the expense of conducting their business."[44]

In the spring of 1781, Congress unanimously elected Morris to the newly created office of superintendent of finance, the top economic post in the Continental administration (Figure 6). His charge was "to Examine into the State of the Public Debt, the Public Expenditures and the Public Revenue, to digest & report plans for improving & regulating the

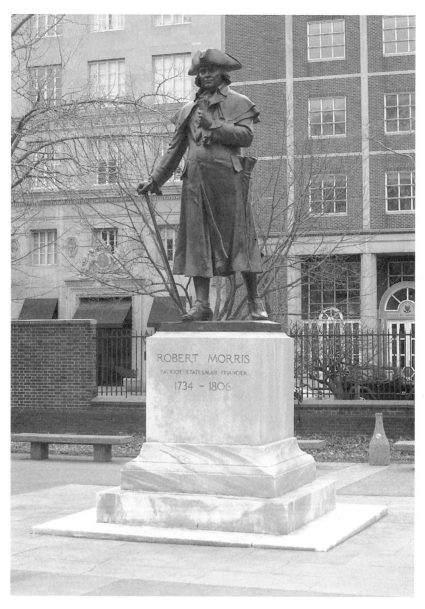

Figure 6. Statue of Robert Morris in Independence National Historical Park. Photograph by Ashley J. Hahn, 2008. Though never a member of the Board of Brokers, Robert Morris was largely responsible for shaping the financial system in which it would trade.

Finances & for Establishing order and economy in the expenditure of the Public Money . . . to direct and control all Persons employed in Procuring supplies for the Public Service."[45]

Morris made certain that Congress did not consider his assumption of this post "incompatible with commercial concerns and connections," so that he could continue to operate his mercantile business.[46] The key instrument of his administration was the Bank of North America, chartered by Congress as a quasi-national bank. It was organized at a meeting at the City Tavern, where the founding merchants elected Thomas Willing president and Tench Francis cashier.[47] With shares of stock marketed largely from the tavern, the bank represented the first true initial public offering (IPO) in America.

Postwar Market Making

Wars are run on debt, and the American Revolution was no exception. Investing in the repayment of that debt at war's end created the first full-scale securities market in the New World. It would be housed, to a great extent, in Philadelphia. It was in Philadelphia that Congress announced the end of hostilities with Britain—on April 11, 1783, at the State House, now Independence Hall. Shortly thereafter, however, the national government decamped—eventually winding up in New York, although it would return to Philadelphia some seven years later. With its departure, and with the nation's economy contracting, Philadelphia's economy virtually collapsed. The peace-generated boomlet that nearly doubled the number of mercantile houses in Philadelphia in 1783 turned to ruin only a year later.[48]

One of the businesses that failed was the City Tavern, which was sold in 1785 at a sheriff's sale. Its new owner leased it to Edward Moyston, the former steward for Robert Morris, who offered cuisine "in both the French and English taste" and provided "all Daily and Weekly Papers for the Perusal of his Customers."[49] It seems clear that Moyston was alert to the nascent market in government securities and aimed to preserve the tavern's role as Philadelphia's exchange.

He succeeded. The reborn City Tavern would house much of the securities market. In North America, investment in stock had previously been limited to a few merchants and propertied individuals, but this would soon change. As remittance for provisions, quartermasters had sold bills of exchange, issued by the French government, at a discount, introducing speculators to the benefits of liquid, interest-bearing public bonds that made many investors hungry for other sorts of securities such as bank stock.[50]

But along with the expansion of the investment market and investing activity came expanded opposition. Critics of speculation—and of cities—abounded in early America, particularly among men who derived their wealth from the land and from slave agriculture, including George Washington, Thomas Jefferson, and James Madison. To these detractors, Robert Morris responded, "He who wants Money to commence, pursue or extend his Business, is more benefited by selling Stock of any Kind (even at a considerable Discount) than he could be by the Rise of it at a future Period." Though he did not believe in totally "free" markets, Morris adopted the rhetoric of freedom, arguing that "Every Man [is] able to judge better of his own Business and Situation, than the Government can for him."[51] Urban merchants, in turn, spread this message to their colleagues and customers, generating the buzz that spurred the market's growth. In early 1784, for example, Samson Fleming, a Philadelphian and a shareholder in the Bank of North America, wrote to his friend William Edgar in New York, remarking, "It is an amazing Advantage to have Stock in Bank, for a man who has Commercial Views. He can take out & put in as reason directs." Finding this sort of liquid investment attractive, Edgar bought fifty-five shares.[52]

To take advantage of the new market for securities, certain merchants in Philadelphia and New York began to specialize in brokerage. As far back as 1781, the transplanted New York merchant Haym Salomon had advertised in the Philadelphia press, citing his services as a dealer in bills of exchange on Holland and France. Robert Morris subsequently engaged him to broker the majority of the foreign loans for the Revolution.[53] In June 1784, Salomon and his partner, Jacob Mordecai, began advertising in New York, touting Salomon's role as "Factor, Auctioneer & Broker to the Office of Finance" and boasting of their ability to "make remittances to any part of the world, with peculiar facility."[54] The Philadelphian Isaac Franks advertised his services as a "stock and exchange broker" in 1787.[55] Quotations of securities prices appeared in New York and Philadelphia newspapers as early as 1786 and were regularly published beginning in 1789, by which time brokerage was a recognized profession.[56]

American brokers borrowed such English techniques as options, time bargains, and even sometimes third-party "insurance policies" on the lives of public figures such as kings or prime ministers.[57] Speculative contracts thus came to be settled by the payment of price differentials. In 1789, the Philadelphia broker Edward Fox wrote a potential investor in New York, introducing him to this system of trading. "[A] sum of Continental Debt . . . might be sold to be *delivered* in any given time," Fox explained, "that is to fix the price at present, and agree upon a mode of fixing it at the end of the Time,—and then without transferring, or delivering any Certificate to *pay* or receive the difference of price. This is the Common practice in England . . . called *"Stock Jobing."*[58]

While the economy of the United States was generally depressed during the 1780s, though no formal exchanges existed yet, the informal market for securities was relatively active. Between January 1785 and December 1788, the Philadelphia firm of Reed and Forde purchased £1,436 of securities and made sales worth £2,577. Some of these shares were bought for clients; others were purchased on the firm's own account.[59] By 1789, Philadelphia's Clement Biddle and Company was trading stock for a client base dispersed from Virginia to London.[60] Biddle had served as a colonel and as the deputy quartermaster general under George Washington and handled the first president's business affairs in Philadelphia. The following year, he would join Matthew McConnell and other revolutionary officers, wholesalers, and public figures to found the Board of Brokers.

While the securities market in the late 1780s included stock in banks, canals, turnpikes, bridges, insurance companies, and a handful of manufacturing concerns, the most active trading by far was in certificates for government debt and land claims in the so-called Western Reserve. Thousands of veterans who received these claims as deferred payment for their services sold them to investors speculating on the promise of repayment. A relatively small number of northern merchants bought up most of the outstanding public debt, giving rise to the U.S. early financial elite.[61]

Most of these same merchants also acquired vast tracts of land, where they immediately became planners, developers, and boosters, shaping the economic development of western Pennsylvania, New York, Ohio, and other territories. Thomas Willing's son-in-law, the U.S. senator William Bingham, epitomized this trend. After accumulating an initial fortune running guns from the Caribbean for Robert Morris, Bingham bought up all the Continental currency he could in the 1780s, then forced Alexander Hamilton to redeem it for federal debt certificates on par. Bingham and his allies, including William Cooper, coordinated their purchase of upstate

New York and northern Pennsylvania lands, where development projects like Binghamton and Cooperstown contributed to the rapid proliferation of small cities across the interior in the early republic.[62] Bingham bought two million acres in the future state of Maine, though the westward thrust of settlement and improvement projects (and the rocky soils of New England) made this a less urbanized landscape. Instead, Philadelphians would get their lumber from the woods of Maine and build vacation homes and yacht clubs along the coast.

Though many of their investments failed financially, politically engaged "insider" financiers effectively underwrote the networks of transportation, communication, and land development that urbanized the early United States. The big cities, especially Philadelphia and New York, remained the main centers in this economic geography, coordinating or threatening the viability of different improvement projects.

Of course, the economic relationships among capitalists were almost never simply economic. Deploying deliberate social networking strategies, the financial elite reinforced their position—and their cities' position—in the financial world through marriage. William Bingham's two daughters, for example, married into the Baring family, whose London firm was one of the two banks that would handle the Louisiana Purchase transactions.

These sorts of transatlantic connections enabled big city brokers and their European allies to control much of the early American securities market. A few men with access to large amounts of cash succeeded in accumulating some 80 percent of all federal debt stock issued in Massachusetts. The New York merchant William Duer and seven or eight of his associates held more than 15 percent of the combined state debts of Virginia and the Carolinas. Many sold shares to correspondents in Europe. Investors in Holland, for example, bought nearly $3 million of U.S. government stock.[63]

When the federal government formed in New York in April 1789, certificates for its debt traded at 15 percent to 23 percent of nominal par value, and it remained unclear whether or how the national and state debts would be repaid. Robert Morris, by then a senator from Pennsylvania, called for a new issue of securities for which holders of the old stock could exchange their claims, a plan endorsed by Alexander Hamilton, the secretary of the Treasury. James Madison of Virginia led a group of congressmen wary of securities speculation who supported a two-tier system that favored the original holders of these claims, who were primarily former soldiers. In late 1789, the market for government stock rebounded and prices rose in anticipation of a vote on the national debt. Philadelphians in the government, such as Robert Morris and Tench Coxe, the assistant secretary of the Treasury, funneled information about the New York market to the Quaker City. Edward Fox reported in December that "the Rage of the Day is the purchase of Stock."[64] When Madison's plan was defeated by a vote of 36 to 13 in the spring of 1790, the market for government debt appeared secure.

Beyond the financial mechanisms for funding the national debt, the new nation's securities market would be profoundly shaped by the locus of the federal government. As the largest cities with the most developed social institutions, Philadelphia and New York enjoyed distinct advantages over potential sites in the South or New England. In June 1790, however, the Virginian Thomas Jefferson brokered a deal in which another Virginian, James Madison, agreed to support the New Yorker Alexander Hamilton's proposals for a national bank and the assumption of state debts by the federal government. In return, Hamilton pledged to secure votes from New Englanders, whose states suffered the greatest war debts, for the establishment of the permanent national capital just across the Potomac River from Virginia. Here Jefferson set aside his mistrust of financial markets for his goal of giving Virginia proximity to the national center. He would deal with the national bank at a later date. The federal government would reside in Philadelphia for a decade, from the end of 1790 until it moved to Washington in 1800. With the arrival of Congress and the establishment of the Bank of the United States, Philadelphia was left with a decade-long window of opportunity to secure its place as the nation's financial capital.

2

National Capital:
The Board of Brokers' Founding Generation

Matthew McConnell's name is nowhere listed among the ranks of America's financial founding fathers.[1] As a major in the Continental army, he had been badly wounded during the war and had been awarded a pension by Congress. Augmenting this income, he kept a modest shop at 66 Chestnut Street, operating simultaneously as a dry goods merchant, book dealer, and notary public. He was not a fabulously wealthy merchant like Robert Morris, but he was much more than a simple shopkeeper (Figure 7).

Indeed, McConnell's ambitions were international in scope. In 1787, he and his wife authored *An Essay on the Domestic Debts of the United States of America*, "giving an account of the various kinds of public securities . . . with the provision made and proposed for payment of the interest and principal thereof by federal measures, and of those adopted by individual states."[2] To this they appended "A Statement of our Foreign Debts," probably the first true balance sheet of the nation. While the McConnells may have profited from its sales, this publication had less to do with Matthew's bookselling vocation than it did with his nascent career as a financier. His particular interest was the new nation's war debt of some $77 million. In an era when the country's gross domestic product totaled just $200 million, the challenge of underwriting this debt required new financial instruments and institutions.[3]

Three years later, in the spring of 1790, McConnell and nine other merchants established the Philadelphia Board of Brokers.[4] The express purpose of this first stock exchange in America lay in taking advantage of the city's

Figure 7. Portrait of Matthew McConnell. CIGNA Collection, National Museum of American History, Smithsonian Institution. Matthew McConnell, the Board of Brokers' first president, was part of a group of merchants concerned with capitalizing the newly independent nation's war debt.

impending role as the national capital. On the eve of Congress's transfer from New York to Philadelphia in August that year, McConnell penned a quick letter to Assistant Secretary of the Treasury Tench Coxe, a fellow Philadelphian. He enumerated their city's imminent advantages as both a political and financial center: "that the seat of Government will always be the governing Market, that people in every part of the Union & of Europe will look to it for the prices, and that a great part of the certificates for sale will travel that way as to a common centre, and as the fountain head both of information & of the money of the union."[5] Coxe's business partner, Nalbro Frazier, would soon join the Board of Brokers, along with other merchants seeking an organized forum for making new markets that capitalized on this position.

Frazier, McConnell, and their colleagues enjoyed more than a fair shot at making the board the nation's leading securities market, and thus the main trading partner with the financial centers of Europe and the wider world. In addition to housing Congress and the president, their city would be home to the new national bank. Yet becoming the financial capital of the republic meant more than just hosting the Bank of the United States. It required establishing the city's private banking and brokerage firms and institutions as the dominant players in an emerging national economy.

In 1790, the shooting war had been over for some time, but the competition to be the United States' financial capital was just heating up. Philadelphia and New York vied against one another head-to-head for the prize. In the fall of that year, three new series of federal debt were issued—thanks to Robert Morris and Alexander Hamilton—creating a large and relatively secure national market for public securities. Brokers in Philadelphia and New York organized auctions for the stock, becoming the principal markets for government scrip. They reached out to a slowly expanding investing public at home and abroad that was eager to put its money in other ventures as well, including private bank and insurance stocks, public works, new trade routes, and land development.

Philadelphia and New York stockbrokers competed against more than just one another. Even as the growth of the securities market leveraged the national debt and spurred new economic activity, it stirred a public backlash against speculation that was never far below the surface. Much of the new nation harbored deep suspicion of these metropolitan centers and their financiers. In this climate of competition and insecurity, the Board of Brokers innovated on three key fronts—expanding the reach of its markets, self-regulating those markets through an evolving system of governance, and managing information flows through technology. These would all be enduring factors in sustaining the stock exchanges of Philadelphia, New York, and other cities around the world.

The First Brokers

The first membership roll of the Philadelphia Board of Brokers included Clement and William Biddle, George Eddy, James Glentworth, Matthew McConnell, James McCuragh, Thomas McEuen, Thomas Newman, Thomas Orr, and Andrew Summers Jr. Soon after its founding, a dozen more men joined their ranks: Nicholas Arnous, John Donaldson, Nalbro Frazier, Thomas Greeves, T. G. Laroche, Richard Hill Morris, James Musgrave, Mark Prager, Norton Pryor, George Taylor Jr., Kearney Wharton, and Israel Whelen.

These men were not the city's most powerful capitalists, though their personal connections reached the highest levels of government and international finance. Their diversified political, civic, and economic development activities helped expand the institution and its markets. All of the board's original members were merchants, and many were involved in the public affairs of the city. Wharton was president of Philadelphia's Common Council in the 1790s. Pryor was its public recorder of deaths from 1791 to 1815.[6] Eddy, Whelen, Frazier, and Wharton were among the first subscribers to the Bank of North America.[7]

Several members of the board leveraged military service into profitable public positions. James Glentworth, who succeeded McConnell as the Board of Brokers' second president in 1791, served as a captain in Washington's army and became Philadelphia's tax collector following the war. The board's third president, Israel Whelen, though a Quaker, had been the city's purveyor of public supplies during the Revolution and was a commissioner of the Continental Congress, "in which capacity he signed the first issue of Continental currency. . . . He rose by degrees to the rank of commissary-general of the army, and was a financial agent of the government, in which capacity he made large remittances to Antwerp and Amsterdam." From his office at Fourth and Market Streets, he developed a substantial trade in gunpowder with France and acted as the Philadelphia agent of London's Phoenix Insurance Company. Whelen was a member of the Pennsylvania Senate and a customs collector for the port of Philadelphia; he was appointed federal purveyor of public supplies by President John Adams. He and Matthew McConnell were founding directors of the Bank of the United States.[8]

Like McConnell, Glentworth, and Whelen, Clement Biddle was an active revolutionary. Born into a family of Quaker merchants, he served as deputy quartermaster general and later as commissary general, supplying the Continental troops in the Philadelphia theater of the war. He joined the attack against the Hessians at Trenton and was chosen by Washington to receive the swords of the surrendering German officers. By the time the nation's capital moved to Philadelphia, Biddle was running a large trading house, "engag[ing] in business as a notary public, and [becoming] well known in commercial circles for his ability in adjusting marine losses."[9] In 1793–94, he authored the first list of the city's citizens, the *Philadelphia Directory and Register,* akin to a combination of today's white pages, yellow pages, and social register, which must have proved a useful survey for his commercial interests.[10]

The brokers' connections not only resulted in an intense concentration of activity in the city, but they also fostered extensive networks that linked them to markets around the world. The most important of these markets, of course, sat just ninety miles to the north. The securities auctions in New York and Philadelphia complemented and stimulated one another. Inter-market arbitrage proceeded apace, evidenced in the behavior of prices and in the publication of price quotations from both markets in the newspapers of each city.[11] Express stagecoaches facilitated trading between the two cities. In the early 1790s, observers reported as many as twenty expresses carrying brokers back and forth across New Jersey on busy days.[12]

The two markets initially operated quite differently. Where New York's early stock auctions were public, held in the street under a buttonwood tree, the Board of Brokers constituted a private association of stock traders officially licensed by the City of Philadelphia.[13] Simply establishing a marketplace was not enough for them, because outsiders observing the auctions could privately sell securities at a lower rate, thereby undercutting their business. The board's original ten members therefore established regular hours of operation at a fixed, closed site—which suggests that they appreciated the values of secrecy and regulation.[14] While they continued to conduct some of their business "out of doors," the board's space and hours offered its members a new measure of security in trading.[15] With a set of rules, a president and secretary elected annually on March 4, and a $30 admission fee, it was a self-perpetuating and controlling organization that, so long as it was reasonably open to membership or was secure in its monopoly, could sustain some measure of control over the market.[16]

Banking on an Urban Financial Center

The presence of federal financial institutions in Philadelphia was largely responsible for driving the growth of the capital market and the fevers of speculation that sustained it. As the financial historian Richard Sylla has noted, "When countries are newly establishing or reforming themselves, the state's financial requirements and policies *determine* the ways in which private financial institutions and markets emerge and develop."[17] Although the Board of Brokers and the Bank of North America made Philadelphia the foremost financial center in the United States, these self-interested institutions could not meet the larger needs of a federal financial system. Instead, Alexander Hamilton designed a national bank whose actions could cross state boundaries, capitalizing and catalyzing the economy of the entire republic.

The federally chartered Bank of the United States caused considerable controversy, sparking a persistent debate about the future of the republic and the character of its economy. Thomas Jefferson feared the expansion of urban financial interests at the expense of the agrarian concerns of his native Virginia. Despite using Hamilton to further Virginia's interests in the location of the new capital, he had long argued that the national bank was an unwise foundation that was little better than gambling. Jefferson condemned the rapidity of the bank subscription as evidence of his fears: "You will have seen the rapidity with which the subscription to the bank were filled, as yet the delirium of speculation is too strong to admit sober reflection. It remains to be seen whether in a country whose capital is too small to carry on its own commerce, to establish manufacturers, erect buildings, &c. such sums should have been withdrawn from these useful pursuits to be employed by gambling?"[18]

Jefferson's misgivings notwithstanding, under the Federalists George Washington and Alexander Hamilton the Bank of the United States was chartered by Congress in February 1791 for a term of twenty years. Its new building was constructed on Third Street in Philadelphia between 1794 and 1797 (Figure 8). As a semi-public institution, it was authorized to trade in foreign exchange, and it acted as a fiscal agent and depository for the government, which owned twenty percent of its stock—a good investment.

Hamilton's plan allowed securities for the federal debt to be transferred into stock in the bank. With $65 million in federal bonds offered for sale by the Treasury, another $12 million in bonds distributed among foreign

Figure 8. William Birch, *Bank of the United States, in Third Street, Philadelphia*. Steel engraving, 1799. Print and Picture Collection, The Free Library of Philadelphia. Just a block from the City Tavern, the Bank of the United States was one of the few federal institutions that remained in Philadelphia.

creditors, and $10 million of bank stock issued between 1790 and 1791, the government created the "nucleus of a national capital market."[19] As the hot IPO in the summer of 1791, the Bank of the United States' 6 percent bonds (known as "stock" at the time) traded at 20 percent above par by the fall.[20] Investors in London and Amsterdam bought up close to half of these securities within a decade, funneling European liquid capital across the Atlantic and into the coffers of an institution controlled by Philadelphians.

Despite its national purpose, the bank's charter gave overwhelming control to local interests, setting the stage for future calamity. Of its $10 million capital, $5.7 million was reserved for the parent bank in Philadelphia, while the balance was divided among eight branches in other cities, from Boston to Charleston. Eleven of the bank's twenty-five directors—including its first president, Thomas Willing—hailed from Pennsylvania, with six from New York, three from Massachusetts, and one each from Maryland, Connecticut, Virginia, and South and North Carolina.[21]

But while Philadelphia's financial elite was pleased about the Bank of the United States, the city's brokers were far less approving of the idea of a national currency based on a decimal system of dollars and cents. Congress in 1792 had called for construction of the U.S. Mint to give the new nation its own coinage and to replace the French and Spanish coins that were the international units of trade, as well as symbols of nations. The mint was erected in Philadelphia at Seventh and Farmer (now Filbert) Streets, in a metal-working district that is still discernible in present-day Jewelers' Row (Figure 9). It was equipped with specialized tools, and was placed under the direction of the scientist and mechanic David Rittenhouse.[22] The city's stockbrokers, however, whose market remained closely tied to that of London, resisted the new coinage for the entire decade. It wasn't until November 1, 1800 that "the brokers gave notice that thereafter they intended to buy and sell public stocks for dollars and cents, and they published books for the use of those accustomed to the old style of computation."[23]

While the mint operated on the industrial outskirts of the city at Seventh Street, Second and Third Streets were built up as Philadelphia's—and indeed the nation's—central financial district. The United States Treasury Department sat on Second Street. A block west, on Third Street between Chestnut and Walnut, stood the Bank of the United States. The building's pedimental sculpture was said to mark the beginnings of an American national style. It held a sculpted American eagle, its wings outspread with talons of one foot grasping the arrows of defense while the other held a cornucopia of plenty. One newspaper claimed that it "may safely be pronounced the masterpiece of Philadelphia, for beauty and grandeur of architecture."[24] Around the corner stood the plain brick Bank of North America. In the middle of it all was the old City Tavern, renamed the Exchange Coffee House, headquarters of the Board of Brokers and of the new nation's first securities market (Figures 10 and 11).

Making the Stock Market

The Philadelphia Board of Brokers and its members played multiple roles in shaping the economy of the new republic. Stock brokerage was initially too small a business for the first board members to be able to abandon

Figure 9. Unknown artist, U.S. Mint, First Building, 1792. Lithographic reproduction, ca. 1913. Print and Picture Collection, The Free Library of Philadelphia. Located on the outskirts of the built-up city at the time, the mint helped make Philadelphia a center of specialized manufacturing.

their other mercantile pursuits. In fact, the two often ran on parallel and mutually beneficial tracks, with commodities trading networks helping to spread the geographical reach of securities markets—and vice versa. In the 1790s, the board member Mark Prager, for example, corresponded in Dutch, French, and English with merchants in Boston, New York, Trenton, Wilmington, Baltimore, Washington, Virginia, Charleston, New Orleans, St. Croix, Lisbon, Madeira, Tenerife, Hamburg, and especially Amsterdam. Illustrating the value of family networks in early modern business, he traded with his brother in Calcutta and their father in London, shipping wine, wheat, flour, corn, pipe stave, rum, and other commodities around

BANK OF PENNSYLVANIA, *South Second Street* PHILADELPHIA.

Drawn Engraved & Published by W Birch & Son Nichaminy Bridge

Figure 10. William Birch, *Bank of Pennsylvania, South Second Street*. Steel engraving, 1799. Print and Picture Collection, The Free Library of Philadelphia. The City Tavern is at the left, across the alley from the Bank of Pennsylvania, part of a growing regional banking sector whose securities traded on the Board of Brokers.

the Atlantic and Indian Oceans. They also cultivated an active international trade in bills of exchange, bank stock, and U.S. debt. The Pragers' letters were filled with regular quotes of stock prices and currency exchange on the markets of Philadelphia, London, and Amsterdam.[25] Similarly, Clement Biddle's correspondents and clients included brokers in Baltimore and New York as well as investors in England and Switzerland (Figure 12).[26]

The practice of securities brokerage at the time covered a sophisticated

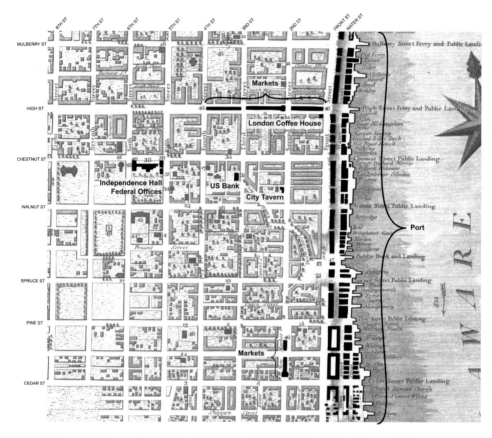

Figure 11. Excerpt from John Hills, *Map of Philadelphia*, 1797. Library of Congress. Markets and selected institutions are highlighted (by Susan Snyder and Christy Kwan). As the national capital in the 1790s, Philadelphia developed a diverse complex of public and private financial institutions that enhanced regional economic development.

range of financial services. For a fee, brokers acted primarily as intermediaries in the purchase and sale of stock. They also traded the subscription rights to forthcoming public offerings, which could be particularly lucrative in an era with few shares on the market. Again building on their experience in trading commodities and futures contracts, many early brokers engaged in more speculative transactions like short sales, put and call options,[27] and other types of transactions. The Board of Brokers member James McCur-

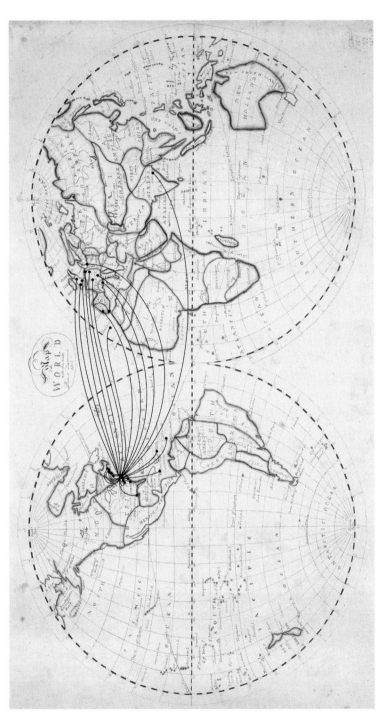

Figure 12. Mary Van Schaack, *Map of the World with the Most Recent Discoveries*, 1811. Library of Congress. Selected cities with which Board of Brokers founding members traded are highlighted (by Christy Kwan). With correspondents and sometimes family in cities around the Atlantic and beyond, members of the Board of Brokers connected Philadelphia's financial market to the wider world.

ach, for example, specialized in currency. His advertisement in the *Political and Commercial Register* in 1805 boasted, "He has always bills of exchange, for sale—Buys and sells all kinds of stock, furnishes money on the shortest notice for negotiable paper, &c."[28]

Like many colonial merchant houses, securities brokers traded both on their own account and for affluent clients—other merchants, widows, and "those too busy with retirement, gentlemanly agricultural pursuits, or politics to spend time in active trade."[29] The work was sufficiently remunerative. Evidence from the letters and account books of Biddle, Glentworth, Prager, and Wharton suggest that board members maintained a steady commission rate of 0.25 percent from the 1790s to at least the 1830s.[30]

While trading activity on the early Board of Brokers was minuscule by today's standards, the relatively few available securities on the market attracted enough interest to drive prices up at a rapid rate. The financial historian Robert Wright has estimated that trading volume in Philadelphia "was at least $1.5 million per year in the early 1790s."[31] Even in the months before the establishment of the board, in the spring of 1790, Clement Biddle traded thousands of dollars of stock per week, and Matthew McConnell reportedly sold $10,000 of U.S. debt certificates in a single transaction.[32] In 1791, the chartering of the first Bank of the United States ushered in the nation's first bull market, and activity and prices soared. As Andrew Barnes, a chronicler of the stock exchange, later wrote:

On July 5 of that year as high as $35 was paid for scrip of this bank on which but $25 had been paid in, and the next month, the stock with $50 paid in rose to $200, with a subsequent quick drop to $145. Stock speculation became very active about this time. When the Schuylkill and Susquehanna Navigation Company was brought out in 1791, with 1,000 shares offered at $400 a share, there was a rush to get in, and the issue was forty times over-subscribed, so that it was necessary to make distribution by lot. The Delaware and Schuylkill Canal Navigation Company, with 2,000 shares at $200, was largely over-subscribed the same year, and in the case of the Philadelphia and Lancaster Turnpike Company, another promotion of the same year, 2,276 shares were subscribed for on a total issue of but 1,000 at $300. . . . Shares with $300 paid in rose in a few days to $1,000.[33]

The buzz around these stocks reflected the market's transition from a primary focus on federal bonds to a more diverse portfolio including stock in financial, insurance, and infrastructure corporations. As trading volume and prices gained momentum in 1791, in early November Philadelphia brokers expanded their use of forward and futures contracts, which helped hedge some of their risk.[34] On a particularly active day the following March, in 1792, trading on the board included "sixty-three different transactions, consisting of 104 shares of the Bank of North America and the United States Bank, and $54,500 in Government bonds," a considerable sum for that era.[35] By that time, enough brokerage activity was taking place that the Board of Brokers rented a separate room in the Exchange Coffee House, as the City Tavern was now known, and the morning papers began to report on "Sales of Stock, Last Evening."[36] This information helped standardize securities prices in the broader market, fostering confidence among investors and inter-market arbitrage.[37]

Panic and Epidemic

But the financial markets did not run entirely according to Alexander Hamilton's and Matthew McConnell's plans. Overspeculation in the young market, particularly in the federal debt, brought about the nation's first financial panic in the spring of 1792. It left many large investors bankrupt, most famously the first assistant secretary of the Treasury, New York's William Duer, whose attempt to drive up stock prices had caused the collapse. Federal institutions lacked the power to prevent such a disaster. In response, the legislature of New York made public auctions of securities illegal, leading to the Buttonwood Agreement and the founding of the New York Board of Brokers, later the New York Stock Exchange. Remarkably, New York brokers continued to trade out of doors, under the buttonwood tree, shading themselves from the sun but exposing their transactions to non-member traders who threatened to undercut their markets.

Outside of New York, however, the downturn of 1792 may not have been a true crash, argues the financial historian Edwin Perkins. "American investors were still getting their feet wet" in the new markets, he claims. "The upswing was too short-lived and the number of issues traded and speculators involved were too few." Rather than a true market collapse, the panic of 1792 was, in Perkins's view, "a justifiable market reversal," a correction rather than a disaster.[38] Philadelphia was among those markets that escaped the collapse. Indeed, to judge from Matthew McConnell's sizable taxable wealth of £1,201 in 1794, the city's brokers appear to have weathered the panic with relatively little trouble.[39]

Nevertheless, the flowering of securities speculation in the early 1790s, like the South Sea Bubble earlier in the century, inspired sharp criticism centered around the beliefs that stock trading added nothing to the national wealth, that speculators were generally dishonest, and that speculation encouraged political corruption. In the summer of 1791, a correspondent of the *Philadelphia General Advertiser* argued that "the obvious tendency of that evil spirit of speculation which has so long raged amongst us . . . is to divert the active capital of our country from its proper channel (the support of commerce and agriculture) to a most pernicious one, that of ministering to the aggrandizement of a host of adventurers."[40] In the midst of the panic of 1792, another correspondent charged that, among all types of business, stock trading encouraged "more numerous instances of fraud and deceit than any other which could possibly be mentioned."[41] A writer in the *National Gazette*, having witnessed William Duer and other public figures pushing up the price of federal bonds and the stock of the national bank, asked, "Can anything be more disgraceful to the councils of a free country, or more loudly call for the indignation of a virtuous people?"[42]

Despite the public outrage at the scourge of securities trading, particularly among farmers and artisans whose livelihoods derived from land and labor, the greatest damage to Philadelphia's economy and its financial markets came not from economics but from epidemiology. The yellow fever outbreak in the summer of 1793 killed about 10 percent of the city's approximately forty thousand inhabitants and left all business at a standstill for one hundred days. Benjamin Rush, the region's leading physician, diagnosed the fever as a distinctly urban problem whose treatment included the ineffective strategies of purging and bleeding, and a more effective retreat to the countryside.

When Rush called for the wholesale abandonment of the city, Matthew McConnell dashed off a cordial but direct letter in response. For the stockbroker, Rush's theory was "a dangerous one to advance if not true considering the consequences that might result therefrom to the city as the seat of the government"—not to mention its commercial and financial losses![43] President Washington and the federal government eventually escaped for the summer to Germantown, outside the city (where they and the city's banks would transfer operations during another outbreak of the disease in

1798). The economic impact of the epidemic of 1793 has been estimated at $2 million, but this figure fails to account for the many ships laden with cargo and correspondence that were diverted from Philadelphia to New York, Baltimore, and other ports.[44]

Growing a Regional Financial Sector

Still, the capital market proved remarkably resilient. Despite panic and epidemic, the city's capitalists used banks, insurance companies, and the securities market to expand their influence in Pennsylvania as well as the nation. Thomas Willing and other locally based directors of the Bank of the United States were intimately involved in the Bank of North America. The two banks dominated the region's financial sector in the 1790s, enjoying considerable profits. Between 1791 and 1800, the Bank of North America paid yearly dividends between 10 percent and 13.5 percent.[45] Its directors advanced $160,000 to the Commonwealth of Pennsylvania in 1792. Two years later, they financed the army of twenty thousand sent against the Whisky Rebellion of farmers and small traders in the western part of the state who mounted an insurrection against taxes, creditors, and agents of inflation.[46]

The same financiers who controlled the Bank of North America founded another vital engine of economic growth when they converted the Universal Tontine Association into the Insurance Company of North America in 1792. With an initial offering of sixty thousand shares at $10 par, this new company was designed to overcome the shortage of capital among individual local underwriters, who previously had struggled to compete for larger contracts with the agents of big London companies. Marketed by Samuel Blodget Jr., and Ebenezer Hazard, its initial subscription attracted immediate attention. In just eleven days, Hazard reported forty thousand shares taken.[47]

With Matthew McConnell a founding director of the Insurance Company of North America, an active secondary market for its stock grew quickly on the Board of Brokers. Board member Andrew Summers specialized in the company's stock, buying or selling more than twelve thousand shares in the late 1790s and early 1800s.[48] The City of Philadelphia, seeking to support regional growth, bought large blocks of the company's stock, presumably on the advice of publicly connected brokers.[49] The board also traded the stock of other insurance companies, including the Mutual Assur-

ance Company and the Philadelphia Contributionship, which wrote the
city's earliest fire insurance policies. Beyond their stock issues, these companies stimulated the region's stock market through their investment in bank
and transportation stock. With its ample capital and access to insider information, the Insurance Company of North America pursued this strategy
aggressively, reaping huge profits and paying dividends between 6 percent
and 15 percent in its first decade.

The three big institutions—the Bank of the United States, the Bank
of North America, and the Insurance Company of North America—made
Pennsylvania's financial sector an oligopoly for a time, limiting access to
capital for entrepreneurs outside the relatively small circle of the institutions' directors.[50] The state legislature responded in 1793 by granting a
twenty-year state charter to the preexisting Bank of Pennsylvania, with a
capital of $2 million. In addition to its headquarters in Philadelphia, the
Bank of Pennsylvania had branches in Lancaster, Pittsburgh, and Easton.
In its new form, the institution became a de facto arm of the state, which
subscribed for fully half of its initial stock offering. Capitalists associated
with the Bank of North America, including Matthew McConnell, bought
up a large proportion of the remaining shares, and the Insurance Company
of North America took on $40,000 of Bank of Pennsylvania stock, continu-
ing to exercise great influence in the market. By charter, however, the legislature had assured itself a $500,000 line of credit at a steady 6 percent
interest, together with the right to appoint six of the bank's thirteen directors. The state made the bank its fiscal agent, assuring a constant stream of
deposits as the proceeds from frontier land sales were transferred from the
state treasury to the bank.[51]

Other state-chartered banks and insurance companies helped grow the
capital market, too. By 1800, a Philadelphia business directory listed
twenty-eight securities brokers in the city—not all of whom were members
of the Board of Brokers[52]—ready to handle the business in stocks. Bank
stocks represented reasonably secure investments, as the relative scarcity of
shares in the 1790s and early 1800s maintained stock prices above par.[53]
Equally important, however, were the shares of companies established to
push back the frontiers of the American economy.

Improving the Republic

The post-revolutionary era witnessed a great land rush west, coupled with
public and private works of transportation and communication aimed at

overcoming geographic isolation and integrating the continent's markets. The expanding investment community eagerly speculated in land and funded the internal "improvements," as they were called—roads, canals, and bridges to connect with the interior. These were the physical manifestations of economic development in the early republic.

Real estate speculation, for Philadelphia's merchants and financiers, enabled the growth of agriculture, extractive industries such as logging and mining, and markets for urban products in the interior. To these ends, William Davidson, Thomas Hale, and Thomas McEuen, members of the Board of Brokers, speculated in land on the northern tier of Pennsylvania with Henry Drinker, Thomas Willing, and others.[54] Brought into the brokers' orbit by internal improvements and financial services—from the credit and currency discounts of banks and brokers to the underwriting services of insurance companies—these markets and resources promised to sustain the economic life of the city and its port.

For the same reasons, the brokers funneled capital into turnpikes and canals. The first battleground for Pennsylvanians was the Susquehanna River, whose waters threatened to drain the trade of the central and western parts of the state to Baltimore. This river "we may properly call our own," Robert Morris told the state legislature in 1791. If "duly improved," it offered access to "such numerous sources and channels of inland trade, all leading to the port of Philadelphia, as perhaps no other nation or sea-port on the whole globe can boast of."[55] The state legislator Albert Gallatin, a member of Morris's Society for Promoting Improvements who would later serve as Jefferson's secretary of the Treasury, pushed this agenda on the floor of the Pennsylvania Assembly in Independence Hall. The Philadelphia *General Advertiser* reported that Gallatin "dwelt on the advantages of connecting the Western and Eastern waters," arguing that improvements "would draw the Western ports to enrich the Eastern" and warning that, unless something were done, "a great deal of the riches . . . would go down the Potowmack." Turnpikes and canals "would naturally draw and encrease population in the improved parts."[56]

By 1792, the commonwealth had appropriated £5,250 for a passage at the falls on the Conowingo River and chartered the Susquehanna Canal Company and the Schuylkill Navigation, which promised to link Philadelphia to the Susquehanna through a continuously navigable waterway. To prevent boats, barges, and goods from passing out of Pennsylvania, the legislature passed a law threatening fines up to $2,000 for clearing obstructions on the lower Susquehanna near the Maryland border. In Philadelphia, the IPO of the Susquehanna Canal Company in 1791 was so oversubscribed that a lottery was necessary to determine who could purchase shares. The following year, the legislature incorporated the Delaware and Schuylkill Canal, an initiative led by Robert Morris, to dig a canal from the Delaware River to Norristown on the Schuylkill, where boats and barges could link up with the canal to the Susquehanna.

The greatest financial success among early American internal improvements was not a grand waterway but a relatively short road. At the urging of the Society for Promoting the Improvement of Roads and Inland Navigation, in 1792 the General Assembly passed an act incorporating the nation's first major private turnpike, the Philadelphia and Lancaster Turnpike Company, with an initial capital of $300,000. Although its progress was impeded by the yellow fever epidemic of 1793, the sixty-two-mile macadam road was finished in 1794 at a cost about $465,000. Serving a heavy traffic between Philadelphia and the core of its agricultural hinterland, the turnpike's tolls made it a great financial success, and other roads were soon linked to it.[57]

To the market for internal improvement stocks, Philadelphia brokers attracted an investing public of considerable size, including prominent institutional investors. The Board of Brokers president Israel Whelen was among the Lancaster Turnpike's foremost promoters and served as the company's first president, aiding the rapid subscription and active secondary trading in its securities. Even much smaller ventures found great favor in the market. The IPO in 1798 of the Schuylkill Permanent Bridge Company, which promised to link the city of Philadelphia with points west, attracted 427 subscribers. Its largest stockholder was the city itself, which took 2,000 shares in exchange for real estate.[58] The city, the legislature—with its charters and appropriations—and private shareholders together organized internal improvements as public-private ventures.

The Limits of Improvement

Yet economic development was a risky investment. Public and private investors in internal improvements and frontier real estate encountered problems of scale and timing. Canal construction stalled as engineers grossly underestimated budgets, while land speculators routinely went bankrupt as booms turned to busts. Just two years into construction, the builders of the Schuylkill-to-Susquehanna canal had spent all of their paid-in capital of $440,000 and had completed only the fifteen easiest miles of their project. Showing that they had not yet learned their lesson, state legislators granted them permission to raise an additional $400,000 through lotteries to complete the more than one hundred miles remaining to go on the route.[59] The only canal completed in Pennsylvania in the 1790s was a shortcut around the Conowingo Rapids on the Susquehanna, which was intended to ease the transport of up-river produce to join the Lancaster Turnpike at Columbia; ultimately, however, it opened a clearer passage to Baltimore. Although their importance for growing and integrating markets was undeniable, the Board of Brokers and other stock markets understandably shied away from grander projects as the eighteenth century waned.

Perhaps the direst exemplar of risky investing—and a dramatic blow to Philadelphia's financial community—was the case of its most public merchant and financier, Robert Morris. As a U.S. senator in the early 1790s, he had chosen to emulate the landed elite of Europe and the South by abandoning his mercantile business in favor of investment in real estate. Buying on credit, he assembled vast tracts in the interior of Pennsylvania and New York, sometimes in collaboration with the likes of Tench Coxe, the merchant Henry Drinker, and the Bank of North America cashier Tench Francis.[60] These men bolstered their investments by lobbying for favorable land policy and internal improvements.

But in 1798, Morris's debts were called in, and he was caught short. Unable to pay up, he landed in debtor's prison, causing a minor national banking panic in the process. He was liberated from the Walnut Street Prison—across the street from the Statehouse yard—by the national bankruptcy law of 1802. But his fall from financial, social, and political prominence represented a source of embarrassment for Philadelphia capitalists as well as a sober warning about the precarious nature of speculation.[61]

Losing Political Capital, Building New Connections

Morris's failure was compounded by the city's loss of not one but two government capitals. First, in 1799, Pennsylvania's governor and legislature left Philadelphia for Lancaster (only to relocate later to Harrisburg). This move was part of the "Jeffersonian revolution," in which the nation's rural majority took back the presidency from the urban minority represented by John Adams and removed state capitals from the leading coastal cities to places like Springfield, Massachusetts, and Albany, New York. A year later came the expected but still highly controversial transfer of Congress, the president, and the nation's tiny federal bureaucracy to a village with a handful of majestic classical buildings under construction on the swampy banks of the Potomac River.

Although the Bank of the United States, the U.S. Mint, and a relatively robust community of bankers and brokers remained in Philadelphia, the city and its collective ego reeled from these departures. Meanwhile, New York threatened to surpass the Delaware River port in its volume of shipping. Its geography gave it a leg up when it came to overseas trading, with its vast harbor a week closer to Europe than Philadelphia. Competition with New York and the lowly District of Columbia so consumed Philadelphians that they defined their city in its terms. A city directory of 1804 introduced it as "the Chief City of the United States, in point of size and splendour," lamenting, however, that "it now fills but the second rank in respect to commercial importance" and "it must also yield metropolitan precedence to the doubtful policy of *a seat of government, far removed from the chief resort of wealth and population.*"[62]

The region's capitalists responded with two staples of metropolitan economic development—marketing the city and connecting it to networks of information. They engaged the artist William Birch to depict Philadelphia as a vibrant economic center. His book, funded by the subscription of merchants, included colorful images of the city's bustling port, markets, genteel residential streets, public and civic architecture, and the Bank of the United States and the Bank of Pennsylvania. One cautionary plate depicted Robert Morris's unfinished mansion, a reminder of the perils of risk. Birch wrote in his autobiography, "no other work of the kind had ever been published by which an idea of the early improvements of the country could be conveyed to Europe, to promote and encourage settlers to the establishment of trade and commerce which in its early progress when the restless minds of those with capital expected nothing but a Forest. . . ."[63]

Philadelphia brokers also created the nation's first information superhighway. Once the federal government had gone from the city, Philadelphia lost its status as the "fountain head," as Matthew McConnell had put it, of economic information emanating directly from the federal government. It also thereby lost one of its key competitive advantages over the New York stock market. The rapid transfer of information, then as now, was of particular importance to financiers, who depended on current and reliable news for the security of their investments, and who profited or perished from getting information sooner or later than someone else, or from getting it more or less accurately than someone else. Philadelphia brokers had been able to counter New York's position as the first and primary port of call for the majority of ships from Europe—loaded with information—with their greater access to information from Congress and the Treasury Department. But when the federal government departed they became more vulnerable to marauding traders.

Indeed, New York brokers who learned news of commodity and security prices just off ships from London or the Netherlands began hopping on stagecoaches across New Jersey and undercutting the Philadelphia market, taking advantage of what economists call asymmetries of information. In response, members of the Philadelphia Board of Brokers developed a private system of rapid communication between Second Street and Manhattan. They erected towers atop hills across New Jersey, from which men flashed signals using mirrors by day and torches at night. Watching each other with telescopes, these optical telegraph (or heliograph) operators relayed news of stock prices, ship cargoes, lottery numbers, and other information between the nation's two principal markets—reportedly in as little as ten minutes.[64] The nation's first information superhighway allowed brokers, bankers, and merchants in Philadelphia to anticipate the arrival of ships, and to head off any stagecoach passengers peddling fishy trades. They could thus set prices and rates on commodities, currency discounts, marine insurance, and securities to more accurately reflect and respond to activity on other markets, most importantly in New York and London.

The optical telegraph positioned the Philadelphia Board of Brokers as a central node in interregional communications. The speed of this system was remarkable, considering that as late as 1840 it still took an entire week for market information from New Orleans to reach Philadelphia and New York. Its reliability was also noteworthy in an era when passenger pigeons were the only other mode by which sensitive financial information could be communicated rapidly over long distances. (Even in 1850, for example, Paul Julius Reuter still employed carrier pigeons to relay stock quotes from Brussels to Aachen, Germany, while D. H. Craig used the same method to inform Boston brokers of ships and cargoes landing at Halifax, Nova Scotia.)[65] Protective and informative, the Philadelphia–New York heliograph system also came in time to facilitate a wave of new stock issues and financial products that expanded markets both numerically and spatially in the early nineteenth century.

New Institutions and Products

The "Jeffersonian revolution" not only redrew the nation's political map; it also transformed its economy—and in the process helped grow Philadelphia's stock market even more. At the federal level, the Louisiana Purchase created vast new tradable debt, although the market for these securities was initially concentrated in Europe as Napoleon took U.S. bonds in payment to finance his military campaigns. In addition, the opening of the Mississippi Valley to wheat farmers and cotton plantations further spurred migration and transportation projects to settle, improve, and incorporate the new territory into the national economy.

At the regional level, Jeffersonian Democrats spurred a proliferation of state-chartered banks designed to undercut the monopolies of Federalist-allied banks. The move was political as well as financial. Since about 85 percent of the stock of the Bank of the United States was held in England, it was widely suspected of favoring foreign interests—and it certainly supported urban enterprise over rural interests. Similarly, the Banks of North America and Pennsylvania followed insider lending practices that favored overseas shippers rather than local tradesmen.[66] (Even had they wished to offer loans more broadly, they could never have met the enormous demand for short-term credit in a city growing about 40 percent per decade between 1790 and 1820.)[67] To Jeffersonians, these institutions were instruments of political oppression that favored the merchant and financier classes while withholding access to capital from the likes of farmers.

Rather than revolt against the banks, Pennsylvanians tackled the problem of access to capital by chartering new banks oriented toward underserved markets. In 1803, the merchant John Welsh, in collaboration with George Clymer and Mayor Matthew Lawler, organized the Philadelphia Bank, with subscriptions payable at the Exchange Coffee House and a capital of $100,000. The city's established banks opposed this newcomer, and the Bank of Pennsylvania made an overture to the legislature in an attempt to maintain its oligopoly. In return for a payment of $200,000 to the state and other financial concessions, the directors of the Bank of Pennsylvania asked the legislature for an extension of their charter to 1834 with a monopoly clause to prevent the chartering of any other banks in the commonwealth until that date.[68]

The directors of the Philadelphia Bank, however, countered with more favorable incorporation plans, granting the state a "gratuity" of $135,000 and taking $300,000 of the state's 6 percent U.S. bonds at par value in exchange for shares of its much more liquid stock. (The new bank ultimately took a $10,000 loss on this transaction, as the U.S. bonds were selling below par.)[69] The Philadelphia Bank soon boasted over six hundred individual stockholders, including many women and at least one free African American, as well as businesses, governments, and charitable societies.[70] By early nineteenth-century standards, this was a broad market.

The Jeffersonian banks enjoyed wide impacts through connections to both the public sector and the borrowing and investing public. By 1813, the commonwealth would derive a significant proportion of its annual budget from dividends on shares valued at $1.5 million in the Bank of Pennsylvania, $523,000 in the Philadelphia Bank, and $85,400 in the Farmers' and Mechanics' Bank. The charter of this last institution, granted in 1809, stipulated that farmers, mechanics, and manufacturers must make up a majority of its thirteen directors, and that the bank must lend at least 10 percent of its capital to farmers on long-term mortgages at an annual interest rate of 6 percent.[71] The Bank of Germantown, chartered in 1813, boasted a diverse group of customers: "Germantown shoemakers, Philadelphia chairmakers, Roxborough tailors, Chestnut Hill farmers, Manayunk gluemakers, paper manufacturers, stonecutters, and a host of retailers from the Northern Liberties and other north Philadelphia districts, received discounts from the institution," according to the financial historian Robert Wright.[72]

Philadelphia's insurance sector also expanded its ranks and its capital in the early nineteenth century, and this expansion was likewise felt in the stock market. In 1800, the Mutual Assurance Company introduced a new product, a perpetual policy with a single prepaid premium. Although the initial outlay was substantial, policyholders avoided annual payments and their premiums swelled the company's reserve fund, facilitating the growth of its investment portfolio. The first venture established specifically to underwrite life insurance policies, the Pennsylvania Company for Insurance on Lives and Granting Annuities grew out of a meeting at the Exchange Coffee House in December 1809.[73] Its initial offering of $500,000 in stock at $100 par was heavily oversubscribed within a month. Since policy sales were comparatively slow, the company functioned primarily as an investment club for its shareholders, and it joined other insurance concerns in swelling the supply of floating capital on the Board of Brokers.[74]

The Insurance Company of North America remained the dominant concern in its sector, driving the development of an "Insurance Row."

Located on Walnut Street in the block west of Front Street, this new district was strategically positioned between the industry's financial backers in the banks and brokerage houses of Second Street and the shipping offices, wharves, and portside warehouses of its principal clientele. In 1808, the Insurance Company of North America bought its fifth property on the block, portions of which were rented to the Delaware Insurance Company and to a young attorney by the name of Nicholas Biddle.[75] Other neighbors engaged in marine underwriting included the recently established Insurance Company of Pennsylvania and the Union, Phoenix, Marine, and United States Insurance Companies.

Whatever their political intentions, the region's new banks and insurance companies helped grow its stock market with new securities issues, new investors, and the occasional new product. Andrew Summers, a member of the Board of Brokers, saw his business grow in 1806–7 when he traded close to $900,000 in insurance, bank, and transportation stocks, as well as three forms of government debt. This was a significant increase over the $510,000 Summers handled between 1798 and 1806, which had earned him only about $1,300 in commissions. In 1809 alone, the board's largest brokerage house, that of Clement Biddle and Company, handled more than $1.3 million in securities.[76]

Even as their regional market expanded, however, Philadelphia capitalists faced new and daunting challenges from Washington and New York. The Jeffersonian revolution enabled state-chartered banks to blossom, but it challenged the authority and the charter of the Bank of the United States and its Quaker City directors. At the same time, the winds of global trade began to blow away from the Delaware River port, undermining its hold on American commerce. With the city's position as the nation's financial capital under fire, the Board of Brokers took on an even more significant role in promoting and underwriting economic development.

3

Trade Wars and Bank Wars:
The Board of Brokers in the Early Republic

Lewis and Clark's Corps of Discovery was initiated and financed by the federal government in Washington, but in practical terms it was launched from Philadelphia. Lacking a scientific community or a manufacturing sector in the District of Columbia, Thomas Jefferson sent Meriwether Lewis to the Quaker City to prepare for the expedition. At the American Philosophical Society and the Pennsylvania Hospital, the city's intelligentsia taught him the basics of botany, navigation, and emergency medicine. Between lessons, Lewis walked up and down Philadelphia's commercial thoroughfares with Israel Whelen, the president of the Board of Brokers and the federal purveyor of public supplies (Figure 13).

Whelen and Lewis visited dozens of workshops and stores, spending over $2,000 for some 3,500 pounds of provisions and equipment. Their purchases included 500 brooches and 72 rings, vermillion, red lead, ribbon, beads, and bells to use as gifts for Indians. They bought medical supplies, compasses and a gold chronometer, 130 rolls of pigtail tobacco, 30 gallons of Strong Spirit Wine, and 193 pounds of dried soup. Only in Philadelphia could they find an urban economy and institutions so diverse and advanced to prepare Lewis for his journey.[1]

For Israel Whelen, this shopping spree signified far more than the simple execution of his federal duties. For Philadelphia capitalists and scientists, Lewis and Clark's expedition promised to push back the frontiers of knowledge and trade. The Board of Brokers, ever more concerned with internal improvements, would have a literal map on which to chart the expansion of markets in the interior. The plant and animal species, Indian

ISRAEL WHELEN,

BORN DECEMBER 13, 1752.

DIED OCTOBER 21, 1806.

FROM THE ORIGINAL PICTURE BY

SHARPLESS ABOUT 1798.

Figure 13. Portrait of Israel Whelen. From Philadelphia Stock Exchange, *Souvenir History, Album of Members, Gallery of Men of Affairs* (Philadelphia: Philadelphia Stock Exchange, 1903). Like other early members of the Board of Brokers, Israel Whelen played multiple roles in public and private institutions of economic development at the local and national levels.

objects, and maps and notes from the Corps of Discovery would be brought back to Philadelphia at the end of the trip. Local museums still house these artifacts.

Just as Philadelphia merchants viewed the War of Independence as a commercial revolution, for Whelen and fellow brokers Lewis and Clark's journey was about economic development. Before, during, and after the voyage, they poured vast sums of capital into turnpikes, canals, and banks that reached westward. Despite this investment, the Board of Brokers and fellow Philadelphia capitalists lost the race to dominate the markets and resources of the interior. Instead, New York would reap most of the economic benefits of the nineteenth-century American West. This was partly a result of geography, as western Pennsylvania's mountains proved much harder to cross than the route west through New York.

The simple story about Philadelphia in the early republic is that it lost the political capital to Washington, the Erie Canal confirmed New York as the nation's commercial capital, and the loss of the Bank of the United States ended its tenuous position as the financial capital. Yet this is reading history backward, from the perspective of the winners. When reading it forward, taking seriously the initiatives of Philadelphia capitalists, a more complicated, contested story emerges.

The Board of Brokers and its members played vital roles in shaping the economic geography of early nineteenth-century America. As they had in the 1790s, they helped define what it meant to institutionalize the financial sector. This became especially significant as Jefferson closed the national bank in 1811 and then, after its subsequent restoration, Andrew Jackson killed it in 1836. This left nominally private institutions like stock exchanges a greater responsibility to regulate the American economy. In this era of bank wars, trade wars, financial panics, and exuberant westward expansion, the struggles of the Board of Brokers and fellow Philadelphia capitalists reveal much about the underlying issues at stake in the nation's early economic development. As the institutional landscape of federal and local finance remained fluid and contested, the board and fellow capitalists sought to reassert their position in the young republic and its markets.

Jefferson's Revenge, Girard's Bank

The demise of the Bank of the United States had been a long-held goal of Thomas Jefferson. He had consistently opposed not just the concept of the bank itself but also its founder, Alexander Hamilton, whom he accused of being unable "to give a clear view of the excesses of our debts beyond our credits, nor whether we were diminishing or increasing the debt."[2] A Jeffersonian Congress decisively defeated the bank charter's renewal in 1809, and the charter officially came to an end in 1811—a blow to Philadelphia's influence over the country's currency and long-distance money flows. All that was left was the building on Third Street and the bank's considerable resources, which now had seemingly nowhere to go and certainly no authority to operate.

Into this organizational vacuum stepped Philadelphia's wealthiest citizen, the shipping merchant Stephen Girard, the nation's first millionaire. Between 1808 and 1811, he had been forced to repatriate his assets in the midst of Jefferson's embargo against Britain and the intensification of the Napoleonic wars. Girard did this by converting the large balance he held with his London correspondent, the house of Barings Brothers, into $1.8 million worth of stock in the Bank of the United States. He then purchased the building on Third Street and the adjacent cashier's house from the government for about one-third of their original cost. In May 1812, he reopened the building as his own private bank and counting house. This allowed Girard to capitalize his shareholdings at par, while at the same time he continued to collect dividends and earn interest and discount fees from his own bank.[3]

Though never a member of the Board of Brokers, Girard profoundly influenced the context of its market, helping to keep the city's economy liquid. Starting with capital of $1.2 million, his bank embarked on a series of initiatives that would stabilize the Philadelphia region's financial sector and its place in the nation's financial system. To begin, Girard retained the officers and clerks of the Bank of the United States at their old salaries and held onto most of the old bank's customers. The new bank also handled all of the old trustees' financial affairs, including $5 million in specie. It continued to perform a central reserve function for rural banks like the Farmers' Banks of Lancaster and of Reading. All these rural banks had to do was keep an account at Girard, and it would cash or deposit the banks' promissory notes so that they could retain their par value in the city.[4] On the strength of Stephen Girard's shipping connections, the bank also gained a large share of the business of the U.S. Customs House.[5] Finally, Girard joined with New Yorkers John Jacob Astor and David Parish in forming the first true investment syndicate in the United States, which controlled much of the federal finances by pooling purchases and subcontracting sales of government bonds. Many of these securities would be exchanged on the Board of Brokers, as federal debt continued to comprise a large portion of its market.

The Girard-Astor partnership proved particularly important when the government in Washington, now lacking a national bank, found itself incapable of financing the War of 1812. The Bank of North America and other institutions aided in the subscription of $17 million in Treasury notes and $63 million in government bonds to pay for the war. But the financial crisis brought on by Jefferson's and Madison's foreign policies ultimately caused the banks to suspend specie payments.[6] Teaming with Astor, Girard intervened to buy $10 million of the federal loans and sustain the war effort. Ironically, the two financiers occupied the role that the Bank of the United States, in whose former home the Girard Bank resided, would have served had its charter been renewed.[7]

Brokering the Republic

The demise of the Bank of the United States presented other opportunities for Philadelphia's stock traders. For one thing, all of the members of Philadelphia's Board of Brokers benefited handsomely from a regional banking boom in the wake of the national bank's closure. In 1814 alone, the Pennsylvania legislature authorized the creation of forty-one new banks—thirty-seven of which actually opened—with an aggregate capital of $17 million.[8] Their stock traded on the board, expanding its market considerably. As these smaller regional banks as well as behemoths like Girard's took on many of the banking functions abdicated by Washington, brokers and stock exchanges took on other key tasks of managing the nation's financial sector.

One thing that made cities the command and control centers of the nineteenth-century economy was the way in which stock exchanges and other urban financial institutions regulated their own markets—and by extension the capital underwriting economic development. Although state and local governments regulated a wide variety of economic activities, the economy of the United States was still young and rather unstable. In a specie-poor environment, financial transactions of all sorts were based on trust, almost always executed with pieces of paper (IOUs).

Part of the Board of Brokers' significance lay in the regularity and security it could offer investors. Its members met from noon to two in the afternoon and from six to eight in the evening. To boost trading volume and prevent outside attempts to undercut the market, the board kept its doors closed, and all members were required to be present unless ill health or out-of-town business kept them away.

The power these attributes brought to the board's ability for market making was felt well beyond Philadelphia. Brokers in New York soon recognized the advantages of this system, especially when their own less regulated organization fell into crisis in 1817. The New York Board of Brokers voted to send a committee headed by William Lamb to Philadelphia to learn about its exchange; the initiative was urgent enough that Lamb deferred his honeymoon to make the trip. Upon his return, the New York board copied Philadelphia's rules on membership, commissions, and closed trading in a room at 40 Wall Street.[9] Clearly, there was benefit to be gained in self-regulation, and member firms and their clients felt a distinct advantage over non-member brokers and their customers.

The case of one Philadelphia investor and her broker, gleaned from a court case, reveals the extent to which this self-regulation mattered to investors. In 1825, one George Tyson, a broker who was *not* a member of the board, called on a widow named Mary Stewart, and "in the course of conversation she mentioned that she had about a thousand dollars, which she should like to invest if she could do it advantageously." The widow Stewart had dealt with Tyson before, yet when he recommended bank stock, she at first objected, "as the late difficulties in the Bank of Northern Liberties," a small local concern, "had made her timid." Tyson left, then returned an hour later, saying, "there was a gentleman at the Coffee House, who had twenty shares of Commercial Bank Stock, which he was willing to part with, and advis[ed] her by all means to purchase them." The widow asked her broker to sit down, but he "said he could not stay, as the gentleman was waiting to receive an answer. After some hesitation, she handed him her check-book and he filled up a check for 1022 dollars 55 cents, the price of the stock, and his own commission, payable to himself or bearer." In return, "Tyson gave her a bill of stock purchased by him for her, and left her, saying he would come the next day with the certificate."

When two or three days passed "without his appearing, Mrs. Stewart called upon him to ascertain the cause of his delay. He evaded her inquiries." Ultimately, the widow learned that Tyson had made no transfer but "had drawn the check, deposited the money in his own name at the Bank of Pennsylvania, and afterwards drawn out the greater part of it, at various times, for his own use." In his subsequent trial, Tyson was duly convicted and quickly imprisoned for what legal minds of the day termed "constructive larceny."[10]

Constructive or not, Tyson's ability to so easily perpetrate this crime upon an investor raised a broader point about the structure of the market— namely, that outside the Board of Brokers, there were no institutional mechanisms that could effectively police trading activities. The converse was equally true: had Mary Stewart conducted her business with a board member, she would have been assured of at least standardized commission rates and the recording of all transactions on paper in a closed and closely monitored forum.

Partly because of this security, some non-member brokerage firms in Philadelphia made extensive use of member firms' services. Alexander Lardner, for example, who invested in securities on behalf of family members as well as other clients, contracted with Thomas Biddle and Company in amassing holdings in concerns including the Schuylkill Navigation, Pennsylvania Insurance Company, Pottsville Bank, Commercial Bank, Philadelphia Bank, Farmers' and Mechanics' Bank, Bank of North America, Bank of the United States, Union Canal, and New Orleans Canal and Bank Company[11]—a sizable portfolio. In addition to these clients, the Board of Brokers itself became an investing club of sorts. While most of its revenues went toward paying rent and other expenses at the Exchange Coffee House, a portion of its membership fees was invested in securities on behalf of the association.

Security and liquidity weren't the only advantages of self-regulation. The Board of Brokers soon found that so long as it regulated itself, it was shielded from much of the state regulation that accompanied incorporation. It remained a licensed but unincorporated—and relatively small— association of traders.[12] This contrasted starkly with the London Stock Exchange, where until 1870 the City of London set policies, managed the inclusion of new members, and policed trading activity[13]—all of which mitigated risk and attracted great numbers of traders.[14] Membership in the Philadelphia and New York boards, however, hovered around twenty individuals and firms for most of the early national period.[15]

Virtually all of the hundreds of stock exchanges founded in nineteenth-century North America followed the organizational model of the Philadelphia board. From Baltimore to Toronto to Los Angeles, exchanges remained private, unincorporated associations that wrote their own rules.

Most, including Philadelphia and New York, admitted new members by both election among the membership and the purchase of existing seats on the board.

By January 1818, the Philadelphia board had a roster of eighteen members: Nicholas Arnous, William J. Bell, Thomas Biddle, William Davidson, Thomas Greeves, Thomas Hale, Thomas McEuen, Richard Hill Morris, the board president James Musgrave, Samuel and James Nevins, Mark Prager, Andrew M. Prevost—a lieutenant colonel in the War of 1812—George Rundle, George Taylor Jr., William M. Walmsley, John Wharton, and Brittain White. While the new names indicate a considerable amount of turnover, the presence of Arnous, Greeves, Morris, Prager, Taylor, McEuen—a founding member—and Musgrave, who remained the organization's president for most of the 1810s and 1820s, represented a strong measure of continuity.[16]

There was also continuity of a sort in the generational succession at the brokerage houses of Thomas Biddle and John Wharton, who took over their fathers' posts on the board, and who often traded together. Indeed, Biddle, Wharton and Company was the largest brokerage house in Philadelphia, trading 72,534 corporate shares worth more than $5.2 million as well as $5.4 million in government debt in 1817.[17] That banner year saw not only a boost in internal improvements investment in response to the Erie Canal, but also the return of the national bank.

The Second Bank of the United States

The federal government's inability to capitalize the War of 1812 was enough to convince Congress and President Madison to charter the second Bank of the United States in April 1816. Organized by the Philadelphian Alexander J. Dallas, then secretary of the Treasury, the second bank echoed the first in its operation. Three-fifths of the bank's capital would be privately held, with the remainder allocated to the federal government. Its twenty-year charter would expire in March 1836 unless renewed.[18]

When stock in the second Bank of the United States was offered for sale beginning in July 1816, the Girard Bank on Third Street served as the central locus for the subscription. It was no accident that the Quaker City was again the headquarters of the national bank, directing the flow of capital among branches in other urban centers. After all, Pennsylvanians dominated the Treasury Department throughout the early nineteenth century.

Almost from the beginning, the Board of Brokers enjoyed close ties with the second bank, although the consequences were not always fortuitous. The bank found little early success—thanks both to poor management and to the panic of 1819. Principally a result of an unfavorable balance of trade with Great Britain, as well as inflationary credit policies that led to rampant land speculation, the panic was exacerbated by overspeculation in the bank's stock. In August 1818, when the bank moved to curb inflation through a policy of note contraction, calling on the state banks to redeem weighty balances owed to its branches, it virtually ensured a general panic. By the following year, some twenty thousand Philadelphians were reportedly out of work, out of a total labor force of sixty-four thousand.[19] Although the economy recovered in 1821, many state banks and businesses blamed the national bank's policy for their failure. State legislatures in Maryland and Tennessee even began imposing taxes on the Bank of the United States.

While the bank itself lost considerable sums in the panic, land foreclosures in the West sowed the seeds of its renewal, as it seized a vast amount of real estate in frontier states in liquidation of its debts at a time when land values had hit rock bottom. When the panic ended and real estate values rose sharply, the bank sold high and recouped its losses. It made many enemies in the process.[20]

Following the panic, the next two bank presidents, Langdon Cheves (1819–23) and Nicholas Biddle (1823–36), tightened the institution's lending practices, protecting the capital markets and strengthening the U.S. dollar. Their conservative fiscal policies also made the bank's stock a sound investment.[21] Both men had strong ties to the Board of Brokers. Cheves had served with Israel Whelen as a customs collector in the port of Philadelphia, while Biddle was the first cousin of board member Thomas Biddle. These relationships again gave the board prime access to the nation's central bank and monetary policy.[22]

In 1824, the bank proclaimed its strength and soundness when it opened its second headquarters, in the form of a Greek temple, on Chestnut Street. Not far away were the offices and warehouses of the U.S. Customs department and the U.S. Mint—all signaling the city's continued role as the financial capital of the republic.[23] Linked to these institutions by ties of business, family, and self-interest, Philadelphia's brokers rekindled their national aspirations down the street at their coffee house exchange.

The Urgency of Improvement

With opportunities presented by the return of the bank, and challenges posed by New York's Erie Canal, Philadelphians gained renewed interest in internal improvements. At the federal level, Secretary of War John C. Calhoun had established the Board of Engineers for Internal Improvements and had prioritized a long list of proposals according to their commercial, military, and postal utility. In a careful effort to boost his presidential prospects, Calhoun designated projects in every state, raising hopes throughout the nation and fueling interest in canal stocks at an otherwise low point for the market.[24]

In Pennsylvania, the legislature issued a flood of new charters for works that promised private profit and public utility. By 1837, it had chartered 261 turnpikes, 103 bridges, 23 canals, 27 other transportation companies, 19 water companies, and 89 railroads—all incorporated after 1825—in addition to 85 banks and 41 insurance companies.[25]

These charters reflected the new sense of urgency Philadelphians felt as the race for interior trade heated up, with Pennsylvania vying against both nearby Maryland and distant New York. Maryland's Susquehanna or Tide Water Canal was draining Pennsylvania exports through Baltimore. Meanwhile, the Delaware and Hudson Canal across New Jersey, financed by New York investors, threatened to carry off the agricultural products, timber, and coal in the eastern part of the state.

Indeed, New York seemed well poised to capture inland markets and resources at the expense of Philadelphia. The city on the Hudson had decisively surpassed its rival on the Delaware as the nation's foremost port in the wake of the War of 1812, when British manufacturers dumped surpluses of textiles on the New York market. Aided by liberal New York State auction legislation in 1817, New York City became a haven for commodities traders who had previously dealt in Philadelphia or Boston. Also in 1817, the state legislature funded the Erie Canal, and New York merchants launched a line of packet ships between Britain and the United States, replacing old seasonal sailing patterns with year-round commercial service. A group of Philadelphians headed by the merchant Thomas Pym Cope responded with their own transatlantic line in 1821, and another syndicate soon established a coastal packet for trade with the South.[26] But by 1825 the Erie Canal linked the Hudson River to Lake Erie at Buffalo. Philadelphians realized that their city was still far behind in the race for markets and resources in the Great Lakes—including northwestern Pennsylvania—and in the Ohio and upper Mississippi Valleys, where farms and cities were springing up like mushrooms.

The political economist Matthew Carey took the lead in articulating a way to counter New York's advantage, reigniting the passion of Philadelphia for canals above all. His campaign in 1821 to revive the Chesapeake and Delaware Canal aimed to recapture the produce of the Susquehanna Valley from Baltimore. But his major thrust, starting in 1824, was his call for a canal from Philadelphia all the way to Pittsburgh, where the Ohio River offered access to the Mississippi.

Writing under the pseudonym "Fulton"—an allusion to Robert Fulton, who left Pennsylvania to pioneer steamboat service in New York harbor—Carey stressed the urgent need for a route across the Appalachians. He presented statistics illustrating New York's commercial growth and claiming a 40 percent decline in Pennsylvania exports since 1817. In newspapers and before the legislature, Carey insisted that the investment required for a project of this magnitude could not be "undertaken or completed by private subscription. It must be executed by the state, as the Erie and Champlain canals have been."[27] At the same time, the Society for the Promotion of Internal Improvement and the newly formed Franklin Institute for the Promotion of the Mechanic Arts sent the architect William Strickland, the designer of the Second Bank, to England to study the civil and mechanical engineering of canals and railways.[28]

A spate of canals built during the 1820s sought to connect eastern and western waterways (Figure 14). Though most failed from the outset or gave way to rail transportation, their construction brought on a torrent of state debt financing. By 1838, Pennsylvania was home to 789 miles of completed canals, with another 134 miles under construction.[29] Their routes and subcontracts did engage many rural communities in economic development projects, strengthening their connections to the metropolitan center of Philadelphia.[30] Nearly all were backed by corporate stock and state bonds that made up a significant portion of the Board of Brokers' market.

Other concerns traded on the board likewise invested in frontier expansion and improvements. By 1829, the Bank of Pennsylvania held $1.76 million in 5-percent state bonds tied to public works, $8,557 in Conestoga Turnpike and Navigation stock, and outstanding loans to the Union Canal, Schuylkill Navigation, and Delaware and Chesapeake Canal companies.[31] The Insurance Company of North America not only bought canal stock; it

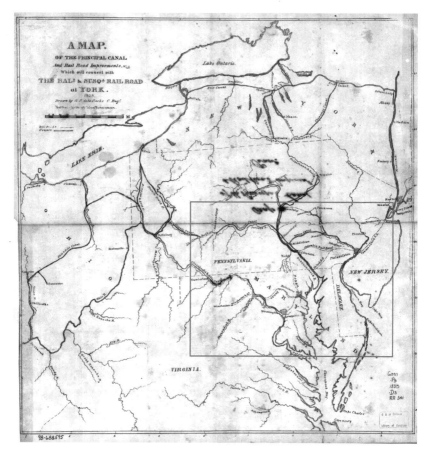

Figure 14. *A Map of the Principal Canal and Rail Road Improvments [sic], Which Will Connect with the Baltimore & Susquehanna Rail Road at York*, 1825, drawn by G. F. de la Roche. Library of Congress, Geography and Map Division. The Erie Canal (top) offered New Yorkers far more direct access to the West than did the relatively convoluted routes of canal systems from Philadelphia and Baltimore.

was also the first to offer fire insurance to frontier settlers. For the company's directors, this was their contribution to "the westward march of empire."[32] For the Board of Brokers, underwriting development that extended Philadelphia's economic reach simultaneously helped grow the stock market and reinforce its competitive position on the nation's financial landscape.

The diversification of the market proved key to the board's growth. In the early 1790s, it had been dominated by just a handful of securities: stock in the Bank of the United States, the Bank of North America, the Insurance Company of North America, and Lancaster Turnpike, as well as U.S. debt. By 1834, the city's financial papers quoted prices on seventy-five securities, including the stock of twenty-eight banks, fifteen insurance companies, twenty transportation concerns, and about twenty-four issues of state and federal debt. Insurance company stocks made up just 2.5 percent of the total value of securities traded on the Board of Brokers, while more than 20 percent of the capital on the board was in canal and early railroad securities. Another 20 percent was in bonds tied to public debt. Bank stocks accounted for the remaining 55 percent, with about 40 percent of this capital in the equities of Delaware Valley banks. Another 40 percent was stock in banks in such places as Pittsburgh, Kentucky, Cincinnati, and New Orleans. And the remaining 20 percent was in shares of the second Bank of the United States.[33]

Philadelphia banks, insurance companies, and their allies on the Board of Brokers succeeded in concentrating investment and banking capital in the city. In 1830, more than one-third of the state's thirty-three banks were headquartered in the city and held $11,233,430 of the state's total banking capital of $14,609,963.[34] While the banks of New York held $20.1 million, the main branch of the Bank of the United States, located in Philadelphia, boosted Pennsylvania's total and made the total banking capital in the two states essentially even. But banks and stock exchanges were just two among many forums designed to foster exchange in the early republic.

A Community of Exchange

The early years of the nation witnessed the flowering of an American culture with foundations in numerical knowledge and active urban institutions. Traveling through the principal market centers of the United States at the close of the 1820s, the Englishman Thomas Hamilton encountered what he labeled a "guessing, reckoning, expecting and calculating people."[35] Public and private societies abounded for the exchange of information, ideas, commodities, and financial capital. In addition to the Board of Brokers, Philadelphia was home to lobbying groups promoting internal improvements, scientific and engineering institutes devising new machines and products, and a variety of merchants' associations that organized trad-

Table 1. Exchanges and Economic Associations in Nineteenth-Century Philadelphia: A Selected List

Regional Associations	Master Builders' Exchange
Board of Brokers	Oil Trade Association
Chamber of Commerce	Paint Club
Coal Exchange	Produce Exchange
Commercial Exchange (founded as	Quaker City Association (leather
the Corn Exchange in 1855)	manufacturers)
Drug Exchange	Shoe and Leather Exchange
Fire Underwriters' Association	Trades League
Green Room Association (mercantile	
traders)	*National Associations*
Grocers' and Importers' Exchange	Association of the Electrical Trades
Hardware Merchants' Exchange	Book Trade Association
Lumbermen's Exchange	Brick Manufacturers' Association
Manufacturers and Dealers in	Manufacturers' Club
Plumbers' Supplies Association	National Association of
Maritime Exchange	Manufacturers

Source: John R. Dos Passos, *A Treatise on the Law of Stock-Brokers and Stock-Exchanges* (New York: Banks Law Publishing Co., 1905), 16–17.

ing in particular sectors. The board's neighbors in the adjacent private room at the Exchange Coffee House, for example, were the maritime agents of the Green Room Association, a name derived from the color of the walls in their quarters.[36] Local capitalists founded regional and national associations across the nineteenth century (see Table 1).

It had long been common practice for associations of merchants and brokers to meet in coffee houses, private offices, even homes. (The one exception had been the monumental Charleston Exchange, opened in 1771.) But by the late eighteenth century and the early nineteenth, the idea of designated exchange buildings had begun to catch on among businessmen in Philadelphia and other market centers. In the 1790s, in fact, Benjamin Henry Latrobe had prepared designs for a Philadelphia Exchange to stand directly across from his Bank of Pennsylvania building on Second Street. Sketches in the architect's notebooks show an immense structure with a classical colonnade opening into an enclosed but exterior court or "open exchange." The facility was to have contained coffee houses, insurance offices, auction rooms, and a customs house[37]—but Latrobe's proposal found no takers.[38]

Baltimore completed a grand exchange building, designed by Latrobe, in 1820, and this prompted businessmen in Philadelphia to form the Chamber of Commerce the following year.[39] When the young chamber was rebuffed in its attempt to purchase the Exchange Coffee House from its private owners, it invited local architects to submit proposals for a new building meant to house the Board of Brokers and other mercantile associations, commercial offices, and the post office.[40] William Strickland responded with a design that resembled the old plan of his mentor, Latrobe. This plan likewise languished, despite attempts by Thomas Biddle and other members of the chamber to revive it through meetings at the Exchange Coffee House throughout 1826 and 1827.[41]

A Home of Their Own

In 1831, however, Stephen Girard managed to pull Philadelphia's capitalists together to form the Philadelphia Merchants Exchange Company, with the sole purpose of building a central exchange (Figure 15). A broadside for fundraising purposes was published in the *Philadelphia Mercury*, emphasizing the value of the location at the intersection of Third, Walnut, and Dock Streets, between the Exchange Coffee House and the Girard Bank. The building, the broadside claimed, could house activity on all three sides, as it was "surrounded by spacious streets." It would be "contiguous to all the city Banks, in the immediate neighborhood of the Insurance Companies and the Custom House, and quite in the center of the commercial interests of the city."[42] As the Merchants Exchange Company was forming, new elite housing with marble steps and columns was under construction in the blocks to the west. These would be the residences of a growing community of brokers, bankers, and merchants, who in this era still lived within walking distance of their offices.

With a total cost estimated at $175,000, the Merchants Exchange Company "confidently believed that on this expenditure, allowing a reasonable sum for the rent of the Exchange, an income of six percent will accrue to the stockholders—certainly not less than five per cent." To raise this sum, the company proposed an issue of 1,750 shares at one hundred dollars each.[43] Some subscribers agreed to pay extra. The Philadelphia Contributionship insurance company, for example, took five shares at five hundred dollars apiece.[44]

Although Strickland was not guaranteed the architectural commission,

Figure 15. Statue of Stephen Girard in front of Founders Hall at Girard College. Photograph by Ashley J. Hahn, 2008. The school Girard established through his will, with a budget of $2 million ($50 million in 2007 dollars) for construction under the supervision of Nicholas Biddle, was the second most expensive building in America when it opened in 1847.

he took the risk of publicly exhibiting a new design to boost interest and investment in the project. It attracted enough attention that by the late fall of 1831, a board of managers had been established to oversee an architectural competition. Nine plans were submitted, and it began to look as if Strickland might lose his bet. But in one of the last acts of his life, Stephen Girard awarded Strickland the commission on November 22—a reward for his role in promoting the project as well as his design.[45]

Even Girard's sudden death—a horse-car ran him down—did not slow the venture. Two days after Girard died, in fact, on December 28, Strickland wrote to Italy to commission monumental column capitals "to be executed of the best Carara [sic] Marble"[46]—from the same quarries that Michelangelo mined for his *David* and other sculptures.

In February 1832, the cornerstone of the Merchants Exchange foundation was laid twenty feet below ground, on a day selected to coincide with one of the nation's secular holy days, the one hundredth anniversary of Washington's birthday. Emphasizing the significance of the event, President Andrew Jackson made just his second visit to the city since his days as a young congressman in 1797–98, while Governor George Wolf arrived from Harrisburg.

Civic pride was in evidence in the grand parade that passed through the city and paused at the site of the new exchange for the cornerstone-laying ceremony. In addition to the directors and stockholders of the Merchants Exchange Company and their distinguished guests, the procession included elaborate floats. One had a twenty-four-column structure representing the union of twenty-four states. Another took the form of a naval ship complete with crew, pointing to the new exchange's importance in overseas commerce. Still others referenced the region's productive and processing sectors with craftsmen striking medals, carving wood, and butchering animals.[47]

Construction proceeded rapidly for so large a project. In November 1833, the *National Gazette* announced the placing of the last stone, as "fifty workmen at the top gave a hearty 'three times three.'"[48] In celebration of the progress, the architect and his master mason, John Struthers, hosted a dinner attended by all 140 of the men who had worked on the building. One of the project's masons, I. R. Chandler, paraphrased what was said of the Roman emperor Augustus in his toast to William Strickland, proclaiming that the architect "found us living in a city of brick, and . . . will leave us in a city of marble."[49] The total construction expenditure came in at

$159,435, on budget and on time, though fundraising continued in order to cover the costs. As late as March 1834, significant funds were still needed. The board of the Philadelphia Contributionship agreed to take an additional $10,000 in Merchants Exchange stock, provided that "the Mutual Assurance Co. take an equal sum at the same rate."[50]

Strickland's choice of a combination of "democratic" Greek and imperial Roman elements in his classical design for the exchange exemplified the image that Philadelphia capitalists sought to present to the rest of the nation. As the self-described "Athens of America," Philadelphians claimed ownership of the democratic nation's birth, but also tied their fortunes and identity to the imperial march of American capitalism across the continent.

Within, the exchange boasted the most modern comforts of any American building. Separate furnaces isolated in the basement not only heated the post office, which occupied nearly half of the ground floor, but also the exchange and reading room, which took up half of the second story. Hollow cast-iron columns carried the heat from the basement to the exchange above and in the process also warmed the public hallways by radiation. Like Strickland's earlier trip to Britain, these new heating and mechanical systems hinted at the city's rising industrial economy.

Life at the Exchange

As the exchange building neared completion, businesses began taking leases on the offices that opened onto Dock and Walnut Streets and for the rooms on the second floor. Construction was completed just in time, for in late March 1834, sparks from a nearby chimney ignited a fire that destroyed the wood shingle roof and much of the upper floor of the Exchange Coffee House.[51] As a result, it was decided to open the new exchange for public inspection the following day, Sunday, and by the middle of the following week, records and papers of its various tenants had been moved from the old building.

Two additional days were allowed for public inspection of the building, and on Thursday, March 27, 1834, the Merchants Exchange officially opened for business.[52] As one of the foremost architectural and mercantile landmarks in the nation, it became an instant attraction for visitors to the city. It also immediately became the central node of the region's networks of communication, information, financial transactions, and business services. From the United States Post Office on the ground floor, letters to be shipped overseas could be deposited in bags bound for specific ships. On the second floor, the Mercantile Library reading room provided a full complement of books and newspapers and was open to all merchants by subscription.

The building's lantern, a feature usually regarded as a decoration, served the communications needs of both brokers and commodities traders. Situated on the building's east end, the lantern illumined views of the harbor, making it possible for a clerk armed with a telescope to identify arriving ships by their flags and to sell cargoes before docking according to the original shipping manifests. The lantern may also have served as the new terminus for the private optical telegraph system of signal towers between Philadelphia and New York, relaying price quotes and other commercial and financial information between North America's two principal markets (Figure 16).

Tenants of the exchange offered a variety of commercial services. Insurance companies occupied many of the ground floor spaces. M. Thomas and Sons Auctioneers advertised their various sales of "Real Estate, Stocks, Furniture, Books, Stationary, Paintings, Fancy Goods, &c."[53] The skills of the business world could be acquired at C. A. Wilson's Philadelphia Mercantile Academy; its rooms on the third floor were "open for the benefit of those wishing to improve in Book-Keeping, Writing, Arithmetic, and higher branches of Mathematics," with separate instruction "apartments for Ladies."[54]

The private rooms surrounding the main floor of the exchange and the library on the upper stories were rented by such trading associations as the maritime Green Room Association, the Board of Brokers, and, by the 1840s, the commodities traders of the Commercial Room Association.[55] The Green Room Association had been located in the southeast room of the Exchange Coffee House, and its members somehow assumed that their prized location would be transferable to the new exchange. The space they sought in the new building, however—facing the port at the closest point to the river—had already been rented to the Philadelphia Board of Brokers.[56] The haggling went on through 1834 until February 1835, when the difficulty was finally resolved. The Green Room Association got its preferred space while the Board of Brokers was placed in a room initially intended for the Union Insurance Company. Both groups retained access to the lantern.[57]

Despite conflicts over prime space in the new building, the presence of multiple commercial forums in their private spaces illustrates the value

THE NEW STOCK EXCHANGE, formerly the Merchants' Exchange, Dock, Walnut and Third Streets

Figure 16. Merchants Exchange. From Moses King, *Philadelphia and Notable Philadelphians* (New York: Moses King, 1902). The caption of this photograph from 1902 announces the Stock Exchange's return to the Merchants Exchange building. It operated there from 1834 to 1876 and again from 1902 to 1913.

Philadelphia capitalists placed on the proximity and association of different business groups with one another.[58] Shortly after its official opening, the Merchants Exchange Company in April announced rules that set hours to attract as much of the trading community as possible on a daily basis. The *Commercial Herald* reported that, "following the model of other cities," the company believed that "the dispersed locality of the places of business render it particularly important that the traders of this community should meet at a certain time." One o'clock in the afternoon was thus "fixed as the hour of the High Change, when Merchants, Manufacturers, and all other persons engaged in buying and selling, are particularly requested to attend." The directors of the Merchants Exchange urged capitalists to remain "for at *least five minutes* at the hour . . . designated" and to "exert themselves to procure the assembling of as many of the trading community as possible."[59]

Befitting its central position, the exchange became the place where the account books of local institutions were placed for review; it also served as the headquarters for subscription to public issues of stock and for petitions regarding all manner of economic questions.[60] Even as the exchange was being built, the most pressing of those questions was once again the impending loss of the national bank.

The Battle for the Bank

After its difficult beginnings in the 1820s, the second Bank of the United States successfully carried out its directors' stated mission: "the restoration of the currency, the maintenance of the general credit, and the accommodation of the internal and foreign trade of the country."[61] But the election of another agrarian populist, Andrew Jackson, in 1828, brought to the White House a hard money advocate hostile to banks and bank notes.

The new president was not alone in his dislike of the bank, although he developed a singular animus toward Nicholas Biddle.[62] Western bankers, farmers, and land speculators took exception to the bank's continued restraints on note issues by banks west of the Appalachians. Eastern bankers—apart from the Philadelphia group that controlled the bank—resented its monopoly on federal deposits and its interstate network, through which it could preempt their transfer of funds and dominate the market in bills of exchange. Urban laborers, "residual Jeffersonians[,] and leveling democrats" opposed the bank's soft money, to which they attributed panics and unemployment.[63]

Jackson challenged the bank early in his presidency. In 1829, Biddle refused to remove Jeremiah Mason, a friend of the president's bitter rival, U.S. senator Daniel Webster, from his post as the Portsmouth branch director. Old Hickory responded by publicly questioning the constitutionality of the bank's charter, signaling an apparent intention to follow Thomas Jefferson's precedent and let it expire.[64] The following year, Jackson and Biddle made a private accord to defer the renewal of the bank's charter until after the presidential election of 1832. Convinced, however, that the president intended to shut the bank down, Biddle joined with Jackson's main political enemies in Congress, Webster and Henry Clay, to introduce a re-chartering bill. Proponents of the bank issued pamphlets in favor of the institution, pointing up its importance to the nation's economy. Even Boston capitalists, who had no branch of their own, celebrated its "promotion of the great interests of AGRICULTURE, MANUFACTURES, and COMMERCE."[65] The bill passed both the House and Senate in early 1832, but the president vetoed it.

Following his reelection, Jackson took further steps to dismantle the bank. In 1833, Jackson and his cabinet pressured Secretary of the Treasury Albert Gallatin into withdrawing almost $8 million of the federal deposits from the bank. A committee of the bank's directors charged that Jackson had mounted "a combined effort to render the Institution subservient to political purposes."[66] Then, in January 1834, Jackson called on Secretary of War Lewis Cass to direct Biddle to surrender all military pension accounts—a sizeable portion of the government's money in the bank—to the War Department. When Biddle refused, alleging that the action was illegal, Cass suspended pension payments. Angry veterans, many of whom had served under Jackson in the War of 1812, could not believe that the president would withhold their money. Instead, they, the Democratic press, and much of the public blamed the aristocratic banker of Philadelphia for this fiscal embarrassment.[67] The way was clear to dismantle the bank.

Fallout and Depression

When Congress allowed the second bank's charter to expire in 1836, Philadelphia's financial elite once again lost the power to determine national monetary policy, manage federal finances, and leverage them into regional economic development. They also forfeited control over the second bank's network of branches, through which they had shaped lending and economic development in the South and the West.

But the void in public finance and regulation had an impact well beyond Philadelphia and its merchants, financiers, and Board of Brokers. The absence of a federal fiscal agent supporting a sound currency, together with rampant land speculation on the frontier and overborrowing for internal improvements, resulted in the panic of 1837 and a deep, long, and widespread depression. All areas of the market collapsed, from transportation companies to real estate and farming, from state and federal bonds to private banks and insurance companies.

Nicholas Biddle managed to salvage the institution, in a way. In 1836, he gained a state charter and incorporated the capital stock of the national bank into the Bank of the United States of Pennsylvania. By April 1839, the new bank's assets included over $17 million in corporate stockholdings, and its own stock remained a popular investment.[68] The bank's loans extended beyond its supply of specie, however, and this only contributed to the increasing financial instability of the country.

In an attempt to reign in speculation, Congress issued the Deposit Act and Specie Circular of 1836, which required payment in gold or silver on all sales of government land. The subsequent contraction among U.S. banks led to numerous business failures and, perhaps more importantly, the Bank of England's decision to curb credit for American banks. When the Bank of England instructed Liverpool shipping agents not to accept bills of exchange on certain British banks tied to American interests, it sparked a collapse in the market for foreign exchange. The banks of New York and Philadelphia subsequently suspended specie payments on May 10 and 11, 1837, setting off the financial panic and depression that would last well into the next decade.[69]

The long duration of this depression was partly due to the wide range of market sectors affected. In addition to real estate, banking, and insurance stocks, troubles with internal improvements and the state bonds that helped finance them contributed to the breadth and depth of the crisis. Canals, in particular, were veritable money pits for the corporations and states that built them. Engineers consistently lowballed their cost estimates. Regular maintenance demanded unanticipated expenditures. In many states the expediency of digging links to each legislative district, in order to obtain politicians' votes, meant that capital for internal improvements was spread too thin. The Pennsylvania geographer Charles Trego complained in 1843 that "a system of management directed by party politics, and the employment of swarms of public agents as a reward for political services, without due regard to their character or qualifications," had drained the commonwealth's coffers and bloated its payroll. "The present deranged condition of the State finances, and the utter prostration of the credit of the commonwealth," he lamented, "have now put a stop to the further prosecution of the public works."[70]

Courting further disaster, Pennsylvania and other states responded to the banking crises of 1836 and 1837 by overborrowing. This contributed to the collapse of the capital market for internal improvements—particularly in the West and the South—in the summer of 1839 and resulted in another four years of deflation and depression.[71] Early in the 1840s, nine states defaulted on their debts. Pennsylvania was able to resume payments only by enacting a property tax.[72] By 1843, however, the state's debt amounted to over $40 million, and the market for both canal stocks and state bonds on the Board of Brokers continued to suffer.[73]

Banks resumed specie payments in 1838 and bank stocks traded above par on the board in that year. In March 1839 Nicholas Biddle resigned his post as president of the Bank of the United States of Pennsylvania. "Few events could be expected to excite greater sensation in our city," affirmed the *United States Gazette*. "When yesterday it was announced [at the Merchants Exchange] that Mr. Biddle had resigned his office men looked astonished." Some expressed surprise "that anyone would voluntarily lay down a salary as large as eight thousand dollars" per year. Biddle announced he was leaving "the affairs of the institution in a state of great prosperity," but with so much of the bank's capital tied up in state bonds and internal improvements, its position was precarious. The banking panic of February 1841, which brought more severe losses than the panic of 1837, resulted in the failure of the bank seven months later.

The nation's longest depression to date inspired a host of public and private reforms. An act passed by the legislature in 1841 voided all contracts for sales of corporate stock or government bonds in which delivery of the certificates "may be executed or performed at any future period exceeding five judicial days next ensuing the date of such contract." By limiting investors' ability to speculate without paying in their capital, this statute, explained a Pennsylvania judge, was "a remedial law of great importance" and should be "construed so as to suppress the mischief which the Act was intended to prevent."[74]

Philadelphia's commercial associations likewise underwent contraction that reflected the business failures and limited opportunities of the depression. Membership in the maritime Green Room Association fell from a high of forty-eight in 1835 to twenty-nine in 1847, as shipping slumped and many merchant houses went under. It would only revive in the mid-1850s.[75]

Although records of the Board of Brokers' membership are lacking for this period, its trading activity clearly suffered with the depressed state of the entire market. Stock trading volume on the board declined from 565,656 shares in 1835 to just 33,593 shares in 1842. The financial historian Robert Wright has identified a "strong shift toward bond trading in the wake of the Panic of 1837," as Philadelphians sought more secure investments.[76]

New York's securities market had been somewhat more active than

Philadelphia's as early as the 1790s. However, with the Quaker City's loss of commercial status and the national bank, the depression years of 1837 to 1840 saw the volume of shares traded on Third Street amount to only 14 percent of the volume on Wall Street.[77] Clearly, the city could no longer sustain its position as the nation's financial capital, and its brokers' misfortunes reflected that decline.

Still, the institutional apparatus the brokers had developed between the War of 1812 and the panic of 1837 to capitalize and organize the construction of turnpikes and canals would prove a formidable platform for revival of the city's stock market. The board would soon underwrite a new generation of economic development projects. The railroad was on the way, and, together with coal and iron mines, this would spur manufacturing and further integrate the markets and resources of the nation. Without a national bank, and with Pennsylvania's abolition of lotteries to raise capital, stockbrokers and exchanges would expand their roles in the regional and national economy, fueling the industrialization of America and the globe.[78]

4

The "Workshop of the World":
Industrial Capital and Industrial Revolutions

If Nicholas Biddle symbolized Philadelphians' desperate and vain attempts to hold onto a past in which their city was the nation's financial capital, his cousin Thomas Biddle represented the future of the region and its Board of Brokers (Figure 17). Thomas's firm was founded on capital originally accumulated in the colonial trade of the merchant-brokers John and Clement Biddle. Most of his clients likewise hailed from the region's colonial elite. Yet, beginning in the 1820s, Thomas and his colleagues on the board spent much of their time investing in the future, not simply preserving their wealth in conservative purchases. In the second quarter of the nineteenth century, they helped engineer the dramatic restructuring of the region's economy. In the process, they helped make Philadelphia the foremost industrial metropolis of the United States, the "Manchester of America."

Having survived the depression of the 1830s, Thomas Biddle and Company enjoyed a strong reputation both in Europe and the United States.[1] Through its investments, the firm and its clients gained controlling interests and directorships in coal mining, canal, and early railroad companies. For such major investors as General George Cadwalader, Biddle's services included representing clients at meetings of the shareholders and directors of these corporations.[2] Biddle and other prominent firms with transatlantic connections also funneled European capital into the recovering American economy and its new growth sectors.[3] In these ways, members of the Board of Brokers coordinated industrial finance as consummate insiders.

Figure 17. Portrait of Thomas Biddle, by the painter Thomas Sully, 1828. Courtesy of Geoffrey Biddle. Thomas Biddle's life (1776–1857) spanned the city's shift from a mercantile economy to an industrial one, and his firm's investments in mining, railroads, and real estate helped spur that transformation.

Biddle and his colleagues played a focused, particular role in industrialization. They did not invest in manufacturing, which remained the province of smaller financial arrangements. Instead, they underwrote the real estate, transportation, communications, and energy infrastructure that shaped the course of industrial development on a grand scale. In this sense, their well-regulated market served a public purpose, as the Board of Brokers helped make up for the lack of a national bank, integrating the national economy in an era when new states and cities were popping up across the North American continent.[4]

The Energy Revolution

Historians who write about stock exchanges portray the nineteenth century as essentially an era of railroad finance. Philadelphia financiers capitalized the largest railroad company—ultimately the largest corporation—in the world, the Pennsylvania Railroad, which came to dominate the nation's industrial heartland. But railroads were only part of the story. Equally important for the city's status as the "Workshop of the World" were the anthracite coal mines in its hinterland.

The discovery of rich veins of hard anthracite coal in Lehigh and Schuylkill counties outside the city catapulted Philadelphia's manufacturers and financiers into the industrial age. The boom set off an energy revolution. As early as 1814, the entrepreneurs Josiah White and Erskine Hazard observed that "with Lehigh Coal it takes 5 bushels per day of twelve hours to heat and roll one thousand pounds of iron for wire. With Virginia [bituminous] Coal it takes 20 bushels for the same, and as well twice the time and twice the cost in labor for the quantity of product."[5] Pennsylvania's superior coal touched off an energy boom, inspiring frenzied investment in eastern Pennsylvania's mines, mining towns, canals, and—in time—railroads to connect the coal fields of the Schuylkill and Lehigh valleys to the city.

White and Hazard captured much of the coal trade through their Schuylkill Navigation Company, which made the river navigable by barge. Funded with Stephen Girard's help, it was completed in the summer of 1824.[6] The company inaugurated the route with canon salutes, speeches, and the launching of three boats of politicians and "distinguished guests." A fourth vessel carried agricultural implements downriver from Reading to Philadelphia, symbolizing farmers' continued connection to the city.[7] The city government immediately put in sizable orders for anthracite to heat its gas and water works. The following year, mechanics made the first successful attempt to generate steam with anthracite at an ironworks in Phoenixville, fifteen miles up the Schuylkill River from White and Hazard's wire mill at what is today the East Falls section of Philadelphia. Steam engines could now run hotter with less coal, generating more power to drive the region's factories.

The lawyer James Dundas, a director of the Philadelphia Savings Fund Society and the president of the Commercial Bank, was the largest individual investor in the anthracite region. His broker, Thomas Biddle and Company, kept him abreast of stock market conditions on a regular basis, informing him of trading activity and of going prices on the exchange.[8] Dundas and Biddle encouraged fellow bankers and brokers to put their money in anthracite, effectively capitalizing the energy source behind the region's simultaneous manufacturing boom.

By the late 1820s, a veritable coal rush was on. As the industrial booster Edwin Freedley later noted, "The news of fortunes accumulated by piercing the bowels of the earth . . . aroused an enthusiasm less wide-spread than that which fevered Europe upon the discovery of silver in Mexico . . . but certainly not less intense." Backed by millions of dollars in stock, "capitalists, arm-in-arm with confidential advisers, civil engineers, and grave scientific gentlemen, explored every recess, and solemnly contemplated the present and future value" of every inch of the coal lands. Barges poured tons of anthracite into the city, which in turn sent north workers, manufactured goods, and even prefabricated wood houses. "Thus *whole towns* were arriving in the returning canal boats," Freedley exclaimed.[9]

On the heels of the coal boom came the construction of immense iron forges, which were among the greatest consumers of coal. While iron manufactories continued to raise capital through private partnerships, the Board of Brokers listed the iron mining concerns. As in the case of coal, the capital funneled into iron mining had important multiplier effects in the economy of Pennsylvania and the United States. As the Pennsylvania state geologist Charles Trego put it, "A pound of iron in its various changes from the ore through the furnace, bloomery, forge, rolling-mill, steel manufactory, and then into fine cutlery, watch springs, and the thousand other delicate and useful articles made from it, employs hundreds of men, and is increased by their labour in value almost equal to its weight in gold."[10] Though the Board of Brokers did not underwrite these steel manufactories until later in the century, the markets it made for coal and iron mines, canals, and railroads laid the foundations of the manufacturing economy Trego described.

Capitalizing an Industrial Heartland

Early nineteenth-century industrialization inspired a flowering of institutions and a concentration of financial and human capital within Philadelphia. Neither the dollars nor the people who invested them stayed home, however. Local bankers and brokers traveled themselves, sent colleagues, and corresponded with trusted agents who looked into investments in other regions. On the Board of Brokers, Philadelphia capital found its way into private and public sector securities that spread the city's influence across the industrializing continent.

In the decades following the bank war, the stock markets of New York and Philadelphia traded an increasing number of securities for non-local concerns.[11] Like their counterparts on Wall Street, the brokers at the Merchants Exchange on Third Street established links to the economies of the South and the West, where agriculture and manufacturing were booming. In the 1840s, the Philadelphia Board of Brokers listed securities for banks, governments, and railroads in western Pennsylvania, New Jersey, Ohio, Indiana, Illinois, Kentucky, Tennessee, Mississippi, and Louisiana.[12] While New York financiers pursued longer-distance strategies to control the agricultural and timber markets of the West via Chicago, Philadelphia's brokers remained focused primarily on developing and linking the nation's foremost centers of mining and manufacturing through networks of credit and capital, as well as via the iron bonds of the railroads. This resulted in a more intensive pattern of investment in Pennsylvania anthracite, iron, and industrial cities from New Jersey to St. Louis. The small cities dotting Pennsylvania, Ohio, Indiana, and Illinois constituted a dense industrial belt, where demand for coal and Quaker City machines was highest.[13]

Members of the Board of Brokers sought to coordinate investment in this large region's industrial infrastructure. Established houses descended from the board's founders, including Thomas Biddle and Company and E. S. Whelen and Company, invested the fortunes of such elite families as the Cadwaladers and the Biddles to that purpose. Through their extensive activities in the continent's interior, they attracted new generations of entrepreneurs to Philadelphia.

The newcomers engaged in all sectors of the economy. From the coal regions of Pennsylvania came Thomas Dolan, a future textile and public utility magnate, Samuel S. White, a dental manufacturer, and Richard D. Wood, an iron maker. Thomas A. Scott, Henry Houston, and Alexander Cassatt, a native of Pittsburgh, all converged upon Philadelphia in the mid-nineteenth century to help build the Pennsylvania Railroad. Joseph Pew, the founder of Sun Oil, and William Elkins, a future partner in Standard Oil, would come to the city after the Civil War with substantial fortunes to invest in refining and utilities.[14]

Relatively low barriers to entry in the mid-nineteenth century meant that ample opportunities existed for new brokers as well as established firms. Even in the crisis years of 1836 and 1837, some fourteen new broker-age houses advertised in a single local newspaper.[15] W. H. Newbold's Son and Company opened as the economy rebounded in 1844. The Baltimore firms J. I. Cohen and Brothers and Alexander Brown and Sons established branch offices in the Quaker City.[16]

The region's most important new houses, however, were Clark, Dodge and Co., founded in 1837, and Drexel and Company, which opened the following year. Enoch W. Clark came from Boston, where his old firm had gone bankrupt, to join with his brother-in-law, Edward Dodge, launching their firm in an office on Third Street, where two decades earlier Clark had gained his business education in the house of S. and M. Allen and Co. Dealing primarily in currency but also in stock, by 1839 Clark and Dodge were handling close to $1 million in currency and earning some $50,000 a year (almost $1 million in year 2000 dollars)—a substantial fortune for a firm with just a handful of employees.[17] In the absence of a national bank, well-connected financiers like Clark were able to step in to manage and profit from the money market, forming national networks of brokerage that facilitated long distance transfers of funds.

The Austrian immigrant Francis Drexel founded Drexel and Company to exploit many of the same opportunities. After several years of travel in Mexico and South America, painting portraits for aristocrats and government officials, Drexel left his wife and young children in Philadelphia to open a currency brokerage in Louisville in 1837. This burgeoning city on the banks of the Ohio River offered a strategic location between eastern markets and Drexel's source of Mexican gold and silver in New Orleans, just five days away via steamboat.[18]

The following year, Drexel rejoined his family in Philadelphia and opened an office on Third Street between Market and Chestnut. It was a block where commercial and financial capital came together. Late each winter, throngs of merchants from the South and the West arrived in Philadelphia to shop for dry goods along Market Street, and the city's currency brokers discounted the promissory notes they brought to cover their purchases. Brokerage houses specializing in stocks and bonds gravitated toward the block of Third Street south of Chestnut, clustering around the Merchants Exchange.[19] Clark and Drexel would soon expand their interest in securities, joining the Board of Brokers and its well-ordered market.

Regulating the Post-Bank Market

Recently well-ordered, that is. The financial crises of the 1830s and 1840s in fact brought considerable turbulence to the board, which saw fit to take corrective action. As a later publication of the board put it, "The difficulties frequently arising between members at that eventful period, on account of the unnatural activity and fluctuations of the stock market, led to the creation of the Standing Committee."[20] This new group oversaw all applications for membership and invested the board's surplus funds in securities. In 1837, it made substantial amendments to the organization's written regulations, aimed at structuring orderly and attentive trading on the exchange. Daily sessions lasted from 11:30 AM to 1:00 PM, with members required to sit in assigned seats. The president first called the roll, then read through the list of stocks as brokers made markets in one security at a time.

Much of the board's new regulatory framework endeavored to control access to information. Each member was "to report any sale made by him immediately, on penalty of paying ten cents."[21] A clerk was instructed to "transcribe in a book to be placed in the Exchange Subscription Room all sales made during the calls—to furnish to the members a correct list of their contracts—to deposit the book of record in such a place . . . so that no one except the members can have access thereto without permission of the President."[22] Another rule stipulated that "no member shall take out of the room any book, charter or paper belonging to this Board, under penalty of paying fifty cents for the first offence, one dollar for the second, and five dollars for any subsequent offence." Within the board's private quarters, brokers were not to trade in secrecy: "All offers to buy or sell Stock at the Board shall be made in public, and in an audible voice; any bargain made in the room, in a tone of voice so low, that the President decides it to be a private bargain, shall be annulled; and all such transgressors be fined fifty cents."[23]

In addition to these rules of conduct for those admitted to the board, the Standing Committee set specific standards for admittance aimed at protecting Philadelphia and its financial community. The Standing Committee set admission fees at $300 in 1837 and established base rates on commissions to prevent brokers from underbidding one another for potential clients. Members not attending sessions of the board were to be fined "unless sick or out of the city." Any prospective member "moving to this city," the rules declared, "must have had a continued and permanent residence of at least two years before he can be elected a member, unless he be a partner of a member of this Board, when fifteen months will be considered sufficient." The rules further stated that "absence from the city for eighteen months vacates the right of a member to a seat in this Board."[24] In terms of its membership, if not its market, the Philadelphia Board of Brokers would be a strictly local affair.

Many of the rules drafted in 1837 concerned decorum, which had presumably broke down in the panic. "Any member of the Board who shall be guilty of indecorous language or conduct towards another member, while in session," the committee instructed, "shall by a vote of two-thirds of the members present, be suspended from his seat at the Board, for not less than one week, nor more than one month." Repeating this offense could lead to expulsion. To promote the efficient prosecution of business, another rule demanded that "any member interrupting the President while calling the Stocks, by speaking on any other business, shall pay a fine of not less than five cents, nor more than twenty cents for each offence, at the discretion of the President."[25]

One of the more important rules, judging by the severity of the penalty, asserted that "no offers to purchase or sell dividends, or make wagers, shall be permitted in the Board, under penalty of fine, from *one* to *five* dollars, at the discretion of the President."[26] The Commercial Room Association, which met next door to the Merchants Exchange, had no such compunction. Its members filled their ledger primarily with records of bets on presidential elections, impending federal policy, and general economic trends—the very kind of speculative gambling the Board of Brokers now forbade as it tightened its focus on stocks and bonds.[27]

This well-regulated market—and the opportunities it held—attracted a growing membership. By the time Abraham Barker joined the board in

March 1845, it included forty-two brokers, five of whom—Thomas Biddle, James Musgrave, James and Samuel Nevins, and George Rundle—had been members for more than a quarter of a century. With its numbers doubled, the board introduced sales on time, a departure from the requirement of immediate cash transactions. By 1844, there were two meetings daily, one beginning at 10:30 AM and lasting an hour, the second beginning at 1:30 PM and lasting half an hour. Sometime in the antebellum period, the group outgrew its room on the third floor of the Merchants Exchange. Barker reminisced much later, "Stocks went up, and we went down to the second floor and in the board room had desks, after which we moved into [the second floor] rotunda which we adorned with barbaric splendor."[28]

Members of the Board of Brokers were able to draw from a well of resources pooled by all the occupants of the Merchants Exchange. The Statistical Society was founded in 1845 "to collect and publish correct statistics of the Arts-Manufactures-Commerce-Population, and the wealth invested in various industrial pursuits."[29] The magnetic telegraph, which in 1846 brought an end to the old heliograph to New York, soon linked the exchange to major cities across the United States.

Ready data and communications links to other markets: the equation restructured the financial market's operations in time and space, as the board began to encourage its members to follow and trade on other markets. To support the idea, it printed ledgers for members with not only the securities list of the Philadelphia board but also sections for brokers to record transactions in Cincinnati, Louisville, St. Louis, Nashville, New York, and Baltimore.[30] Responding to this growth of market information, in 1851 Abraham Barker began printing daily records of sales for his colleagues. Soon thereafter, the board's clerks took over this function.[31]

Meanwhile, all of this expanding activity led to more revisions of the rules, especially where decorum was concerned. In 1850, the board came down more explicitly on the use of profanity—which in that era included the word "devil." Speak profanely, the new rules decreed, and you were to pay a penalty of one dollar. Whistling carried a fine of ten cents. Putting one's feet on the rounds of a chair or spilling ink cost the offender fifty cents. The more serious transgression of winding the board's clock without permission from the president was punishable by a fine of five dollars.[32] One new rule stated that "a member throwing a cushion, cracker, or any other article in the room, at another, or locking the door when any members are within, is finable five dollars."[33]

There was a saving grace to all these penalties for bad etiquette, however, which the rulebook made clear should be considered neither petty nor onerous. "The fines forming a large portion of the revenue of the Board," the rulebook explained, "and being essentially necessary to meet its expenses . . . are to be considered, in most cases, more as voluntary contributions for those objects than as punishments for transgressions." Most of these sanctions, it continued, "imply no censure whatsoever. It would be desirable they should be submitted to without unnecessary discussion, and without wasting the time of the Board, whose chief object is the rapid transaction of business."[34] That, indeed, was the point, and by the mid-nineteenth century, Philadelphia's stock brokers had developed a quick and orderly exchange in the most important securities for American industrialization.

The Railroad Revolution

If coal initiated the industrialization of U.S. stock markets, the railroad boom of the 1840s and 1850s completed this revolution. Railroads embodied Philadelphia capitalists' greatest ambitions, as they fanned out across the country to capture markets and resources. Their webs of tracks promised to funnel trade into the city while linking the region's factories to consumers in the interior. Railroads were the first "modern" corporations, with complex managerial hierarchies that organized legions of engineers, clerks, mechanics, conductors, and laborers spread out across immense territories.[35] These gigantic workforces, coupled with large stocks of equipment and mammoth issues of securities, made the railroads vast pools of human, mechanical, and financial capital designed to profit from the integration of American markets. They imposed what the environmental historian William Cronon calls a "logic of capital" across the continent.[36]

In large measure, stockbrokers made this transportation and corporate revolution possible. They helped float railroad stocks and bonds on exchanges, to which they attracted enough investment capital to make profitable markets in those securities, and thus sustain the value and viability of railroads. The exchanges of Philadelphia, New York, and other cities would introduce new listing standards, requiring listed companies to provide more information on their finances, giving investors a greater sense of security and new ways to compare investment options.[37]

Individual brokers and clients' investment decisions were, of course, vital to the development of railroads. Between the 1830s and the early 1840s, the firms of Biddle, Whelen and Co. and Thomas Biddle and Co. invested hundreds of thousands of dollars in railroads that linked Philadelphia to Baltimore and the Susquehanna Valley. Thomas and Edward Biddle convinced their cousin Nicholas to borrow more than £20,000 from the Bank of the United States to buy stock in the Philadelphia, Wilmington and Baltimore Railroad (PWB).[38] Their colleagues in Drexel and Co. and Clark, Dodge and Co. soon made floating railroad bonds a major part of their business, as well.

The Biddle firm also purchased large properties along these lines, where passenger stations, freight depots, and factories would be built. On the Susquehanna, it procured corporate charters from the Maryland legislature for bridges whose securities were floated in separate issues.[39] With ownership of this key link in the network of connections between East Coast cities, the Biddles and their clients controlled much of Maryland's and Delaware's economic development.[40]

The booster Edwin Freedley claimed—with only slight exaggeration—that Philadelphians accounted for fully half of the $160 million invested in the nation's canal and rail infrastructure between 1820 and 1857.[41] By 1855, the Philadelphia Board of Brokers was listing securities for a dozen railroads, including the Camden and Amboy Railroad of New Jersey, the Philadelphia and Reading Railroad, the Long Island Railroad, and the PWB. Together, these lines wrested control of the most important continental shipping routes—including the coal trade—from canals, with local concerns like Edward Biddle's Lehigh Valley Railroad and Josiah White's Schuylkill and Lehigh Navigation Companies controlling the southern anthracite trade.[42]

The region's most important new venture—and Philadelphia capital's greatest achievement in the nineteenth century—was the Pennsylvania Railroad. Built along the route of the disastrous Main Line Canal, its capital dwarfed that of all other American corporations. By 1854 it linked the city to the Ohio River and the markets of the Mississippi Valley, as its directors poured money into tracks that linked the myriad mines and manufacturers between New England, Baltimore, and St. Louis.

While New York's railroads raced to Chicago in order to drain the agricultural and natural resources of the Great West, the Pennsylvania Railroad's system was known for its "compactness," keeping competitors out of its territory, and the "careful safeguarding of its dividend position," according to the economist William Ripley.[43] It reinforced Philadelphia capital's pattern of concentrated investment in the industrial heartland, and in a move that rationalized the movement of goods and capital across that landscape, it introduced standard time zones to the United States in the 1870s. The "standard railroad," as it branded itself, thus profoundly affected people's experiences of time, space, and markets.

The railroads' tracks articulated the economic geography of the industrial North and its cities (Figures 18 and 19). Factories clustered along the rails, and in turn, neighborhoods of workers' and managers' homes, stores, and churches were built around the plants. Rail lines that radiated out from the largest cities supported the development of elite "railroad suburbs," such as Philadelphia's Chestnut Hill and Main Line. There, railroad directors, financiers, and other prominent businessmen settled, in part to escape the coal-burning factories and immigrant laborers of growing working-class districts. Lines from the coal fields arrived directly at piers on the Delaware and Schuylkill rivers, making the city a major coal port. In the districts of Kensington, Richmond, and Southwark, the so-called iron triangle of coal, iron, and railroads encouraged the growth of steel mills and machine works on the former sites of colonial shipyards. Metal supplanted wood, and smokestacks—of factories as well as steamships—soon replaced clipper masts on the skyline of these and other waterfront neighborhoods.

A New Landscape of Exchange—and of Exchanges

The railroads also remade the global geography of finance, as their voracious appetite for capital constantly required fresh sustenance. Across Europe and North America, established stock exchanges responded—and new ones emerged.

On the exchanges of London, New York, and Philadelphia, for example, railway securities drew new investors and brokers into the market just at the moment that the national debts of Britain and the United States were declining. These securities enabled the rise of a class of *rentiers* who lived off their real estate holdings and the dividends collected from railroad stocks and bonds, providing the economic base, according to the industrial historian Eric Hobsbawm, "for the Victorian spinster and the Victorian aesthete."[44]

Railroad-building schemes designed to serve growing industrial regions also encouraged the foundation of new stock exchanges in other cities.[45] In

Figure 18. "An Assembly Line 26,000 Miles Long." From the Pennsylvania Railroad Company, *One Hundred Years: Ninety-Ninth Annual Report*, 1946. This map from the twentieth century illustrates the network of mining and manufacturing cities linked by the Pennsylvania Railroad by the late nineteenth century.

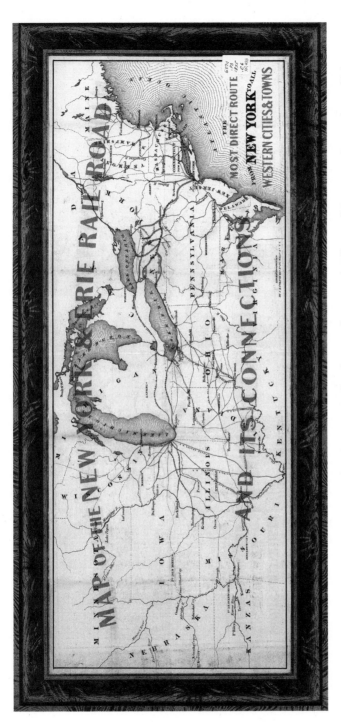

Figure 19. *Map of New York and Erie Rail Road and Its Connections* (J. H. Colton, 1855). Library of Congress, Geography and Map Division. In contrast to the Philadelphia-based railroads' dense concentration of tracks in the industrial heartland, New York railroads competed to reach Chicago, the gateway to the West.

Britain, the "railway mania" of 1843–45 gave birth to exchanges in Manchester, Liverpool, Glasgow, Edinburgh, and Aberdeen.[46] The pattern was repeated across North America; as the railroads and industry spread, local capitalists founded exchanges from Baltimore to Toronto to Denver. Of the nearly 250 stock exchanges founded in the United States in the nineteenth century, most were aimed at making railroad hubs and commercial metropolises of such places as Centralia, Ohio, and Spokane, Washington. Many of these exchanges quickly disappeared, but the major urban centers of the continent maintained exchanges into the twentieth century.[47]

Nineteenth-century exchanges fostered distinct patterns of economic development in the continent's diverse regions.[48] New Yorkers funneled European capital into railroads that solidified their hold on America's new breadbasket in the Midwest and reinforced their dominant position in ocean shipping and the Atlantic cotton market.[49] With profits from commissions, shipping fees, insurance premiums, and interest on loans, they made their city the foremost money market in America.[50]

Midwestern stock markets helped build railroads and local banks that jockeyed for control of trade between the East and the West. This was the strategy of Cincinnati, Cleveland, Indianapolis, Louisville, and St. Louis, which all aspired to be the chief gateway between New York and the Great Plains. The ultimate winner in this battle, however, was Chicago, and its most prominent commercial institutions were its Board of Trade and Mercantile Exchange, not its stock exchange.[51] In fact, the Chicago Stock Exchange was founded late, in 1882, after the absence of a central forum for raising capital hindered the progress of infrastructure and real estate ventures that were rebuilding the city after the Great Fire of 1871. (An Illinois law limiting the exchange of railroad securities had discouraged Chicagoans from starting an exchange, heightening their dependence on New York.)

New Orleans capitalists founded a stock exchange to complement that city's more prominent Cotton Exchange, financing railroads and banks that enhanced its preeminence in cotton shipping. But, for the most part, the South depended upon northern capital to support its overwhelmingly agricultural economy, as the majority of southern planters—at least, before the Civil War—concentrated their investments in land and slaves. In response to his uncle's recommendation to purchase stock in the Mississippi State Bank in 1818, for example, the planter Sam Steer explained that "for a young man just commencing in life, the best stock in which he can invest capital is, I think, Negro stock."[52]

In New England and Canada, the Boston, Montreal, Providence, and Toronto stock exchanges combined railroad and mining securities with early stock issues for industry. Machine makers and mammoth textile mills in Massachusetts and Rhode Island were among a very small number of U.S. manufacturers with publicly traded stock in the antebellum period.[53]

In the more speculative economy of the western states, stock exchanges were developed in reaction to dramatic events that necessitated new institutions to foster and regulate investment. The San Francisco Stock Exchange grew up to finance the mining enterprises, banks, insurance companies, and railroads that served the Gold Rush. At the end of the nineteenth century, Los Angeles brokers founded an exchange to capitalize the city's oil boom. Black gold also gave rise to stock exchanges in Texas.

But these were all regional exchanges. It was the New York exchange and the Philadelphia Board of Brokers that made legitimately national markets. In the second half of the nineteenth century, the main technological instrument through which they did so was the telegraph. The communications revolution it spurred, like the heliograph before it, would restructure trading at the exchange on Third Street.

The Communications Revolution

Foreseeing the consequences of Samuel Morse's magnetic telegraph, the Philadelphia broker William Bridges sold the heliograph between the Merchants Exchange and Wall Street for $3,000 in 1843.[54] The following year, Morse laid his first line between Baltimore and Washington. Two years later, in 1846, a cable connected Newark, New Jersey, to a telegraph office in the Merchants Exchange. Couriers and optical telegraphy filled the missing link between Newark and New York.[55] Soon service linked Boston, New York, Philadelphia, Baltimore, Washington, Cleveland, Toledo, Detroit, and Chicago.[56]

Communications companies quickly became popular investments on the Board of Brokers and other exchanges. Backed by ample capital, and with far smaller expenditures than the railroads, magnetic telegraph networks quickly proliferated. More than fourteen thousand miles of cable traversed North America by 1852. In 1866, the transatlantic cable linked London and New York, and five years later cables connected England to

India and Australia. Where ships and railroads previously carried information on voyages lasting days or weeks, these new networks revolutionized global communications. Brokers could now transcend time and space, transferring capital, price quotations, and crop reports almost instantaneously.

Philadelphia's earliest telegraph link to the west, the Pottsville Telegraph Line, ran along the tracks of the Philadelphia and Reading Railroad. In April 1847, the *Public Ledger* newspaper announced the erection of the first post in the line; it connected the Merchants Exchange to the Reading's offices on Fourth Street. The post was "surmounted by a spread eagle, handsomely gilt," a gesture to the riches of the national market it aimed to reach.[57] As the most direct transportation routes between major cities, railways provided logical rights of way for telegraph wires. In return, telegraphy boosted the managerial capacity of American railroads, improving scheduling and allowing carriers to respond promptly to shifting demands for freight. The marriage of railroads, telegraphs, and capital enabled Quaker City brokers to make markets from the Atlantic to the Pacific.

New Names, New Places, New Money

Drexel and Company had opened its first branch office in the early 1840s, the Chicago firm of Drexel and Smith. At the end of the decade, responding to the California Gold Rush, Francis Drexel set up the house of Drexel, Sather and Church in San Francisco, handling the deposits of California's largest mining company as well as many individual prospectors. Like its Philadelphia partner, this firm provided credit and paper (IOUs) for Bay Area merchants to purchase equipment and finished goods from Europe and the East Coast. Since most miners were new to financial matters and starving for a safe place to keep their gold, few demanded interest. It made for a lucrative business, which the Drexels maintained until 1857, shipping gold to the East Coast and Europe via Panama and their bank on Third Street.[58]

Reaping hundreds of thousands of dollars annually from their gold business, the Drexels positioned themselves as Philadelphia's largest floaters of railroad and U.S. government bonds. As the main investment bankers for the Pennsylvania Railroad, they held a privileged position on the Board of Brokers. Their Wall Street house of VanVleck, Read, Drexel and Co., formed in 1855, gave them a strong presence on the New York market. By

1857, Francis Drexel was counted among Philadelphia's twenty-five millionaires, together with Thomas Biddle and E. W. Clark. Few among this elite group owed their fortunes to colonial landholdings and merchant shipping. Rather, it was the financing of the Gold Rush, the railroad boom, and the expansion of industry that accounted for most of the wealth of these twenty-five citizens.[59]

Enoch Clark followed a similar path to prosperity (Figure 20). He established branch houses in New York, St. Louis, and New Orleans, with additional partnerships in Boston, Springfield, Illinois, and Burlington, Iowa—all of which were soon linked by railroads and telegraphs. When his brother-in-law Edward Dodge retired, the firm became E. W. Clark and Co. Then, in 1842, Clark partnered with a twenty-one-year-old from Sandusky, Ohio, named Jay Cooke. Four years later, as the United States conquered Texas and adjacent territories through the Mexican War, Cooke used his contacts in Washington to gain a sizeable government bond business for the Philadelphia firm.[60]

From their office on Third Street, Cooke carried on a regular correspondence with his father and brothers in Ohio, who kept him abreast of current prices and supplies of western land, chickens, turkeys, fish, and other commodities.[61] With the firm's financial backing, these relatives made substantial land grabs in Iowa, Kansas, and Nebraska. Jay Cooke also helped expand Clark's business in western securities, corresponding with bankers and public officials in budding urban centers from Dubuque to St. Louis.[62] Some of the government and utility bonds from Kentucky, Missouri, and Iowa listed on the Philadelphia Board of Brokers in the 1840s and 1850s likely arrived via these connections.

Brokers and the Antebellum State

Such bonds represented a new and powerful instrument of growth for Philadelphia's exchange—and for other exchanges as well. Where the founding generation of the Board of Brokers had tied itself to the fortunes of the new national government, the mid-nineteenth-century stock market profoundly shaped—and was shaped by—state and city governments. The board and other exchanges traded state and municipal bonds that, in turn, gave governments capital to invest in transportation companies, gas and water works, and other "private" improvements of public import. Complementing the railroads, telegraphs, and mining investments that shaped Philadel-

Figure 20. Portrait of Enoch W. Clark. From Thomas Scharf and Thompson Westcott, *History of Philadelphia, 1609–1884* (Philadelphia: Everts, 1884). With the help of Jay Cooke, a transplant from Ohio, the firm of E. W. Clark and Co. brought much of the Midwest into the economic orbit of Philadelphia and its stock market.

phia's relationship with other cities and regions, underwriting this infrastructure gave the board yet another role in the development of the industrializing metropolis.

The consolidation in 1854 of the City of Philadelphia with the twenty-nine other boroughs and townships of Philadelphia County led to a wave of such spending. With the city slated to assume the outlying districts' debts, the townships increased their debt by $4.5 million in the month before consolidation took effect. Germantown took out a loan for $100,000 to build a town hall. Southwark secured debt financing for a new park. Kensington borrowed $150,000 to fill in the valley of the Cohocksink Creek to make way for new homes and factories. Northern Liberties and Richmond borrowed $500,000 each to purchase stock in railroads that promised to stimulate local commerce and enrich the businesses of local politicians.[63] The city bonds that covered this debt were all listed on the Board of Brokers.

The city and state governments, in turn, invested in companies engaged in regional economic development. The Commonwealth of Pennsylvania purchased $100 million worth of shares in railroad and canal corporations that it chartered before the Civil War. This dwarfed the $8 million invested by the Massachusetts legislature and the $23 million expended by the much younger state of Missouri.[64] City hall and the statehouse were the most important backers of the mighty Pennsylvania Railroad, which was truly a public-private venture. The city of Philadelphia made the largest subscription to the railroad's initial offering in 1846, paying $2.5 million for 50,000 shares, a quarter of the total stock. The commonwealth and other cities and towns expecting to benefit from the new route likewise took subscriptions. A decade later, after pouring tens of millions of dollars into the Main Line canal and portage railroad system, the legislature ceded it to the railroad for the relatively meager sum of $7.5 million.[65]

State legislatures also insisted on regulating the industrialization they fostered. To this end, their most important legal tools were the corporate charters granted to railroads, mines, and manufacturers. These charters articulated the rights and responsibilities of private entities, capping railroad freight rates, establishing mining enterprises' rights to assets buried deep under the earth, and setting the amount of capital they could raise through public offerings of stock. Of course, the railroads' own lawyers drafted most of their charters, which gave transportation companies broad powers to shape economic development, including eminent domain that allowed them to restructure land use patterns within and between cities.[66]

States and cities also regulated brokers. A Pennsylvania law of 1861 required all brokers and private bankers to submit yearly disclosures and pay a 3 percent tax on their earnings; the receipts went toward paying off the state's debt. The act imposed a fine of one thousand dollars for noncompliance and imposed a licensing fee on each firm.[67]

Brokers lobbied public officials for help, as they had since the days when they mingled at coffee houses. When a tornado and flood depressed the market for cotton in Mississippi, a group of twenty-three Philadelphia brokers, merchants, lawyers, and insurance companies wrote to their congressmen from Pennsylvania. This group represented Philadelphians who owned nearly half the stock of the Agricultural Bank of Mississippi, which was heavily invested in cotton. The capitalists urged their elected officials to protect "the innocent stockholders of this state" with a "special indulgence of government" in the form of more time for the bank to pay off its loans. This, they claimed, "will not only prevent further sacrifices, but will aid in restoring the usefulness of the Bank to the Community, and [revive] the value of the stock and thereby enable the stockholders in some degree to retrieve their losses."[68]

In another case, in 1855, Thomas Biddle and Co. wrote to the state senator Eli Kirk Price, asking the legislature to make Pennsylvania state bonds more easily transferable. "The reason for this wish," Biddle explained, was "first that many persons in this country who invest in Penna. securities dislike to hold Coupon Bonds from the fear of losing the amount they represent by their being stolen, burnt, or lost at sea." This would benefit investors as well as the commonwealth itself, he argued. "It is very desirable to encourage European and English investment, and with the ample provision for sinking fund, Penna. loans should command a higher estimation in those markets if adapted in shape to the views of investors."[69] Predictably, brokers sometimes found state intervention onerous and lobbied against proposed legislation.[70]

Though fluid and contested, the securities markets that supported nineteenth-century industrialization were necessarily regulated by exchanges and by the state. Jay Cooke and his friends amused themselves by drafting joke laws that made ridiculous demands. One such "act" proposed that "in order to distinguish brokers from the honest portion of the population, every broker shall clothe himself in a pair of scarlet pantalons with a black stripe down the left leg[,] a green coat with metal buttons and a cocked hat."[71] Cooke knew as well as any other nineteenth-century investment banker, however, that public and private capital depended upon one another for liquidity and security in the American market. That would become dramatically apparent during the Civil War, when Cooke and his colleagues on the Board of Brokers would combine federal and corporate finance to underwrite the Union victory.

5

Bankrolling the Union, Building the Metropolis

Philadelphia sits just above the Mason-Dixon Line in more than simple geographic terms. Throughout the Civil War, it was a hotbed of "Copperheads," northerners who sympathized with the Confederacy. Beyond anyone's feelings about politics and slavery, economic ties to the South complicated Philadelphia capitalists' position on secession, as well. On the eve of the war, the city's merchants held over $24 million in collectible debts from southern borrowers.[1] On top of this, its financiers were heavily invested in banks and business ventures from Virginia to New Orleans. Local industrialists depended on southern cotton, timber, and chemical products, as well as on southern customers for their manufactures. So there was a sense in which secession held potentially disastrous economic consequences.

Yet Philadelphia was also a center of the abolitionist movement, led in part by Abraham Barker, a member of the Board of Brokers (Figure 21). Together with Jay Cooke and other prominent capitalists, Barker joined the Union League, which rallied Republican businessmen to support the northern war effort—and which Copperheads nearly succeeded in burning to the ground. Barker put his talents to work for the Union, heading the Finance Committee of the Philadelphia Supervisory Committee for Recruiting Colored Regiments. His committee raised over thirty thousand dollars for the organization's Free Military School on Chestnut Street and its training ground, Camp William Penn, on the northern outskirts of the city. Initially located on Jay Cooke's land in the early suburb of Chelten Hills, the camp was moved to a nearby farm belonging to the family of the

ABRAHAM BARKER

Figure 21. Portrait of Abraham Barker. From Philadelphia Stock Exchange, *Souvenir History, Album of Members, Gallery of Men of Affairs* (Philadelphia: Philadelphia Stock Exchange, 1903). Abraham Barker was a member of the board from the mid-nineteenth century to the early twentieth, when this photo was taken.

abolitionist Lucretia Mott, since Cooke's property was too hilly for proper marching exercises. After the war, the village of LaMott would grow up there, one of the first African American suburbs outside a northern city. Cooke, Barker, and other financiers would build their suburban estates nearby.[2]

Philadelphia brokers contributed to the war effort far beyond the regional level. Without a national bank, Treasury Secretary Salmon Chase and the northern states depended almost entirely upon private bankers, merchants, and railroad companies to furnish capital, supplies, and transportation for the Union war effort. Once again, in the mold of Robert Morris and Stephen Girard in earlier conflicts, it was a Philadelphia capitalist, Jay Cooke, who would be *the* financier of the Civil War (Figure 22).

Cooke and his colleagues on the Board of Brokers profited considerably in the process. The city's overall economy proved exceptionally resilient and flexible, as financiers, manufacturers, and railroads adapted their enterprises to the exigencies and opportunities of the wartime economy. The wealth they accumulated during the war would build the postwar metropolis.

Underwriting the Union

In April 1861, Pennsylvania's "Treason Bill" officially severed economic ties with the South. The act forbade residents of the state from doing business with the Confederacy, condemning anyone who "knowingly and wittingly shall aid or assist any enemies in open war against this State or the United States by joining their armies, or by enlisting, or procuring, or persuading others to enlist for that purpose, or by furnishing such enemies with arms or ammunition, or any other articles, for their aid and comfort," including ships, food, or currency.[3]

In May 1861, the Commonwealth of Pennsylvania appointed Drexel and Company and Cooke's new firm, Jay Cooke and Company, to procure bids for a $3 million bond issue to fund the state's part in early war efforts.[4] Cooke and Drexel printed handbills appealing to "the patriotism and State pride of Pennsylvanians in this hour of trial."[5] Within a month, the loan was oversubscribed, finding purchasers at par among banks, manufacturers, and individuals throughout the commonwealth. Subscriptions ranged from $300,000 to as little as $50.[6]

JAY COOKE

Figure 22. Portrait of Jay Cooke. From Moses King, *Philadelphia and Notable Philadelphians* (New York: Moses King, 1902). Like Robert Morris and Stephen Girard before him, Cooke took advantage of Philadelphia capital's federal connections to underwrite a war.

That summer and fall, northern banks lent the U.S. government upward of $100 million. In exchange, the banks took Treasury bonds that they marketed to the public. But by the end of the year, after a succession of lost battles and gloomy reports from the front, the banks and the public had lost confidence in the Union's capacity to repay its notes. This resulted in a run on specie and a suspension of bank payments. In February 1862, Congress responded with the Legal Tender Act, creating new paper currency—greenbacks—secured by Treasury bonds instead of specie.[7] For the remainder of the war, the Union issued bonds and greenbacks to cover the massive costs of the conflict. (The Confederacy followed a similar strategy, initially contracting for paper currency printed by the National Bank Note Company of New York, since the South lacked the engravers and materials to print its own notes.)[8]

Amid the fiscal crisis of 1861, Treasury Secretary Chase recognized that northern banks alone could not underwrite the war. Jay Cooke devised a solution and pitched it to his close friend Hugh McCulloch, the controller of the currency under Chase. Cooke proposed an innovative investment marketing campaign to sell bonds to ordinary citizens in denominations as low as ten dollars, with the option for payment in monthly installments. To lend weight to this untried scheme, he wrote Chase that Drexel and Co. would join Cooke and Co. in opening "a first class banking Establishment in Washington, *at once* trusting to our energy, capital & credit for success, as well as those natural advantages that would legitimately & honestly flow towards us from your personal friendship & the fact that our firm was ardently & fully with the Administration."[9]

With Chase's backing, Cooke and Drexel opened this office in February 1862, and Cooke enlarged his headquarters on Third Street. Unleashing a torrent of patriotic advertising, Cooke recruited a national sales force of twenty-five hundred men, including brokers in cities throughout the North. In smaller towns without private banks or brokerage houses, he employed merchants and community leaders. Cooke printed reams of handbills, posters, and educational literature that introduced the bonds to Americans unfamiliar with securities investment. He opened Working Men's Savings Banks, which functioned as night sales offices for laborers who could not purchase bonds during working hours.[10] This massive marketing campaign drew the middle classes into the market for the first time, broadening the social and geographic footprint of the securities industry.

It also helped win the war. With Cooke's help, the Union paid for the war with $2.6 billion in bonds, $431 million in greenbacks, and $236 million from taxation and other sources.[11] "The Yankees did not whip us in the field," insisted one Confederate leader. "We were whipped in the Treasury Department."[12]

The Civil War and Corporate Finance

They were also whipped on the factory floor, in banks and stock exchanges, and along the railroad tracks of the industrializing North. Philadelphia's Board of Brokers found gain in it all. While the National Banking Act of February 1863 created a system in which New York became the nation's central reserve city, Philadelphia's banks and brokers nevertheless profited from the new system as capital concentrated in northern cities increasingly found its way into the stock market. The Philadelphia brokers Jay Cooke and Co. and E. W. Clark and Co. took advantage of certain provisions of the act to incorporate the First National Bank of Philadelphia with a capital of $1 million. The new bank did a large business thanks to its association with the Union's most prominent financier.[13]

Philadelphia's railroads were perhaps the greatest beneficiaries of the wartime economy, and their shareholders profited, too. With the most extensive transportation networks along the Mason-Dixon Line, the principal theater of war, the Pennsylvania Railroad and the Philadelphia, Wilmington, and Baltimore Railroad (PWB) moved tens of thousands of troops. Their freight cars carried millions of tons of supplies from local textile mills that shifted their production to make blankets and uniforms, from metalworkers that turned out guns and ammunition, from pharmaceutical manufacturers that made medical supplies, and from grocers and butchers in the Philadelphia area who supplied food. During the war, the mileage of railroad tracks in the commonwealth increased by more than 40 percent. The expansion paid off; by 1864–65, the Pennsylvania and the PWB were paying dividends of 10 percent.[14]

It was thus little wonder that railroad securities attracted new investors. Encouraged by their aggregate profit of over $11 million in 1861, the Philadelphia Bank had increased its holdings of transportation securities from $46,000 to $600,000 by 1863.[15] The railroads used their capital to buy coal lands and mining companies and to purchase or start up their own iron and machine works to furnish rails, bridges, locomotives, and replacement parts. They were now much more than just transportation enterprises, and they quickly became the first corporations to engage in mergers and acquisitions of their rivals on a large scale.

All of this growth spurred a boom in the U.S. financial sector in general and in the Philadelphia exchange in particular. In the years just after the war, while Europe's industrial powers were slumped in "the Great Depression," Americans enjoyed a "Gilded Age."[16] Jay Cooke's war bond campaign had had a lasting effect; the middle-class investors it brought into the market stayed there. In New York, the Open Board of Stock Brokers, which in 1869 would merge with the New York Stock Exchange, initiated the practice of continuous sales by brokers occupying individual stations on its trading floor—giving a major boost to the scale and pace of trading. Exchanges around the country soon abandoned the practice of calling stocks and bonds for bid one at a time.

The roles of investment bankers likewise changed, as they increasingly took an active role in managing the firms they capitalized. Jay Cooke and Co. was the leader in this trend, most notably in its underwriting of the Northern Pacific Railroad.[17] But Cooke was by no means the only firm on the Philadelphia Board of Brokers that was enjoying good times.

The Postwar Board of Brokers

Board members enjoyed such success during the war that they rewarded themselves by initiating a lavish annual dinner in 1865 (Figure 23). The mood was light, and brokers printed playful poems celebrating their accomplishments in making markets.[18] Guests at the dinner included General George Meade, the hero of Gettysburg and a Philadelphian; Commodore J. B. Hull, the commander of the Philadelphia Navy Yard; Mayor Morton McMichael; and brokers from the exchanges of Boston, New York, and Baltimore. The menu included oysters, turtle and julienne soups, salmon and lobster, six kinds of roasts, sweet breads, croquettes, chicken salad, *suprème de volaille*, terrapins, five types of game, five desserts, and eleven kinds of wine.[19]

The dinner celebrated more than just the wartime profits from railroad and bank stocks, for Quaker City brokers had also spent the 1860s capitalizing the world's first oil rush—in northwestern Pennsylvania. In 1865 and 1866 alone, stocks for more than twenty-five oil-drilling companies traded on the Board of Brokers, including Eureka Oil, Big Tank, Upper Economy,

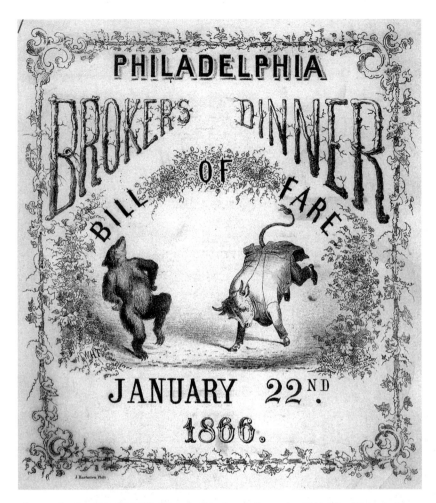

Figure 23. Cartoon from the Board of Brokers' dinner in 1866. The Historical Society of Pennsylvania. The Civil War bond market, western Pennsylvania oil boom, and expansion of railroads fueled growth and prosperity at the Board of Brokers in the late 1860s.

and Royal Oil. Their names suggested their ambitions.[20] As in the earlier anthracite boom, Philadelphia capitalists established transportation companies like the Philadelphia and Oil Creek Railroad to incorporate the oil region into the city's orbit. Together with electricity, this new energy source would soon support the rise of mass production, the automobile, and the consumer society of the twentieth century—what American historians term the Second Industrial Revolution.

In the late nineteenth century, oil and coal stocks enjoyed such popularity that the Board of Brokers established an annex for mining stocks. However, its most active markets remained in railroad securities and city and state bonds, as new issues continued to grow its list in the postwar decades.[21] At the same time, the city's brokerage community expanded its ranks and its connections to other markets. Many new houses, such as Bioren and Co. and H. F. Bachman and Co., held seats on both the Board of Brokers and the New York Stock Exchange. Bachman also traded on the New York Cotton and Coffee Exchanges.[22] Other Philadelphia financiers migrated west. Joseph R. Wilkins, for one, was instrumental in founding the Chicago Stock Exchange in 1882 and served as its chairman until 1904. His fellow Philadelphian Charles T. Yerkes introduced "methods of high finance" in Chicago, where he boosted the capital of street railway systems by a factor of ten.[23]

Jay Cooke and A. J. Drexel expanded their power across the Atlantic after the war. Cooke joined with his friend Hugh McCulloch, the former controller of the currency, to found the London house of Jay Cooke, McCulloch and Co., which developed strong ties to the Rothschilds.[24] Although Francis Drexel had died in 1863, his son Anthony, who had joined his father's firm in 1838 at the age of thirteen, formed the Paris firm of Drexel, Harjes and Co. in 1867 (Figure 24). Four years later, Drexel allied with Junius Morgan of London's leading investment bank, Morgan, Grenfell and Co. They formed the Wall Street house of Drexel, Morgan and Co., run by Junius's son J. P. Morgan, who became Drexel's junior partner.

In 1872–73, A. J. Drexel built a new headquarters at 23 Wall Street. The Washington-based newspaper *National Republican* remarked that "in New York, it is regarded as somewhat of an affront that Philadelphians, and not New York, should be the men to make this bold venture. The great banking house of Drexel & Co. that is to rise upon the newly purchased site is to be a monument of Philadelphia enterprise, which fairly throws New York enterprise into the shade, in this case at least."[25] Drexel's friend, President Ulysses Grant, even assumed a subservient position in his relationship with Philadelphia's foremost financier. Drexel refused the former general's offer to serve as secretary of the Treasury. Instead, he immersed himself in growing his New York office and floating bonds, primarily for the Pennsylvania Railroad.

Figure 24. Portrait of Alexander J. Drexel. From Thomas Scharf and Thompson Westcott, *History of Philadelphia, 1609–1884* (Philadelphia: Everts, 1884). Though not as public as Jay Cooke, Drexel exerted even greater influence upon late nineteenth-century finance, from railroads and government bonds to real estate.

To accommodate the rapid growth of its membership and trading activity, the Philadelphia Board of Brokers again initiated innovations in its operations. Like the New York exchange, it introduced the new technology of the ticker tape around 1867, allowing stock prices to "stream" continuously in the marketplace. In 1868, the board altered its rules to allow brokers to sell their seats on the exchange, creating a market for membership itself. The entrance fee for new members was raised from $2,000 to $5,000, reflecting the increased value brokers associated with the seats. In 1870, to facilitate transactions, the board established the first stock exchange clearing house in America (the NYSE would not create one until 1892). At the end of the trading day, each member sent a sheet detailing his purchases and sales to the Clearing House, which balanced his accounts and transferred the shares.[26] It handled only stock, not bonds, but the volume of clearings suggests that it was immediately put to good use. In 1881, just shy of 24 million shares, worth a total of $1.2 billion, passed through the Clearing House.[27]

The explosive growth of the board signaled not only the strength of America's postwar finance and industry but also the excessive speculation that has historically accompanied the world's greatest economic booms. New middle-class investment capital and the watering of railroad stock sent prices to unsustainable heights. The party came to an end in 1873, when the collapse of the Northern Pacific Railroad touched off a panic, ruined Cooke's banking empire, and brought on a severe depression.

Half a century later, in his *Autobiography of an Idea*, the architect Louis Sullivan still remembered the sounds and sights of the collapse. At the office of his mentor, Frank Furness, at Third and Chestnut Streets, "there came through the open windows a murmur, barely noticed at first; then the murmur became a roar with wild shouting." Rushing to the window, Sullivan saw "far below, not pavement and sidewalks, but a solid black mass of frantic men, crowded, jammed from wall to wall." The offices of Jay Cooke and Co., a few doors away on Third Street, had closed. "The run on the banks had begun," Sullivan recalled; "credit had crumbled to dust . . . men were ruined, and insane with despair . . . this panic would spread like wildfire over the land leaving ruin in its wake everywhere."[28]

The flames of the panic were fanned by the telegraph.[29] Just as the crash of 1929 would be heard on radio and the collapse in 1987 seen live on CNN, the fall of the market in 1873 could be read on the ticker tape at the

Board of Brokers and in numerous offices in the business district, accounting for the instantaneous buzz on the street.

The failure of Jay Cooke and Co. had far-reaching effects on the leadership of North American investment banking. E. W. Clark and Co. held a large interest in the Northern Pacific, and it, too, went bankrupt in 1873. Though the firm was quickly reconstituted, it lost considerable influence nationally and internationally. With Cooke out of business, J. P. Morgan took over as the U.S. Treasury's primary agent for marketing its bonds. A. J. Drexel, a very private person himself, left such high-profile marketing functions to his junior partner, as he had previously to Cooke.[30]

The Philadelphia Stock Exchange

Despite these shifts and the deep depression of the 1870s, the market revived, and Philadelphia's financial sector continued to grow. To provide some measure of security in the industry, the Board of Brokers started a Gratuity Fund that by the end of the century provided five thousand dollars to brokers' families on the occasion of each member's death. This social insurance was one result of brokerage becoming a larger, more formal, and specialized profession. Institutional changes likewise followed.

In December 1875, in the midst of the depression, the board changed its name to the Philadelphia Stock Exchange. The following July, on the nation's one-hundredth birthday, it departed the Merchants Exchange and moved across Third Street to larger quarters in a building constructed for it by the Girard Estate, which remained a major force in the city and its financial community. Designed by James Windrim, a graduate of Girard College, the new stock exchange was literally hidden behind the Girard National Bank, which still occupied the old structure of the first Bank of the United States.[31] This location—at the center of the financial district but without a presence on the street—reflected both the increasingly crowded nature of the downtown and the exchange's traditional desire to keep its proceedings private.

The new building helped the institution expand. When Thomas Sherry left his job as a traveling acrobat to become a page at the exchange in 1880, it counted more than two hundred members. The heads of firms continued to trade on the floor; A. J. Drexel, Abraham Barker, and the others were there in person, easy to spot. Unlike the New York exchanges, where brokers traded at separate posts, Philadelphia's members still gathered around a single long table to trade as the president called out each stock and bond in order. Sherry recorded these transactions, and at the close of trading he carried his log to a printer to produce the daily market report. (That wasn't all Sherry did. On his retirement at the age of sixty-seven in 1930, he assured a newspaper reporter that he had never traded in stocks, but he admitted that he had provided "entertainment for members at the Exchange's annual Christmas parties with his acrobatic feats"—at least in his younger days.)[32]

Despite the persistence of these and other traditions, the growing pains were evident, and in February 1880, the exchange met the challenge by altering its structure of governance. In place of votes taken by the full body of members, the new Governing Committee gained full authority over operations. It was composed of the president, secretary, treasurer, and twenty-one elected members with rotating three-year terms. Subcommittees reporting to the Governing Committee included the following: Building, Finance, Admission, Arrangements, Arbitration, Constitution, Commissions, Elections, Business Conduct, Floor Trading, Insolvencies, and the Stock List.[33] In 1884, the Committee on the Building arranged for the installation of a fan and electric clocks on the trading floor. Two years later, the Governing Committee voted to hire a stenographer and typewriter and to purchase a typewriting machine. Fire- and "burglar-proof" vaults for the Clearing House were installed in 1888. The next year, the exchange improved occupational conditions further when it procured an automatic water cooler "operated by a patented device necessitating the payment of one cent for a glass of water."[34]

Technology did present problems, however. Some telegraph companies leasing space at the exchange could not resist the temptation to leak securities quotes to "bucket shops" that sold stocks and bonds without the permission of the exchange and without contributing membership or annual fees. The Governing Committee conferred with the New York Stock Exchange and the Chicago Board of Trade in an effort to cut off ticker service to bucket shops nationwide. Ultimately, the Philadelphia Exchange simply expelled several telegraph operators from its facility.[35]

The incident, however, revealed just how interconnected the industrial world had become—and how challenging it would be to regulate the flow of financial information in the face of those interconnections. Information remained the lifeblood of the stock exchange. Just as the eighteenth-century exchange had found its home in the London Coffee House amid the flood of information around the port and the public market, the nineteenth-century exchange was the center of a new revolution of telecommunications. However the information was transmitted, its security would always be an issue.

And the next innovation in its transmission came very soon. Introduced to the public at Philadelphia's Centennial Exhibition in 1876, Alexander Graham Bell's telephone spread across the United States in the subsequent decade. Bell's American Telephone and Telegraph Company was the star of the Boston Stock Exchange in the 1880s, and the Philadelphia Stock Exchange began listing phone companies in 1884, including the local Bankers' and Merchants' Telephone and Telegraph Company.[36] As suggested by this concern's name, the new mode of communication was particularly important for finance and commerce.

By the early 1890s, brokers on the exchange could rent private phone lines linking their Philadelphia offices to the trading floor. Five long-distance telegraph and telephone booths rented for upward of $500 a year—nearly $10,000 in year 2000 dollars—indicating the value attached to the information accessible via these technologies.[37] Unlike the telegraph, telephone service soon reached mass markets of urban consumers. Along with the streetcar, gas, and electrical utilities traded on the exchange, it helped fuel an infrastructure boom that remade American cities and stock markets in the late nineteenth century.

Monopolizing the Metropolis

In addition to the wealth amassed by experienced brokers like Jay Cooke, the Civil War and the simultaneous Pennsylvania oil boom brought a new generation of capitalists to the exchange. These men came from diverse backgrounds but converged in a syndicate that would control much of the postwar city through public and private finance. The butcher Peter Widener built his bank account by procuring lucrative contracts through Simon Cameron, the Pennsylvania Republican boss and the secretary of war, to supply the Union troops with mutton. William Elkins made a killing in the oil fields, then moved back to Philadelphia and sold his refineries to Standard Oil (Figure 25). William Kemble served as an agent for federal revenue stamps during the war. Afterward, as the president of the People's Bank, he managed large deposits for the state.

Together, Widener, Elkins, and Kemble leveraged their financial capital

PETER A. BROWN WIDENER   WILLIAM LUKENS ELKINS

Figure 25. Portraits of Peter Widener and William Elkins. From Moses King, *Philadelphia and Notable Philadelphians* (New York: Moses King, 1902). The "traction twins" capitalized the infrastructure and urban development that made the modern metropolis, underwriting utilities, downtown skyscrapers, and suburbanization.

and political connections into monopoly control of the streetcar, gas, and electric systems that built late nineteenth-century Philadelphia. Dubbed the "All Night Poker Players," they carried on a conversation at their high-stakes card games that would shape the region and its economy into the twentieth century. And they made the Philadelphia Stock Exchange and the New York Stock Exchange into critical vehicles for metropolitan expansion.

Though they used Drexel, Morgan and Co. and Elkins's own investment bank, city hall and the state capitol were equally important to their utility empires. All three men held public office—Kemble as a three-time state treasurer, Widener as the city treasurer, and Elkins as a member of the City Council. They enriched not just themselves but also their allies in the Republican machine.[38] In the 1880s, the city boss Jim McManes held over four thousand shares of their Philadelphia Traction Company (PTC) stock, while the state boss Matthew Quay owned thirty-five hundred shares. These politicians pushed through municipal and state legislation that, according to the transit historian Charles Cheape, "rode roughshod over the attempts of reformers to obtain better service and greater public control."[39]

Widener and Elkins became masters of the merger. The PTC devoured almost all other streetcar lines in the region, becoming the forerunner of the Southeastern Pennsylvania Transportation Authority (SEPTA), the public transit system of contemporary Philadelphia. With their New York partners, William Whitney and Thomas Fortune Ryan, they made waves on Wall Street in 1886 when they paid nearly $3 million for ten thousand shares in the Broadway and Seventh Avenue Railroad Company. They consolidated it into the Metropolitan Street Railway Company, the forerunner of today's Metropolitan Transportation Authority in New York.[40] The presence of these magnates attracted other transit ventures to trade on the Philadelphia Stock Exchange, which listed streetcar companies from Staten Island to St. Louis.[41]

Another important addition to the Widener-Elkins-Kemble syndicate was Thomas Dolan, the head of the Philadelphia-based United Gas Improvement Company (UGI), through which the men took control of the city-owned Philadelphia Gas Works. Incorporated in 1882 and listed on the Philadelphia Stock Exchange, the UGI quickly became one of the largest gas-holding companies in the world, active from Atlanta to Denver.[42] In 1887, it purchased the rights to the Welsbach light, a gas mantle invented in Germany, which the syndicate distributed throughout the United States via its Welsbach Light Company. This concern was one of the first manufacturers traded on the exchange.

Meanwhile, as in the case of streetcar lines, the exchange became a market for the securities of the Boston United Gas Company, the Chicago Gas Company, the Gas Light Company of Washington, D.C., and other such concerns. By the 1880s, it also listed such electric companies as Edison Electric Light, National Underground Electric, and Northern Electric Light and Power.[43]

While gas and electric technologies and the companies that produced them competed with one another for investors and consumers, Philadelphia's chief energy magnates opted not to choose sides in this battle. Instead, they were active on both fronts. As a result, by the end of the nineteenth century, Widener, Elkins, and their utility companies held an all but complete monopoly over the city's utilities. They operated publicly traded corporations under the protection of public regulatory boards that they themselves controlled, while competition for the consumer market had been manipulated into extinction. The syndicate's various securities were, however, among the most stable investments on the Philadelphia Stock Exchange, offering some of the steadiest dividends. The infrastructure they built spurred other sorts of urban ventures to issue stock on the exchange.

Underwriting Urbanization

Like their counterparts in railroad finance, the utility magnates coordinated their investments in transportation and energy with speculation in real estate. They were deeply involved with the Republican machine's contractor bosses, who controlled the region's building trades as well as numerous public offices. Widener and Elkins soon floated real estate investment trusts and construction material companies on the exchange, including their Excelsior Brick and Stone Company, whose products built the walls of city hall and thousands of rowhouse blocks. In addition to immense public works contracts, Excelsior supplied the region's largest developer, William Weightman, with whom Widener and Elkins partnered to build neighborhoods along their streetcar lines in North, South, and West Philadelphia. Political scientists call these sorts of alliances urban growth machines.[44]

In the 1890s, Widener and Elkins led an early exodus of the nouveau riche to the northern suburbs, buying up farms and estates in the vicinity of Jay Cooke's and Abraham Barker's country homes. They demolished older summer houses and erected lavish mansions such as Widener's 110-room Lynnewood Hall, surrounded by three hundred acres with a racetrack and polo grounds. Along their longest streetcar line into the suburbs, they constructed upward of three thousand middle-class homes in a community they named Elkins Park. They marketed the area through Willow Grove Park, a family fairground at the end of the line. They thus used their municipal transit franchise to underwrite suburbanization that would ultimately empty the city of its middle classes.

Other Philadelphia financiers shaped real estate markets from downtown to the swamps of Florida. The stock exchange listed such local landmarks as the American Academy of Music and the Masonic Temple on Broad Street. Subscriptions taken on the exchange financed some of the immense buildings at the Centennial Exhibition of 1876 in Fairmount Park.[45] The Philadelphia Warehouse Company raised capital on the exchange to erect industrial facilities. Other listed development ventures included the Florida Land and Improvement Company, the Southwest Virginia Improvement Company, and the Atlantic and Gulf Coast Canal and Okeechobee Land Company, "organized to reclaim lands in Florida" by draining the Everglades, "and to construct Steamboat Canals &c."[46] Still other concerns, such as the New York City Plate Glass Company, the Asphalt Company of America, and the Vulcanite Portland Cement Company, produced the building materials and technologies necessary for metropolitan and continental expansion. William Elkins's son George sat on the boards of the latter two concerns, offering another hint of the many ways in which urban financiers involved themselves in the rapid development of the late nineteenth-century city.[47]

As stockbrokers' interests in real estate grew, insurance companies developed new services to support the industry. In 1876, Philadelphia financiers incorporated the Real Estate Title Insurance and Trust Company to back titles to property, creating an entirely new type of insurance. Other companies, including the Land Title and Trust and Philadelphia Mortgage and Trust, soon offered the same product and were listed on the exchange.[48] The stock exchange thus played a vital role in the growth and everyday life of Philadelphia and other American metropolises, trading securities that underwrote fire, title, and mortgage insurance; real estate trusts; building materials manufacturers; telephone systems; and street railway, gas, and electric utilities.

Drexel and His Building

Some members of the exchange, such as A. J. Drexel, invested more of their own money in real estate than in stocks and bonds. In addition to buildings and land in Philadelphia, New York, and Chicago, Drexel and his close friend, *Public Ledger* publisher George Childs, undertook the development of suburban communities outside both Philadelphia and New York City. These communities formed part of what the historian Eric Hobsbawm termed "the stockbroker belt," leafy suburbs for the growing corporate and managerial classes that were connected to their downtown offices by commuter rail lines and soon parkways for their automobiles.[49]

Drexel underwrote critical portions of downtown Philadelphia, many of which remain part of the city's life today, including the massive Reading Terminal train station. Arguably his most important real estate investment for the region's financiers was at Fifth and Chestnut Streets, just across from Independence Hall and the adjacent city hall. In 1883, he commissioned a marble banking edifice commensurate with the national status of his firm. Four years later, he added an office tower on top of the building, making it one of the city's earliest skyscrapers. In October 1888, the Philadelphia Stock Exchange moved into the second story of the enlarged Drexel Building. Already Chestnut Street was the city's financial hub, with the offices of numerous banking and brokerage firms. This new edifice gave the district a new anchor. The *New York Times* called it "palatial," marveling at its bank of four elevators (Figures 26 and 27).[50]

The Drexel Building offered important advantages over the exchange's cramped quarters behind the Girard Bank. A new layout for the trading floor included posts where brokers traded each stock individually, as continuous trading recorded by the stock ticker replaced the old daily call system.[51] No longer required to sit at desks or around a table, Philadelphia brokers could engage in mobile trading like their counterparts in New York. The floor was arranged with the securities of particular sectors trading together. Thomas Sherry and his fellow pages still wrote down a record of each transaction, but instead of taking them all to a printer at the end of the day, the records were handed to the ticker operator to be displayed immediately.[52] Telegraphs, telephones, and tickers facilitated continuous communication with other markets, and the exchange again expanded its trading hours.

There was another important innovation for the stock exchange in the Drexel Building. Where the operations of the old Board of Brokers had been private—hidden in the upper rooms of the London Coffee House or Merchants Exchange or tucked behind the Girard Bank—the new Philadelphia Stock Exchange now announced itself visually on the financial district's most prominent thoroughfare. Its large leaded glass windows proclaimed the name of the tenant to the street. Inside, in a marked departure from its traditional guild-like secrecy, an elevated gallery above the trading floor gave the public access to the proceedings of the stock exchange for the first time.

When the brokers arrived for their first day on the new trading floor, according to one eyewitness, "they sang a patriotic anthem with the vigor of voice for which our most active brokers are so justly celebrated, and, after startling the people in the Mayor's office with their stentorian melody and shouts that successfully tested the acoustics of the room, they went to work."[53] Ringing in its new continuous trading system in full view of the

Figure 26. Photo of Chestnut Street business district. From Moses King, *Philadelphia and Notable Philadelphians* (New York: Moses King, 1902). The Drexel Building is the tall one in the center, with the second Bank of the United States to its left and Independence Hall (not visible) just beyond.

ENTRANCE TO DREXEL BUILDING, PHILADELPHIA

Figure 27. Photo of the entrance to the Drexel Building. From Andrew Barnes, *History of the Philadelphia Stock Exchange, Banks, and Banking Interests* (Philadelphia: Cornelius Baker, 1911). Unlike its previous quarters, the Drexel Building gave the Philadelphia Stock Exchange at least a sign on the street.

public and in the city's premier office tower, the exchange exuded confidence. Its markets for mining, railroad, telegraph, and utility securities had helped underwrite the "Workshop of the World." Its city's industrial prosperity seemed secure. Yet dramatic changes were brewing in the worlds of industrial and financial capitalism—changes that would ultimately cast the Philadelphia Stock Exchange into relative obscurity, sever many of its ties to the city around it, and help sink the city's economy. These would be the trials of Philadelphia capital in the twentieth century.

6

Decadence: The Stock Exchange
and the Fall of Philadelphia

On New Year's Eve 1900, Philadelphia opened its new city hall amid roaring canons, a pandemonium of fireworks, and a shower of electric lights. Standing at the intersection of Broad and Market Streets, city hall was the largest and most expensive municipal building in the world, underwritten by bond issues on the stock exchange. The man who arranged much of that financing, Edward T. Stotesbury, was by 1900 the senior partner in Drexel and Company and Peter Widener's personal banker (Figure 28). Over the next three decades, Stotesbury would oversee the transformation of central Philadelphia, including the extension of a grand parkway leading from city hall to the suburban estates that he and the Wideners built as monuments to their wealth. Stotesbury's Whitemarsh Hall boasted 147 rooms, 45 baths, 3 elevators, a movie theater, and grounds that required the daily service of 70 gardeners.

Back at the city's center, on all sides of city hall, Stotesbury's colleagues and clients, the railroads and real estate trusts listed on the exchange, were busy erecting a new downtown. Across the street to the northwest stood the Pennsylvania Railroad's Broad Street Station, headquarters of the largest corporation in the world. To the southeast sat the department store founded by the "merchant prince" John Wanamaker, a landmark of the nation's emerging consumer society. Other signs of this new economy could be found in the corporate office towers rising on Broad Street just to the south and in the automobile assembly plants and showrooms that would soon grow up to the north.

On the brink of the new century, local newspapers celebrated the city's

EDWARD THOMAS STOTESBURY
Drexel & Co., Bankers.   Dir. Phila. National Bank
V.-P. Gtn. Cricket Club.   Dir. various Companies

Figure 28. Portrait of Edward Stotesbury. From Moses King, *Philadelphia and Notable Philadelphians* (New York: Moses King, 1902). As Widener's and Elkins's banker and partner in Drexel and Co., Stotesbury was positioned to shape public and private finance and economic development simultaneously.

mighty industries and speculated on new forms of technological and commercial progress in the coming century.[1] By 1900, the United States accounted for one-third of the world's total industrial output, more than England, France, and Germany combined. Philadelphia financiers had capitalized the coal, railroads, and oil that enabled the city to dominate America's most heavily industrialized regions.

As an associate of J. P. Morgan, Edward Stotesbury helped float loans to China and European powers. Yet unlike Anthony Drexel, who died in 1893, he was clearly the junior "senior partner" in Morgan's financial empire. Stotesbury surely amassed great wealth. By 1927 he was reportedly worth $100 million. But when he died eleven years later, those riches had dwindled to $4 million. The Great Depression played a role in these losses, though Stotesbury's spending habits accounted for far more. Between 1933 and 1938, he withdrew $55 million from his account at Morgan's. The upkeep of his Whitemarsh Hall estate cost $1 million a year, and then there were his mansions in Bar Harbor, Maine, and Palm Beach, Florida, as well as his yacht and fleet of automobiles. In 1936, he told his stepson, who had married Doris Duke and become a devout New Dealer, "It's a good thing you married the richest girl in the world because you will get very little from me. I made my fortune and I am going to squander it [on] myself; not your friend Roosevelt."[2]

The fortunes of Philadelphia and its stock exchange paralleled those of Edward Stotesbury. Although times may have looked good on the surface, their economic power in the larger world was waning. What the crowds that marveled at the new city hall, the corporate skyscrapers around it, and the estates of the region's magnates did not realize is that these lavish monuments signaled not the ascendancy of Philadelphia capital but rather its decadence. Capital was fleeing the region and its stock market, as even the Pennsylvania Railroad made Wall Street its financial headquarters. Local captains of industry and of finance lost control of their firms and their markets, mostly to Manhattan-based conglomerates. In short, the late nineteenth century and the early twentieth saw the Philadelphia Stock Exchange decline in importance, and with it the city's position in the world economy significantly eroded.

Philadelphia would remain a relatively prosperous city until the mid-twentieth century, with an abundance of industrial jobs. Yet the foundations of its wealth, and the regional economy's ability to compete in industry and finance with other cities, their firms, and their institutions, were undermined beginning in the late nineteenth century. Ironically, in the nation's most important manufacturing city, the exchange and its members failed to capitalize on key opportunities in industrial finance—though much of this was due to the manufacturers' own issues. Equally important was Philadelphia capital's failure to invest in economic development projects that yielded more growth and activity than just the contracts of a corrupt municipal government and allied utilities and contractors. Like other institutions and firms in the city, the exchange and its members failed to tap into the rapid corporate restructuring and globalization of the age.

Philadelphia in a New Global Economy

Local capitalists organized to address the problem in the 1880s, founding the Committee on Decadence of the Commerce of Philadelphia. In 1889, John A. Wright, a director of the Pennsylvania Railroad, penned an open letter to the committee's chairman. Not surprisingly, he attributed "whatever of foreign commerce the port of Philadelphia now has, and whatever its market may be as a distributing point" to his railroad. But the port was suffering, and the region's manufacturers were losing ground to cheap labor and mass production in the Midwest. "No building of new railroads into the city," Wright warned, "no building of long wharves . . . can overcome the laws of trade."[3] The cities with greatest access to resources would dominate an increasingly global economy.

At the end of the nineteenth century, America's economic empire expanded to embrace the emerging markets of South America and the Caribbean basin as well as the Pacific. The Spanish-American War of 1898 gave the United States new naval bases and coaling stations to support and protect American ships. From Mexico to the Philippines, the United States supported political regimes that favored the interests of American oil, railroad, mining, rubber, timber, chemical, and agricultural sectors. Herein lay vast opportunities for U.S. capital, which when it reached new markets would help spur massive migrations of working people, as well. Between the 1880s and the early 1920s, immigrants from eastern and southern Europe streamed into northeastern and midwestern cities to labor in the factories and construction trades. Latin American, Caribbean, and Asian workers were likewise drawn to the agricultural and service sectors of the Southwest, the Pacific Northwest, and New York City. Cities large and small throughout the United States advertised themselves to potential immigrants in Europe.[4]

Philadelphia shipping merchants and manufacturers turned their atten-
tions to foreign markets and peoples through a new institution, the Commercial Museum, which was adjacent to the campus of the University of
Pennsylvania (and later became the city's Civic Center). It collected many
of the foreign products displayed at the World's Fair in Chicago in 1893,
exhibiting raw and manufactured goods from around the globe. It held
regular expos and ran an information bureau that educated importers and
exporters about the cultures, products, and markets of the world. With the
shipbuilder Charles Cramp as its president, the Commercial Museum sent
envoys to the governments and chambers of commerce of Latin America
and Asia, striving to expand international markets for Philadelphia manufactures.[5]

Italians, Poles, and eastern European Jews arrived at the Immigration
Station on the Delaware River at Washington Avenue, or traveled south
from Ellis Island. But other cities grew much faster. Chicago had replaced
Philadelphia as the nation's second largest city by 1890. The muckraking
journalist Lincoln Steffens labeled Philadelphia the "most American" of
cities, as it had the lowest percentage of foreign-born residents among the
big cities.[6] Though immigration still helped drive economic growth, compared to other regions (and to earlier eras in its own history), the twentieth-
century Delaware Valley was a less desirable destination for people seeking
economic opportunity.[7]

Part of the problem was that Philadelphia capital's pattern of concentrated investment and economic relationships in the mid-Atlantic region
and the Midwest limited the city's ability to expand its markets at the apex
of what historians call the first great era of economic globalization.[8] Of
course, manufacturers, shippers, workers, and boosters alone could not
make cities and regions succeed in an international economy. As the railroad director Wright pointed out, "Capital, to a large degree, is a deciding
quantity in a struggle for trade."[9] In an era of mass production and mass
markets, business and trade needed the help of investment bankers to gain
a strong foothold in the global economy.

Finance capital was critical to the making of America's new economic
empire. But it was the Empire City, not the Quaker City, which underwrote
it and reaped the benefits, building powerful networks of institutions and
firms with global reach.[10] The financial advantages awarded to New York
by the National Banking Act of 1863 had been reinforced by congressional
legislation of 1867 that made it the market for public sales of Treasury

gold.[11] A syndicate led by J. P. Morgan built the Panama Canal, linking Atlantic and Pacific markets. The Vanderbilts' United Fruit Company and the Wall Street sugar trust, which purchased Philadelphia's sugar refineries, supported puppet regimes in Caribbean island nations and banana republics of Central America. Thus the great migration of labor to places other than Philadelphia also paralleled a migration of capital in the same directions, mostly to and through New York. Indeed, much of this story of decline is about what Wall Street did and Chestnut Street didn't do.

The Great Migration of Capital

The New York Stock Exchange's rise to dominance was aided immeasurably by the panic of 1893. The stock market crash of that year resulted from the failure of the Philadelphia and Reading Railroad, which was controlled by Drexel, Morgan and Co. Anthony Drexel had left the Reading's financial management to his New York partner J. P. Morgan, who pursued an overly ambitious merger strategy that backfired when other railroad magnates retaliated. In the heat of the panic, Drexel died at the age of sixty-six. This left Philadelphia capital without a leader of national stature, and it paved the way for Wall Street to bury Chestnut Street's hopes of maintaining a national market. Morgan, whose father had passed away three years before, took over the helm of the world's most powerful investment bank. Drexel, Morgan and Co. became J. P. Morgan and Co., with the Chestnut Street house of Drexel and Co. as a branch office led by Stotesbury and his colleague George C. Thomas.[12] Philadelphia would no longer be the headquarters of major national brokerage firms.

Morgan used his capital and influence to buy up companies made vulnerable by the four-year depression that followed the panic, leading a "merger movement that lasted into the new century."[13] By the end of 1895, halfway through the depression, more than a quarter of all railroad mileage in the United States was in the hands of receivers, ripe for buyout. More significantly, Morgan and his Wall Street raiders expanded the scale and scope of the industrial mergers they had begun in the mid-1880s, consolidating firms in the United States, Germany, and Britain. In North America, they assembled such conglomerates as Westinghouse, General Electric, American Locomotive, and American Tobacco. The securities of these mass producers were invariably listed on the New York Stock Exchange, which suddenly made huge markets for manufacturing—or "industrial"—stocks.

The Dow Jones Company responded by developing an industrial index and used its *Wall Street Journal* to centralize information on industrial finance. These markets pumped unprecedented financial resources into industry, enabling Manhattan's rise as the corporate and financial capital of the world. As the nineteenth century came to a close, Wall Street had usurped Philadelphia's role as the economic headquarters of America's industrial heartland. Financiers of course followed the money, migrating to the growing office district on the southern tip of Manhattan Island.[14] Brokerage houses in New England, Philadelphia, and the Midwest increasingly partnered with New York investment banks or purchased memberships on the New York Stock Exchange.

Newly formed corporate conglomerates such as John D. Rockefeller's Standard Oil moved their headquarters, increasing New York's critical mass of financial and human capital.[15] From their Manhattan skyscrapers, corporate directors used their burgeoning wealth and management bureaucracies to relocate industrial production. To cut costs and increase profits, they initiated a century-long great migration of factories and jobs from the Northeast to the South and later to Mexico and Asia.[16] At the same time, Delaware Valley financiers failed to attract investment from outside the region. One result of all this was that a rising proportion of factories in Philadelphia and its suburbs became branch plants of corporations headquartered in Manhattan.

Industrial securities soon supplanted the railroads as the "blue chips" of the national stock market—that is, the New York Stock Exchange. In a period of deflation that lasted through the 1880s and 1890s, bond yields fell, making railroads less profitable investments as the real prices of their securities rose. Brokers turned to industrial stocks. The New York firms of J. P. Morgan, Lehman Brothers, and Goldman, Sachs and Co. led the way in floating industrial conglomerates, creating such giants as Union Carbide, U.S. Shipbuilding, and U.S. Steel.[17] The bankers who sat on these companies' boards made sure that corporate policies boosted stock values. Between 1871 and 1926, the total value of common stocks tripled while that of industrial stocks sextupled. Simultaneously, in the words of the economic historian Donald Kemmerer, "investment banking fell into the familiar three-step routine of investigation, underwriting, and selling."[18]

Wall Street's ability to make industrial markets was bolstered by its dominance of American and European government finance. New York investment bankers floated $200 million for the Spanish-American War in

1898. To finance the Boer War in South Africa two years later, Britain chose
J. P. Morgan and Co. as its principal agent. The Russian, German, and
Swedish governments likewise floated their treasury notes on the New York
Stock Exchange in 1900. With these states and their debt now tied to Wall
Street, American bank clearings rose from $86 billion in 1900 to almost
$118 billion the following year. New York institutions accounted for two-
thirds of this business.[19] Even the most prominent European banking
houses were subordinated to the powerful Morgan bank and its American
allies and interests.[20] Stotesbury and his Philadelphia colleagues were, at
best, junior partners to these deals.

With Anthony Drexel's death and the market shifts at the turn of the
century, Philadelphia lost any legitimate claim to being a major financial
center. True, it remained home to the main branch of the U.S. Mint,
though that system had been decentralized with branches in New Orleans,
Charlotte, San Francisco, Denver, and even Dahlonega, Georgia. But Wall
Street's control of corporate mergers and industrial securities around the
turn of the century truly knocked Philadelphia's stock exchange down to
the level of a second-tier or "regional" market.

Becoming a Regional Exchange

Throughout the nineteenth century, the New York Stock Exchange had
been home to the nation's most active securities trading. But until the 1890s
the Philadelphia Stock Exchange and its members had competed—and collaborated—sometimes on a nearly equal footing, making markets that ener-
gized and integrated industrial America while enhancing the city's place
within the nation's economy.[21] To be sure, the increased mobility of capital
and information at the end of the century broke down the mutual dependence of financiers and corporations upon local markets.[22] The decline of
Philadelphia capital, however, was by no means inevitable.

As late as 1890, the Philadelphia and New York stock exchanges resembled one another in the numbers and types of concerns traded on their
floors. But they would soon develop starkly different markets. Over the
next fifteen years, the Philadelphia Stock Exchange's list expanded by 56
percent while the New York Stock Exchange's list grew nearly 450 percent,
capturing most of the period's largest issues of stocks and bonds (Table 1).
By 1906, the only sector in which more concerns traded in Philadelphia
was canals, and whereas the Philadelphia Exchange's canals were remnants

Table 2. Number of Concerns Listed on the Philadelphia Stock Exchange (PHLX) and New York Stock Exchange (NYSE), by Category, in 1890 and 1906

Sector	PHLX 1890	NYSE 1890
Railroads	84	207
Passenger Railways	14	7
Utilities	2	17
Finance, Insurance, and Real Estate	49	6
Manufacturing	4	8
Mining	8	15
Canals	7	1
Public	8	11
Miscellaneous	3	9
Total	179	281

Sector	PHLX 1906	NYSE 1906
Railroads	107	255
Passenger Railways	54	98
Utilities	17	168
Finance, Insurance, and Real Estate	12	144
Manufacturing	54	368
Mining	10	87
Canals	3	2
Public	6	27
Miscellaneous	17	109
Total	280	1,258

Sources: The Manual of Statistics: Stock Exchange Handbook (New York: Goodsell, 1890 and 1906); Philadelphia Stock Exchange, Securities Admitted to the List—Bonds, 1886–1911, and Stocks, 1891–1937 (PHLX Archival Collection).

of an earlier economic era, the Morgan-led route across Panama was a linchpin of the new global economy. By the same token, where Philadelphia's coal and iron mining market stagnated, New York grew its list of gold, silver, and South American copper mines. The Philadelphia Exchange also failed to remain a major oil market after the Pennsylvania fields dried up. The NYSE captured most of the financial action around the world's subsequent oil rushes in Texas, Oklahoma, Southern California, and the Middle East.

Among the stocks of manufacturers, the two markets were beyond comparison. By the turn of the century, Wall Street bankers controlled the underwriting, marketing, and listing of manufacturers across the nation. Local "signature" companies like Cincinnati's Procter and Gamble and Detroit's auto makers still listed on their regional exchanges, but the big conglomerates all listed on the NYSE.[23] J. P. Morgan even gained control of Boston's hottest company, AT&T, transferring the bulk of its trading to Wall Street.

In December 1900, the Pennsylvania Railroad, the great accomplishment of Philadelphia capital, moved its principal stock transfer and registry office from Broad Street Station to New York. Two decades earlier, the Wall Street house of Kuhn, Loeb and Co. had replaced Drexel and Co. as the railroad's principal financier, but the Philadelphia Stock Exchange had remained the main market for its securities.[24] Now, at the turn of the century, the company was found its most active markets on the NYSE. The Pennsylvania cited "large holdings" of its stock in New York, "as well as its importance as a financial centre," as its main reasons for opening the new office.[25] Indeed, the increasing tendency for companies to list on more than one exchange increased capital mobility and ultimately favored New York. By 1906, all of the major railroads and utilities on the Philadelphia market listed their stocks and bonds on Wall Street.

The Pennsylvania Railroad's new stock transfer office made a big splash in the *New York Times*, which proclaimed that the move "means radical changes" for the Quaker City.[26] But the Philadelphia papers barely mentioned the listing, expressing more concern for the hierarchy and prestige of the new appointments to the transfer post in Manhattan.[27] The city's decadence was discernible not only in its loss of capital, but also disturbingly in the apathy or lack of recognition of that loss.

The Limited Offerings of Chestnut Street

In 1903, Lincoln Steffens dubbed Philadelphia "corrupt and contented."[28] The "contractor bosses" and "utility monopolists" of the Republican machine controlled municipal coffers and utilities, raising capital on the stock exchange and running the city for their own private benefit. Their lavish new city hall cost upward of $25 million, the majority of which was paid to contracting firms, quarries, and brickworks owned by local bosses.[29] As Steffens noted, even the Pennsylvania Railroad was in bed with the machine. This allowed the railroad to extend its virtual monopoly as it bought up property, manufacturers, and other lines across the state.

Unfortunately, the success of the railroad and the machine—coupled with the failure of local investment bankers to build markets in industrial securities—made for a rather stagnant market. By the 1890s, the Pennsylvania and Reading Railroads and the utility monopolists accounted for close to half of the total capital listed on the Philadelphia Stock Exchange. Counting the Northern Pacific Railroad and U.S. government bonds, more than four-fifths of the stock exchange's primary listings represented just five large interests (see the Appendix). In this respect, the market was truly "regional," as the trading floor in the Drexel Building lacked a healthy diversity of investment opportunities.

Strangely enough, many Philadelphians were content with this market. Edward Stotesbury and his friends the Wideners were national figures, investing on a broad scale and owning celebrated estates and racetracks from Maine to Florida. In Philadelphia and its stock market, they and their allies consolidated power over what became a closely held fiefdom. They accounted for a great portion of its expansion, with their stakes in utilities around the country.[30] Philadelphia Electric, Philadelphia Traction, UGI, and the Pennsylvania Railroad paid steady dividends as they profited from the protection and favors of government. The big fish in the pond reaped clear benefits, keeping investors reasonably contented, yet the pond itself became an ever more limited economic ecosystem.

These trends were a turn-off for financiers and corporations seeking dynamic markets. For most public companies, the Quaker City was clearly not the place to be capitalized. The city's largest trust, the North American Company, which invested in Pennsylvania manufacturing, removed its $40 million in stock from trading on the Philadelphia exchange in 1903. The exchange's recording clerk plainly noted in his ledger, "Company did not want stock listed on P.S.Ex." Wall Street brokers handled the redemption of outstanding shares.[31]

The few major manufacturers that did list in Philadelphia also listed on the NYSE. This was the strategy of Cramp's Shipyard, Welsbach Light, and the Stetson Hat Company, which took its stock off the Philadelphia list in 1910. Many major regional concerns, from S. S. White Dental Manufacturing to National Biscuit, declined ever to list on the local exchange. In a letter of May 1914, the directors of the First National Bank of Philadelphia concluded that "in as much as the transactions in the stock on the Exchange were so infrequent, there was no advantage in having the stock listed."[32]

The divergent fortunes of Wall Street and Chestnut Street were reflected in seat prices on the two exchanges. Prices paid for membership on the New York Stock Exchange rose from a low of $14,000 in 1896 to a high of $82,000 around 1904, at which time membership was fixed at 1,100.[33] At the Philadelphia exchange, a seat could be bought for less than $3,000 in 1896, and prices hardly climbed as the depression ended. Seats cost considerably more on the Boston Stock Exchange, where membership was limited to 150.[34] In 1899, the Philadelphia Stock Exchange was compelled to reduce the number of memberships from 250 to 230, in an effort to boost demand in a market that lacked enough buyers to keep prices high.[35]

One reason brokers and listings flocked to Wall Street was its favorable commission structure. In 1904, Jacob Berry and Co. of New York, which held memberships on several American exchanges, advertised as follows: "Our [profit] margins under ordinary conditions on the stocks usually active in the New York market are *five* [percentage] *points*. On Philadelphia stocks under similar conditions margins of from *five to ten points* are required" by the Exchange.[36] Brokers on Chestnut Street were further limited by the rule articulated by Horace Lee, the secretary and treasurer, that "no one but a member of the Exchange has ever been permitted to represent an Exchange member on the floor."[37]

However, bigger brokers apparently opted out of the Philadelphia market. While smaller traders gained business by handling their trades, the floor seemed relatively quiet otherwise. In 1897, Abraham Barker shared his concern over these conditions with a reporter:

The partners in the larger and influential banking and brokerage firms in a very marked degree absented themselves from the floor of the Exchange, and as a consequence deprived the Exchange of the combination and the force of their interest and influence. It has resulted in the creation of what is known as "Dollar Brokers," who are employed by the absentees. They are generally gentlemen without extended clientage other than that named. The majority of the members on the floor of the Exchange are what may be termed "Traders," who, in the absence of extended clientage, watch the changing quotations on the blackboard controlled greatly by the operations of the New York Exchange, and I fear as a class reap but a precarious support from the "swapping" of jackets.[38]

As its members sought seats and investment opportunities elsewhere, the Philadelphia Stock Exchange became consumed with regulating inter-market and over-the-counter trading.[39] In 1900, its Committee on Building prohibited all telegraph and telephone communications between members on the trading floor and non-member firms, or even member firms' offices in other cities. Penalties for violation of this rule ranged from five hundred dollars for the first offense to suspension of trading privileges.[40] Limiting members' capacity to communicate in an increasingly interconnected global market constricted local brokers' abilities to make new markets, but then the exchange seemed more concerned with holding onto old markets than with developing new ones. This was not an institution moving forward into the future.

Moving Backward

If you stand still while everything around you is moving forward, you eventually slide backward. This is precisely what happened to the exchange, and to a great degree to Philadelphia's broader economy, as well. Even the institution's physical setting reflected this. While a new downtown of skyscrapers was rising around city hall a mile west of Independence Hall and the Drexel Building, the region's investment bankers made the peculiar choice to remain in the old financial district, disconnected from the corporations that sustained their market. The local historian Nicholas Wainwright portrayed their reactions in a defensive light, calling the "massive office buildings . . . erected" along Fifth Street "a fortified line to defend the traditions of downtown Philadelphia."[41]

Banking and brokerage houses had substantial investments in the area's real estate, which they knew they would devalue if they picked up and left. Yet the logic of staying varied for different classes of capitalists. For the Bourse, built on Fifth Street in 1895 to accommodate the city's commodities traders, it still made sense to locate near the port and shipping offices. For stockbrokers distanced from the corporations and trusts clustered along Broad Street near the new city hall, the old downtown proved a liability.

By the 1890s, the younger members of the Philadelphia Stock Exchange had come to see the future of their business in the new downtown; they began to advocate a move from the constricted space of the Drexel Building. Some members felt that it was wrong to be captive to the Drexel Company, which had sent much of its stock business to New York via J. P. Morgan. In 1900, with the dedication of the new city hall looming, a proposal to build a new exchange at Broad and Chestnut Streets was undercut by "various banks and real estate interests [that] banded together." According to the *Souvenir History* of the exchange, published in 1903, John Lowber Welsh, "on behalf of certain financial institutions and individuals interested in having the Stock Exchange remain east of Sixth Street, submitted a proposition" to purchase and donate to the exchange the old Merchants Exchange building, which it had occupied from 1834 to 1876.[42]

The architect Louis Hickman remodeled the building to meet the new technological requirements of the stock exchange.[43] The *Souvenir History* commemorating the "new" building related that Hickman installed "about 15 miles of iron conduit, thereby concealing all service wires and enabling them to be withdrawn at any time without the slightest injury to the building. In these conduits has been run about 95 miles of service wire."[44] The old boardroom on the second story was adapted as the trading floor, with eight kiosks in the center. At the rounded end of the building, once occupied by the Mercantile Library, Hickman built a rostrum with desks for the president and clerks to survey the trading floor. Along the sides of the room, deep alcoves filled with telegraph and telephone booths provided immediate connections to the wider world (Figures 29 and 30).

The front half of the building incorporated an office for the Clearing House as well as private reading and meeting rooms that recalled the old club-like status of the original Board of Brokers.[45] The exchange remained entirely a man's world, with a women's toilet only on the third floor. Throughout the building, spaces for members of the exchange were carefully separated from those for the public and staff. In addition to a members-only elevator, as the *Souvenir History* proudly announced, "entrance to the Clearing House, the Messengers' corridor and the Visitors' reception room is obtained without annoyance to the members. In the mezzanine story, which is reached by a separate stairway, provision has been made for all the attendants' lavatory, lockers, etc."[46]

The stock exchange sent 2,100 invitations for its opening reception on December 27, 1902, garnering an estimated—and possibly exaggerated—attendance of 2,500 people. Horace Lee, the president of the exchange, announced to the assembled celebrants that "after years of wandering," the exchange's new home "decrees that [Third] street is still to be the financial center of the city" (Figure 31).[47]

Yet the symbolism of the move was potent: the exchange had gone *back*—back to a place and, metaphorically, to a time when it had held sway.

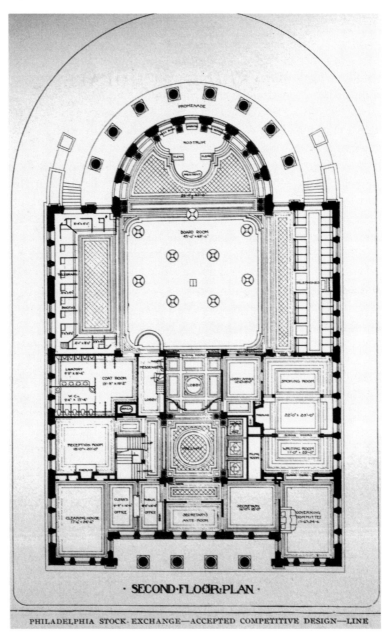

· SECOND·FLOOR·PLAN ·

Figure 29. Plan for the stock exchange on the second floor of the Merchants Exchange. From *American Institute of Architects/T-Square Yearbook* (Philadelphia: AIA, 1900). Hickman's design wrapped telegraph and telephone booths, offices, meeting rooms, and a smoking room around the trading floor.

Figure 30. The new trading floor in the Merchants Exchange. From Andrew Barnes, *History of the Philadelphia Stock Exchange, Banks, and Banking Interests* (Philadelphia: Cornelius Baker, 1911). Beyond the trading stations on the floor, the chairman's rostrum is visible at the far end of the room.

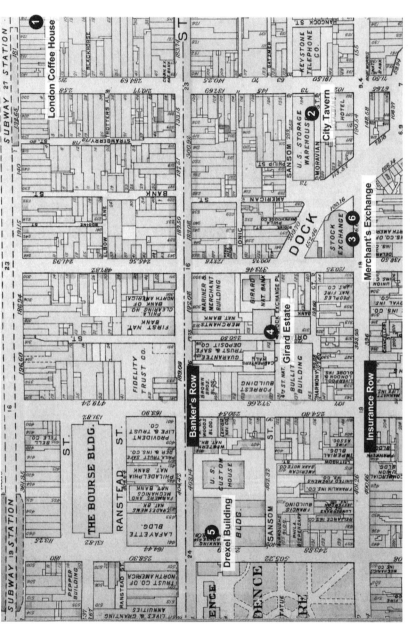

Figure 31. The old financial district, showing the exchange's historic locations. From G. W. Bromley, *Atlas of the City of Philadelphia* (Philadelphia: Bromley, 1910). This atlas illustrates what was left of the old downtown, primarily a group of financial institutions that would soon move a mile west to the new downtown.

The move did not, of course, usher in the glory days again, and within seven years, the question of location at Broad Street was again raised—and again voted down by the members. Two years later, in 1911, however, a proposal for a new building to serve the exchange on Walnut Street just west of Broad prevailed by a margin of 105 to 85.[48] More than forty years after construction on the new city hall had begun and a decade after it opened, the brokers could no longer ignore the limits of their old location.

The Stock Exchange in the New Downtown

The new exchange at 1411 Walnut Street was just one door off the main intersection of the new business district at Broad and Walnut (Figures 32, 33, and 34). Its trading floor occupied the second story, as it had in the Drexel Building, the Merchants Exchange, and even in the old City Tavern. The building's owner, the real estate developer William Deakyne, gave members of the exchange first dibs on its ground-floor retail space and upper-story offices.[49] He also conferred upon the stock exchange the right to reject "undesirable tenants."[50] It seemed a good deal, and at the close of business March 1, 1913, the stock exchange and many of its member firms departed Third Street for 1411 Walnut.

The new building was designed by Horace Trumbauer, the architect of choice among such nouveau-riche Philadelphians as Peter Widener and Edward Stotesbury, and thus sufficiently well connected to big players on the exchange to secure the commission.[51] He announced the anchor tenant to the street, carving "PHILADELPHIA STOCK EXCHANGE" in bold letters above the monumental Corinthian columns that separated tall windows overlooking the trading floor. The upper walls of patterned brick topped by a massive cornice in the Roman Revival style spoke the same architectural language of empire adopted by earlier generations of exchange designers. On the trading floor, Trumbauer copied Louis Hickman's plan for the Merchants Exchange, with the president's rostrum at one end and the boardroom at the other. Offices and phone booths once again lined either side of the floor, and the exchange installed the New York Ticker Service via Western Union telegraphs.[52]

In the towers above the trading floor, the building housed the offices of many traders. Nearby social clubs, oyster houses, tailors, haberdasheries, cigar shops, and bars served members' gastronomic, sartorial, and entertainment needs. The Manufacturer's Club sat next door at the corner of

Figure 32. 1411 Walnut Street. From Andrew Barnes, *History of the Philadelphia Stock Exchange, Banks, and Banking Interests* (Philadelphia: Cornelius Baker, 1911). This early drawing for the exchange's new headquarters shows a solitary skyscraper, though the new downtown was fast growing up in the vicinity.

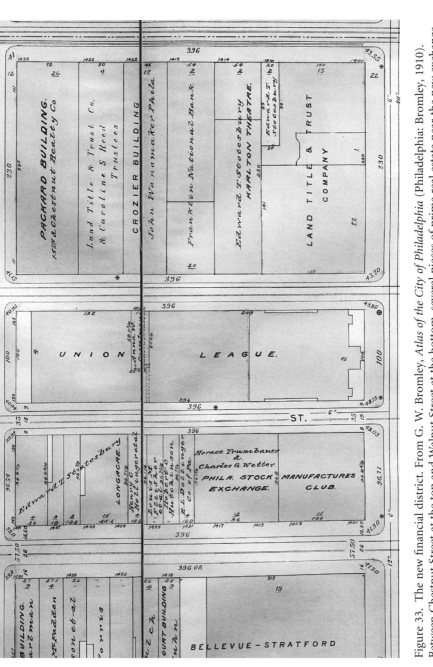

Figure 33. The new financial district. From G. W. Bromley, *Atlas of the City of Philadelphia* (Philadelphia: Bromley, 1910). Between Chestnut Street at the top and Walnut Street at the bottom, several pieces of prime real estate near the new exchange building belonged to Edward Stotesbury. Broad Street is at the right.

Figure 34. Photo of the new downtown along South Broad Street. From Moses King, *Philadelphia and Notable Philadelphians* (New York: Moses King, 1902). A decade before the stock exchange's new building was erected, the office core of the new downtown was already growing up around the new city hall.

Stratford   Bellevue   Lafayette   Land Title   Public Buildings   Beta Girard Trust   Real Estate Trust   North American   Dundas Lippincott House

Broad Street, while the Union League, also a Trumbauer design, and the Racquet Club were a block away. The Bellevue Stratford Hotel across Walnut Street hosted the dinner that inaugurated the new exchange. Guests were issued certificates for one share of "common stock" in "Philadelphia Stock Exchange Punch" and dined on Quaker-style terrapin, sweet potatoes imperial, sherbet financial, and stock exchange ices. There were of course plenty of cigars to go around.[53]

Once again the exchange found itself at the center of things, but the new downtown differed from the old one in important ways. Hotels like the Bellevue and Peter Widener's Ritz Carlton (today the University of the Arts) made Broad and Walnut the main destination for business travelers. Office towers like Trumbauer's Widener Building and the Land Title Building made the area the region's corporate hub. Banks built marble and granite branches, while stockbrokers rented upstairs offices. Unlike those of the colonial era or the nineteenth century, the occupants of these offices commuted via automobile, train, or streetcar from exclusively residential neighborhoods miles away. Many came via the Fairmount Parkway just on the other side of city hall from South Broad Street, the first link in a series of roads that by the early twentieth century linked the white-collar downtown to the suburbs.

Another significant feature of the new business district was what it lacked in the way of businesses. An overwhelming majority of shipping and commodities traders, insurance companies, and even older brokerage houses like Biddle and Drexel remained a mile away in the old downtown between Second and Fifth Streets. Drexel and Co. and other banks would soon build new headquarters around Fifteenth and Walnut Streets, but mercantile and insurance offices declined to join the financiers, trust companies, and other corporations in the new downtown. On the eve of World War I, therefore, the region's business community found itself split along sectoral, social, and geographic lines.[54] Unlike the coffeehouses or Merchants Exchange, which fostered cross-fertilization among merchants, brokers, and corporate directors, the new landscape of Philadelphia capital was fragmented. The disconnect between financial and manufacturing capital caused real damage to the region's stock market and its industrial economy in the twentieth century.

The Industrial Paradox

In 1902, Abraham Barker, by then the senior member of the stock exchange, assured his colleagues that their future lay squarely in the realm of industry. "I am confident you will get your eyes long enough off the ticker," he declared, "so that serious thoughts will devise the ways and means to insure the prosperity of the Philadelphia Stock Exchange and establish it in the first ranks of finance."[55]

On the surface, Barker's vision made perfect sense. With its wealth of factories, technical societies, and educational institutions, the "Workshop of the World" surely had the engineering, institutional, and productive capital that brokers and bankers could leverage with their ample financial capital. Barker proclaimed that the Delaware River would become "the Clyde of America," doing for North America what Glasgow, Scotland, with its Clyde River shipyards and machine builders, did for Europe. He did not seem to realize that it already was that place. Indeed, Philadelphia's Baldwin Works was the largest steam locomotive maker in the world; Cramp's and other shipbuilders made the Delaware the center of steel shipbuilding in the United States; and local machine tool, chemical, textile, and steel manufacturers were international leaders. The entire Delaware Valley, in fact, was still home to such an immense concentration of innovative and profitable manufacturers that capitalizing the region's industry alone represented an opportunity to make substantial markets.

Below the surface, however, this opportunity was limited at best. At the turn of the century, Philadelphia's manufacturers continued to rely on commercial bank loans rather than publicly traded stock for their capital needs, often serving as directors of local banks by the early twentieth century. Investment bankers remained tied to the securities of the nineteenth century, sitting on the boards of different banks, railroads, and insurance companies.[56] Nearly all manufacturing concerns were proprietorships or partnerships, and many could not stomach the prospect of losing corporate control to investment bankers.

The fit between finance and industry was complicated by more than ownership and borrowing patterns. Custom and batch production characterized most of the region's factories, which, unlike mass producers, found little use for extensive systems of bank credit and capital finance designed to underwrite economies of scale. Textile mills, for example, employed more Philadelphians than any other industry, but they typically employed fewer than one hundred hands and served markets for high-end apparel, with limited output and with styles that changed each fashion season. Brokers offered few attractive options for maintaining or expanding such businesses in ways that preserved the flexibility of production so critical to their success.[57] Ultimately, these disincentives limited both the region's pool of robust industrial securities as well as the ability of local manufacturers to compete with mass-producing firms in other regions. The local factories that did serve mass markets for consumer goods, such as General Electric or the automakers along North Broad Street, were often branch plants of companies headquartered elsewhere—and usually capitalized on the NYSE.

When they did get together, Philadelphia investment bankers and factories did not produce especially successful ventures. Bad timing in the issuance of stock and bad investments by manufacturers were part of the problem, as the career and clients of Edward Stotesbury illustrate. In 1903, he bailed out William Cramp and Sons Shipyard, the city's second largest industrial employer, after it failed to find a suitable merger partner.[58] Stotesbury issued stock on the exchange, allowing Cramp to invest in specialized warship technologies. Although it gained large World War I contracts, the shipyard helped create excess tonnage that suppressed demand as commercial shippers converted military vessels after the war. Cramp's overreliance on naval business, coupled with its costly and limited technological focus, curbed the firm's capacity to compete in peacetime markets. The yard closed in July 1927, more than two years before the crash that brought on the Great Depression. Its stock was stricken from the exchange list nine years later.[59]

Or take the example of Philadelphia's largest employer, the Baldwin Locomotive Works. It didn't incorporate until 1909, and then only in response to the financial burden placed upon its partnership by the death of William Henszey, who owned 20 percent of the company. Stotesbury floated $40 million of Baldwin stock on the Philadelphia and New York exchanges and placed other financiers on the board of directors. The company used this capital to refine steam engine production just at the moment when diesel and electric engines began to take over. At the same time, it missed the opportunity to shift from custom design to mass production, and management poured assets into a new suburban plant eight miles south of the city.[60] By the 1920s, its markets and coffers were both depleted. Baldwin removed its common stock from the Philadelphia exchange on October 23, 1929, one day before the crash. Its preferred stock was stricken in 1936.[61] Though production continued for two more decades, Baldwin—like the exchange—would no longer be a major engine of the region's economic development.

Other manufacturers of note listed on the exchange in the early twentieth century, but their markets were often short-lived, too. The streetcar maker J. G. Brill listed $5 million in common stock and $4.6 million in preferred stock in 1907, only to pull it all off the list in 1926. In 1917, Midvale Steel floated $100 million in common stock, but it was removed to New York in 1934 at the request of Midvale's new owner, Bethlehem Steel. Atlantic Refining listed bonds in 1921 but recalled and redeemed them the following year. Other large industrial issues were also victims of poor timing, including Scott Paper, Sun Oil, Alan Wood Steel, Curtis Publishing, and Budd, the auto parts manufacturer, all of which listed on the eve of the Great Depression.[62]

These unhappy marriages of industry and finance showed that the institution was struggling to find profitable connections to other firms and institutions in the region around it. This disconnect helped undermine the exchange's role in regional economic development. And it contributed to a fragmentation of Philadelphia's twentieth-century economic history. While some sectors thrived, they did so in relative isolation, even as other sectors of the metropolitan economy tanked.

World War I was good to manufacturers, but tough for brokers. Delaware Valley shipbuilders, steel makers, munitions manufacturers, textile and garment shops, and oil refineries reaped immense profits by furnishing close to 40 percent of U.S. army and navy supplies.[63] By contrast, local brokers suffered during the war, as the federal government floated bonds through New York. They also had new taxes to complain about. The Philadelphia Stock Exchange had fought off a proposed city business tax in 1913, but Congress and the Pennsylvania legislature imposed taxes on stock brokerage to pay for the war.[64] Every six months, "in order to meet the convenience of the members of the Stock Exchange, two deputy collectors" from Washington visited 1411 Walnut Street "for the purpose of making out returns and taking affidavits in connection therewith."[65] With the outbreak of war, the market collapsed, moving the New York and Philadelphia markets to suspend trading for four months. In an effort to prop up the market, the Philadelphia exchange set minimum prices on certain stocks, including American Gas, General Asphalt, and Pennsylvania Steel, and it suspended many smaller brokerage houses due to insolvency.[66]

Although the stock market came roaring back in the 1920s, Philadelphia and its economy looked somewhat old. The local writer Christopher Morley caricatured it as "a surprisingly large town at the confluence of the Biddle and Drexel families," whose class-conscious ancestor worship took precedence over their waning banking empires. "The principal manufactures are carpets, life insurance premiums, and souvenirs of Independence Hall," he quipped.[67] The region's tourist economy and consumer culture celebrated a quaint colonial past rather than industrial innovation. While the 1920s roared in the mass production centers of Detroit and Chicago and in the white-collar meccas of New York and Los Angeles, the Quaker City virtually fell off the economic map.

To be sure, Philadelphians shared all of the trappings of this decadent decade. In a passage that could have described almost any northern city, the antiquarian Herman Collins recounted how the region's inhabitants awoke to the speculative wonders—and risks—of the stock market. "In the mid-twenties families breakfasted on hopes, lunched sumptuously on paper profits and dined on disaster," he later recalled. "Little else was heard at teas, cocktail parties, golf matches, baseball games, banquets and in railway cars than such words as extra-dividends, split-ups, bonuses, margins, profits, big board, loans, short sales, millions and mergers." Locally and nationally, the market attracted new investors. "Thousands of women who never before had heard the cackle of a stock ticker frequented brokerage offices and thereafter talked learnedly about G.M. . . . G.E. or U.G.I." Stock-holders and the firms they capitalized made quick profits. "By magic of a merger, an ice cream magnate extracted fully $30,000,000, while a promi-nent baker of bread counted securities valued at more than $20,000,000," Collins related. "One stock broker spent $150,000 for new offices."[68]

Although it benefited from national prosperity, the Philadelphia Stock Exchange had become a decidedly regional market. Trading volume grew just marginally in the 1920s, and its share of the national market declined precipitously. The board periodically bought seats to hold off the market in order to sustain their value.[69]

When Eddie Brylawski came to work on the exchange for ten dollars a week in 1924, he found a "lot of décor" but a generally "quiet affair" on the trading floor. The chairman still sat on what Eddie later described as a "throne," looking to levy fines that amounted to Eddie's entire weekly sal-ary for various infractions. A "nice colored fellow" manned a shoeshine and locker room for members—who would remain exclusively white until the 1980s. Smoking was prohibited on the floor, though there were plenty of spittoons. A large cigar lounge and backgammon room just off the floor accommodated brokers' leisure pursuits. Traders also had ample time to play tricks on new members, some of whom came to the exchange from the region's dying textile and garment industries, selling them fictitious stocks in jest.[70] It would take an infusion of fresh talent from outside the region to shake up the stock exchange and put it on some sort of competitive footing.

Side Benefits from New York

Not all of the new members were ex-textile men. In what was perhaps the decade's most fortuitous event for the Philadelphia Stock Exchange, Manhattan's Consolidated Stock Exchange, which made small trades of NYSE-listed stocks, closed down. Several of its traders, instead of absorbing their businesses into the NYSE or the over-the-counter market on Wall Street, decided to move south to 1411 Walnut Street.

One of them was the broker Herbert T. Greenwood, known to friends as H. T. On his arrival in Philadelphia in 1923, he asked the Board of Governors to allow him to become a specialized dealer in the stock of the Pennsylvania Railroad. In return, he offered to buy or sell all orders under one hundred shares—called "odd-lots"—for one-eighth of a percentage point above or below the price indicated on the ticker from New York. Moreover, he would make a market for "round-lots"—trades in denominations of one hundred shares—based on prevailing prices at the NYSE.[71] The exchange launched dealer-specialist trading a year later—in 1924—and expanded it in 1927, giving individual brokers the exclusive right to make odd-lot markets in the major New York and Philadelphia stocks, such as UGI, Victor Talking Machine, and the Pennsylvania Railroad, which was awarded to Greenwood.[72]

This new system remade the exchange from an auction market dependent upon its own list of stocks and bonds to a dealer-oriented market trading equities listed on Wall Street. It was the first regional exchange to make this shift, but other regionals soon followed, becoming what *Business Week* termed "auxiliary markets for New York."[73] Greenwood, and Morris Waber and Harry Dackerman, fellow veterans of the Consolidated Stock Exchange, taught Quaker City brokers how to trade on the coattails of the NYSE. In addition to their odd-lots, Philadelphians learned to take advantage of opportunities arising from the Big Board's de-listed stocks. For instance, when the Canadian Marconi telephone company stock stopped trading on the NYSE in 1928, Walnut Street made a killing. Greenwood, Dackerman, and Waber quickly became the big players on the exchange, helping their clerks purchase memberships. Their new markets, coupled with the buoyant national economy, drove seat prices up to forty thousand dollars by the end of the decade.[74]

To handle the new trading systems, Greenwood initiated another vital innovation at the exchange. In 1924, the Clearing House began processing odd-lot transactions at night and standardized odd-lot execution. Three years later, the Board of Governors incorporated the Stock Clearing Corporation of Philadelphia (SCCP). This unprecedented clearing institution guaranteed the safety of all trades, making big brokerage houses more willing to execute big orders through the small firms on the floor.[75]

A third major change in the Philadelphia market occurred in 1931, when the board approved unlisted trading privileges for all securities listed on the New York, Boston, Chicago, Pittsburgh, and Curb Exchanges.[76] By the following year, brokers on Walnut Street were making markets in such blue chips as DuPont, General Electric, General Motors, Sears-Roebuck, Standard Oil, Warner Brothers, and F. W. Woolworth. Some of these stocks traded on the Philadelphia exchange for the first time, while others—like Atlantic Refining and Bethlehem Steel—returned after an absence. The exchange suddenly created a far broader market, though it was still not a primary market.[77]

Secular Stagnation

On the day the stock markets crashed in 1929, the ticker tape could not keep up with quotes, according to the broker Bob Guarniery, who was a page at the time. Brokers were left to wonder whether their stocks had been sold—and at what price. George Snyder recalled that his father's brokerage house stayed open all night trying to gain a sense of where it stood in the market. Many of the roughly thirty-five members on the floor went bankrupt. Frank Newburger, who came to work for his family firm, Newburger Loeb and Co., in 1929, called it a "physical impossibility" for brokers with overhead to make money in the Great Depression that followed.[78]

Like the rest of the nation, the Philadelphia exchange took a nosedive. The Stock Clearing Corporation reported net losses of around five thousand dollars in both 1930 and 1931. It finished eleven thousand dollars in the black in the recovery of 1933, but it lost more than sixteen thousand dollars the following year.[79] Greenwood, Waber, and Dackerman rescued the exchange from ruin, guaranteeing prices commensurate with the NYSE and thus preserving a modicum of local order flow.[80] Still, Snyder remembered the decade as "desperately quiet" until Hitler's invasion of Czechoslovakia in 1939, when Anaconda Steel "took off like a rabbit," and industrial markets recovered in the run-up to war.[81]

To account for the persistence of the economic depression, analysts posited a theory of "secular stagnation." In spiritual matters, they claimed, there remained room for improvement. But the secular world had reached its economic pinnacle, a veritable endpoint of economic history at which the market would plateau.[82] For Philadelphians, particularly those in finance and industry, secular stagnation offered a convenient and comforting rationalization of their failures to adapt to changing global markets. For the stock exchange, the theory helped explain why its trading volume and market share continued to decline through the 1940s.

Apparent signs of secular stagnation abounded in the Delaware Valley. The region's engineering elite disinvested in technological innovation. Old families cashed out of their manufacturing firms, selling out to national conglomerates. The University of Pennsylvania's Wharton School remained focused on running old corporations. Many Wharton-trained managers ran their families' factories into the post–World War II period, but few of these firms generated significant new patents or lines of business. Research continued at area technical schools, but the links between firms and institutions largely broke down, which had serious implications for regional economic development.[83] In 1933, the Franklin Institute, the nation's foremost technical society of the nineteenth century, abandoned its mission to foster research and technology transfer in the applied sciences. Instead, it became a museum celebrating engineering accomplishments of the past.

For the Philadelphia Stock Exchange, these diminishing opportunities in Delaware Valley manufacturing further restricted the potential for a robust market in local industrial securities. More generally, its members and governors failed to effectively restructure their market by building new networks of firms and institutions as they had before, when the region shifted from a commercial economic base to an industrial one. While the Philadelphia stock market dramatically transformed during the First Industrial Revolution of coal, iron, and railroads, it changed relatively little as the Second Industrial Revolution's big stocks traded mostly on Wall Street.

New Deal legislation helped the exchange, and the markets in general, revive to some extent. In an effort to restore faith and some stability, Congress passed the Securities Act of 1933 and the Securities Exchange Act of

1934. The new Securities and Exchange Commission (SEC) would regulate and foster healthy competition among the nation's exchanges. The SEC would approve all public offerings of securities and regulate each market. In the commission's early years, recalled George Snyder, he and his Walnut Street colleagues felt like distillers during Prohibition. But soon Congress and the SEC aided the regional exchanges by sanctioning unlisted trading privileges in 1936, and by permitting members of the NYSE to trade NYSE-listed securities on the regionals. These decisions spurred the Philadelphia exchange to innovate its trading execution systems—a vital step toward attracting order flow in this more fluid national market. In 1943, the board would admit the SCCP to membership on the exchange, allowing it to broker transactions between other members.[84]

In 1942, Philadelphia actually became the headquarters of the SEC, but for reasons associated with the city's lack of distinction. Weeks after the United States entered World War II, President Franklin D. Roosevelt designated the commission a "nonessential agency" and, in the words of the SEC, "banished it to Philadelphia." Until 1948, when it returned to Washington, the commission occupied the former Pennsylvania Athletic Club on Rittenhouse Square, just four blocks from the stock exchange. In these quarters, "live-in suites with private showers and baths became offices; a swimming pool was boarded up to accommodate files and the stenographic 'pool'; . . . and squash and handball courts provided after-hours recreation."[85] Commissioner Sumner Pike, a sardine factory owner from Maine, used the club's ballroom for holiday celebrations, bond drives, and going-away parties for employees who were drafted into the military. Interaction between the SEC and the local financial community was minimal—and not especially friendly. "None of us wanted to go to Philadelphia," recalled Vivian Shoemaker, a member of the commission's staff, "and we were not very popular up there." Commissioner Byron Woodside remembered an attitude of resentment among locals, claiming that "the newspapers in Philadelphia referred to the SEC in the lower case."[86]

As the commission suffered through its exile, Delaware Valley factories and workers enjoyed a glut of war contracts that obscured the larger forces undermining the region's economy. The Naval Shipyard on the Delaware River employed more than forty thousand men and women, Cramp's reopened for wartime production, and the Baldwin Locomotive Works again shifted production to make tanks, guns, and shell forgings. But Cramp's closed again after the war, and manufacturers around the region faced canceled contracts and striking workers reluctant to let go of inflated wartime earnings.[87]

In the postwar years, national firms such as RCA moved production out of the region, drawn by the cheaper labor, lower taxes, and sweet land deals of cities in the Sun Belt. Simultaneously, Congress and the Defense Department shifted military contracting to the "gun belt" of munitions and aerospace firms mostly concentrated in the South and the West.[88] Philadelphia in turn became part of the Rust Belt, that once-fertile crescent of industrial centers in the Northeast and the Midwest. The deindustrialization and depopulation of the postwar city fueled social and economic crises that continue to the present.

Many factors influenced this decline, and the stagnation of the stock exchange was one of those factors.[89] The lack of a strong capital market represented a competitive disadvantage for a city struggling to attract and retain employers and investors in an age in which financiers played an increasingly large role in building and maintaining firms. Its old mainstays, railroad stocks and municipal bonds, struggled as cars and trucks became the dominant modes of transportation and as Philadelphia endured fiscal crises in nearly every decade of the century.[90] Its new markets in securities listed on the New York Stock Exchange provided a much-needed boost. But these were secondary markets. They did not help the city replace its industrial economy with a vibrant service economy, as the prosperity generated by its members had few multiplier effects in other sectors of the region.

In the first half of the century, Philadelphia's economy and its exchange had less and less to do with one another. As city planning became professionalized and state and municipal bureaucracies grew in this era, private financiers' roles in economic development became more specialized and fragmented, with real estate and public bond finance typically handled by separate firms. Yet, as the region wallowed in mediocrity and its industrial base came crashing down, the Philadelphia Stock Exchange—if not the city around it—would make a series of comebacks in the postwar decades. These revivals would affect financial capitalism profoundly, though they also reveal some of the challenges and limits of Philadelphia's economic redevelopment in the second half of the twentieth century.

7

Revival: Making a Post-Industrial Market

There was no small irony in the disconnection between the Philadelphia Stock Exchange and the region's industrial economy, for one of the last great machines invented in Philadelphia held the keys to the future of financial markets. In the winter of 1945–46, at a low point in the life of the exchange, the world's first supercomputer hummed to life in an old piano factory used by the University of Pennsylvania's Moore School of Electronics. The makers of this Electronic Numerical Integrator and Computer (ENIAC) tried to interest the Pennsylvania Railroad, manufacturers, and the exchange in the new device, but all demurred. They could not anticipate its power to transform business practice. In any case, the exchange's quarters on Walnut Street lacked the space to accommodate ENIAC's nineteen thousand vacuum tubes and switchboards, the size of a tractor-trailer.

Through the 1950s, H. T. Greenwood reportedly resisted computerizing the Philadelphia Stock Exchange. His friends in the printing business thought computers meant their demise, and Greenwood was apparently a good friend.[1] Yet in 1959 the exchange took its first steps into the age of electronic capitalism. Less than half a century later, the former PHLX executive Arnie Staloff could assert without much fear of contradiction that "exchanges are computer companies . . . that's all they are."[2] The transformation had taken place inexorably.

More than the machines themselves, it was what innovators at the stock exchange did with the new technology that made the difference. Computers linked the exchange with other markets, enabled electronic execution of trading, and ultimately led to the development of new products to trade. The exchange still derived most of its market from the primary listings on the New York Stock Exchange, but it came to offer services and investment opportunities not available on the Big Board. These strategies enabled it to survive and even thrive in the second half of the twentieth century. Not only did the Philadelphia Stock Exchange reconnect with the world economy in this period, but it even made a name for itself on the global stage.

New Regional Geographies

If the exchange missed out on the corporate merger movements that made the great industrial securities market of the twentieth century, it nevertheless played a central role in restructuring the landscape of American finance in the decades after World War II. Americans' disposable income had grown from $92 billion in 1940 to more than $231 billion by 1952, and Americans put their money in the stock market on an unprecedented scale.[3] To capture this business in an era of fluid markets, the exchange took new steps to revive its influence throughout the eastern United States. First, it altered its rules to allow members to trade more easily on other markets, as many member firms had joined the NYSE and the American Stock Exchange (AMEX).[4] Then, in May 1949, in the most aggressive move the Philadelphia exchange had made since the nineteenth century, it took over the smaller Baltimore Stock Exchange.[5]

In touting the merger as a union of two important industrial markets, brokers in Philadelphia and Baltimore failed to anticipate the imminent demise of their regions' manufacturing bases. In 1952, George Snyder Jr., the president of the Philadelphia-Baltimore Stock Exchange, celebrated the "awakened spirit" of local manufacturing as it enjoyed an Indian summer of military contracting during the Korean War. "We shall be called upon," he proclaimed, "to furnish financial accommodations for the expanding business in this, America's oldest and newest industrial complex." Philadelphia's financial community had organized an active "Invest in America Committee," Snyder announced, assuming "national leadership in this important activity" of educating new investors and popularizing the stock market.[6]

Ironically, the exchange woke up from its half-century slide just as Philadelphia began hemorrhaging jobs and population—losses that would continue for more than five decades. Since Pennsylvania's first merchants traded at portside coffee houses in the colonial era, the city's exchange and its markets had mirrored—and profoundly shaped—the economic development of the region. Following World War II, however, the fortunes of the stock exchange and the city's economy were separated.

Had it not found new ways to make markets independent of the regional economy around it, the exchange's prospects for surviving the century would have presumably been slim. In 1953, when Tom Cameron moved from Boston to work for his father-in-law's brokerage firm, Hopper Soliday and Co., he found some eighty-four Philadelphia-based companies listed on the NYSE, many of them listed on the local exchange as well. Three decades later, there were just two such firms left on the Big Board.[7] By the end of the century, the city had no locally based commercial banks of consequence, either. The exchange would continue to pay rent in downtown skyscrapers, brokers would patronize nearby restaurants and bars, and the salaries of its growing staff and member firms would sustain many families. But it ceased to be a facilitator of broader regional growth.

In 1951, a short move signaled the increasing distance between the exchange and the city. It departed the second floor of 1411 Walnut Street for the ninth-floor clubroom of the old Manufacturers Club, just next door at 1401 Walnut (Figure 35). The club had folded during the Depression, and the building was now the headquarters of the Central Penn National Bank, itself an amalgamation of earlier banks. Although the new quarters were a heady nine stories above the street, the move up was only in physical terms. Lacking even a plaque announcing its presence at the entrance off the sidewalk, the exchange was as anonymous as it had been in the 1870s behind the Girard Bank (it would get that plaque a few years later).[8] It didn't much matter, though: the business that sustained the exchange's markets would come less from neighbors in downtown Philadelphia and increasingly through the wiring that connected the trading floor to other regions.

In 1953, the Philadelphia-Baltimore Stock Exchange expanded its region, taking over the tiny Washington Stock Exchange. Two years later, it signed an associate membership agreement with the Pittsburgh Stock Exchange, and the Stock Clearing Corporation of Philadelphia (SCCP) absorbed the Pittsburgh Clearing House.[9] Later, the Philadelphia-Baltimore-Washington Exchange (PBW) would formally merge with Pittsburgh, close its trading floor, sell its building, and set up teletypewriter lines that linked its western Pennsylvania members directly to the floor in Philadelphia.[10] In 1957, the PBW signed an associate membership agreement—though it did not merge—with the Boston Stock Exchange, allowing

Figure 35. Members of the Board of Governors of the Philadelphia-Baltimore Stock Exchange. From *Greater Philadelphia: The Magazine for Executives* (January 1959). The governors are lined up in front of the stock quote board at 1401 Walnut Street.

members of each exchange to trade on the other market without incurring extra fees. It would later forge similar agreements with the Montreal and Cincinnati Stock Exchanges and open a short-lived trading floor of its own in Miami.

At the same time, the PBW cultivated a broad network of members and associate members outside the three cities. Board members visited firms in regions without stock exchanges, building relationships and soliciting business.[11] The Stock Clearing Corporation initiated clearing by mail, eliminating the need for distant members to pay other brokers to submit their trades in person. The exchange installed direct phone lines from the Philadelphia floor to Pittsburgh, Boston, Baltimore, and Washington, D.C. Private teletype circuits connected Walnut Street to member firms in Florida, Georgia, Alabama, Mississippi, and the Carolinas, making the PBW the de facto exchange of the fast-growing American Southeast (Figures 36 and 37).[12]

In 1959, the technicians Harry Parker and Paul Cerecino installed an IBM punch card system that enabled the Stock Clearing Corporation to process trades electronically. These "business machines" helped the SCCP clear more than twelve million shares that year, a threefold increase over the number of shares cleared a decade previously.[13] Three years later, the exchange extended its hours to accommodate increased trading.[14]

The Philadelphia exchange's consolidation of regional stock markets in the East was part of a nationwide trend—one that it effectively started. The Chicago, Cleveland, St. Louis, and Minneapolis exchanges combined as the Midwest Stock Exchange in December 1949, taking on the New Orleans exchange a decade later. In 1957, the Los Angeles and San Francisco exchanges joined to become the Pacific Stock Exchange. These markets all took on increased overhead, including large expenditures on telecommunications technology. But the mergers, associate agreements, and new linkages brought to the PBW and to other regional exchanges greater order flow, more access to information, and an ability to compete with the NYSE in more coordinated ways.[15]

One goal of the new conglomerate exchanges lay in repealing or preventing state transfer taxes in Pennsylvania, Illinois, and California, where their clearing houses were incorporated. With the help of the National Association of Securities Dealers, Philadelphia brokers convinced the Pennsylvania legislature to abolish its stock transfer tax in 1957.[16] Soon thereafter, the PBW began issuing marketing pamphlets telling southern

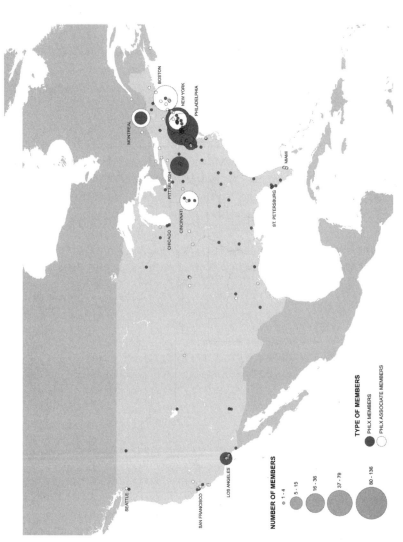

Figure 36. Map of member and associate member firm locations, 1972. Map by Christy Kwan, based on the PBW's directory of 1972. By the early 1970s, the exchange had developed a membership that connected the older regional markets of the Northeast, the Midwest, and eastern Canada with the growing Southeast and West Coast.

Figure 37. Philadelphia Stock Exchange Southeastern Division in Miami, 1976. Philadelphia Stock Exchange records, Historical Society of Pennsylvania. Though short-lived, this office in Miami signaled the exchange's strategy to be the main market for the southeastern United States.

investment bankers about the benefits of trading in its tax-free market rather than in New York, where transfer taxes would have to be paid, or in the over-the-counter markets of their own states.[17] Along with low commission rates and inexpensive membership, the ads proclaimed, this made the PBW a particularly economical place to do business, especially for small traders who lacked the capital to buy a seat on the NYSE.

Despite its renewed initiative to compete on a national stage, the PBW's market had major limitations. Throughout the 1950s and 1960s, it accounted for just 1 percent of the nation's exchange-based trading. Barry Tague recalled that when he came to work on the floor for his father in 1955, "we spent a lot of time sitting around." Only about twenty-five thousand shares traded hands on the average day. Sometimes the biggest action was at the backgammon table, where Eddie Brylawski, Morris Waber, and other high rollers at times won or lost as much money as they traded.[18]

National corporations perceived the PBW as a market of little significance. When the Ford Motor Company went public in 1956, it listed on the New York, San Francisco, Los Angeles, Midwest, and Detroit Stock Exchanges. Alexander Biddle, the executive vice president of the PBW, had gone to Detroit to lobby the company, but to no avail. The exchange finally gained the listing with the help of Walter Annenberg, the publisher of the *Philadelphia Inquirer*, but this embarrassing episode highlighted the difficulties it faced in attracting new issues of stock to trade.[19]

By 1961, only eighty-eight stock issues listed exclusively on the PBW, as members dealt overwhelmingly in NYSE-listed securities. Baltimore and Washington had added only a few stocks to the Philadelphia list, and these were for such regional concerns as the People's Drug Store chain and Potomac Electric Power. More disturbingly, the future of the list looked bleak. Companies going public had largely abandoned the regional exchanges in favor of the over-the-counter market as the place to "season" their equities before seeking a listing on the NYSE or the AMEX.[20] For the PBW, listing industrial securities represented a lost opportunity of the past—surely not a reliable strategy for future growth. Mergers and associate membership agreements had helped it expand marginally, but in order to prosper the exchange would have to find other ways to compete.

Rising from the Valley of the Shadows of the Penn Central

It was fortunate that the PBW no longer depended on railroad stocks and bonds to sustain its market. In the most dramatic event of Philadelphia's deindustrialization, the Pennsylvania Railroad merged with the New York Central in 1968, and the new company went bankrupt two years later. The Penn Central enterprise was an ill-fated and unwieldy transportation and real estate empire whose directors feuded with one another, and even the federal government failed to prop it up. "The wreck of the Penn Central," wrote the *Philadelphia Bulletin* journalists Joseph Daughen and Peter Binzen, "reached far beyond railroads, challenging deep-rooted and basic assumptions of American corporate life." It "raised questions about conglomerates; . . . about the inherent conflicts of interest that arise as a result of incestuous, interlocking directorates between financiers who supply money, managers who borrow the money, and brokers who traffic with both."[21]

Bankers, manufacturers, and thousands of railroad workers were decimated by the demise of the Penn Central and the region's broader deindustrialization. Between 1950 and 2000, the city lost one-third of its population. In the 1970s alone, it hemorrhaged over one hundred thousand industrial jobs. Unlike New Yorkers or Chicagoans, Philadelphians largely failed to replace their once powerful manufacturing base with a diverse and robust base of high-tech and high-paid service jobs.

Yet the PBW largely escaped the disaster, as it had already shifted course toward building a "post-industrial" market with renewed national and global connections. To make this transition, the old, small membership recognized that it needed a fresh generation of members and a larger staff to develop new business. In 1962, Grey Dayton, the president of the board, opined that "in view of the expanded area of the operations of the Stock Exchange, the very substantial increase in transactions in securities, and the problems of management and supervision involved, consideration should be given to provision for a paid President of the Stock Exchange."[22] Three years later, Dayton hired an old friend from school, Elkins Wetherill, to be the first full-time president of the exchange and the Stock Clearing Corporation. His mission, as he understood it, was "to bring the Exchange to life."[23]

Wetherill was an attorney who had served as the chairman of the Pennsylvania Securities Commission, but he had had no experience in the brokerage industry itself. Strangely, this helped make him a good executive. Admitting his ignorance of finance, he later described his role as "sort of like a football coach," pulling together the various constituencies of floor brokers and "upstairs" members who traded via phone or teletype from their offices in Philadelphia, New York, or Miami. Although his name suggested connections to the region's old financial elite, he was actually descended from William Elkins's brother, who also made a fortune in the western Pennsylvania oil boom of the 1860s but whose family then went on to Texas, New York, and Washington, D.C.[24]

Wetherill became the face of the PBW, which did wonders for its public profile. Every evening from 6:20 to 6:22, he delivered a financial report on the local Channel 10 TV news. He forged relationships with the region's business and political communities, sitting on the boards of the Germantown Savings Bank, the Pennsylvania Company, the Chamber of Commerce, and the reformist Greater Philadelphia Movement. In addition, the Board of Governors hired a public relations firm to design advertising campaigns and sponsored lunches with local brokerage houses to solicit their business.[25]

In 1966, the PBW moved out of the ninth floor of the Central Penn Bank building and into the first floor of the city's newest office tower, built by the Provident Bank at 17th and Sansom Streets.[26] Although Sansom was a narrow service street just a half-block north of Walnut, the Provident building sat on the edge of Penn Center. Promoted by the Greater Philadelphia Movement, this new district of concrete and glass office buildings replaced the Pennsylvania Railroad's Broad Street Station and the "Chinese Wall" of tracks that cut across the downtown. The main architect of Penn Center, Vincent G. Kling, designed the exchange's new home (Figure 38).

The rent at 17th and Sansom was nearly double that of the old Mercantile Club, but the Board of Governors saw that the "image of the Exchange would be enhanced by a ground floor location" and by the Provident's willingness to rename the tower "the Philadelphia Stock Exchange Building."[27] The city also obliged, renaming the alleyway along the north side of the building "Stock Exchange Place." The governors signed a fifteen-year lease—with an escape clause that allowed them to break it if the city or state enacted a stock transfer tax. When the exchange moved in on May 2, 1966, the *Bulletin*'s headline explained that the "Opulent Blue-Carpeted Layout Reflects Recent Volume Gains and Optimism of the Members." The carpet would soon be called "carbon blue" for the stains left by carbon negatives of the three-part tickets that traders used to record their transactions—and then threw on the floor to be collected by an evening cleaning crew with a garden rake. With "inlaid cherry desks" at ninety-two dealer positions, the new trading floor was double the size of the old one (Figure 39).[28]

Notwithstanding the traditional trappings of its interior design, the stock exchange's new quarters heralded the technological revolution that was remaking financial capitalism. Sansom Street was a highly computerized market. Brokers' posts faced a massive electronic board that filled the long wall of the room, providing a continuous flow of data from the New York and American Stock Exchanges. Behind the display were 9,920 tape drives, run by 2,580 stacks of plug-in circuit modules that updated the numbers on the board as the market changed.[29] As the PBW's business continued to grow, more computer equipment was needed, and it was soon being stored in what had been the visitors' gallery, a mezzanine balcony above the floor, where tour guides—Wetherill's daughter among them— had welcomed the public to witness the exchange in action.[30]

Together, the new president and the computerized facilities helped build a successful regional stock market just ninety miles away from Wall Street. One strength derived from the PBW's small size, which allowed it to

Figure 38. Drawing of the stock exchange's building on Sansom Street. PBW, *Annual Report* (1967). Philadelphia Stock Exchange records, Historical Society of Pennsylvania. The stock exchange's building on Sansom Street marked the southern edge of Philadelphia's new Penn Center office district, which replaced the Pennsylvania Railroad corridor on the west side of the downtown.

Figure 39. The new trading floor on Sansom Street, ca. 1967. Philadelphia Stock Exchange records, Historical Society of Pennsylvania. The photo was taken shortly after the trading floor opened, just before the arrival of women.

do things that the NYSE could not. "As long as we can keep thinking," observed Wetherill, "we'll keep ahead of the Big Board. They have the disadvantage of being so large they can't experiment without shaking the national economy. We can."[31] He recalled, "If we saw a rule of the NYSE that we could legally work around to get more business, we would do it."[32]

One challenge Wetherill confronted was the threat from institutional investors, pension funds, and investment trusts, which since World War II had increasingly handled investors' money, and even outbid investment banks for contracts to float corporate bond issues. In 1967 the exchange invited securities firms owned by institutional investors to purchase seats. At the same time, it began admitting foreign-owned investment banks to membership. Both of these moves were unheard of, and they gave the PBW a significant—if short-lived—competitive advantage over its rivals. The first institutional member was Nutmeg Securities, which oversaw the State of Connecticut's pension funds. Others included the old Insurance Company of North America and the giant French bank Credit Lyonnais.[33] Wetherill soon added European destinations to his regular jaunts to U.S. cities to recruit new members—leading to his encounter at the Paris airport described in the introduction.

As the number of overseas members rose, Wetherill received a call from Tubby Burnham of the Drexel Burnham bank, based in New York, asking him to a meeting in Manhattan. The head of Morgan Stanley ran the meeting, Wetherill recalled. "He started off by saying he wanted me to know that the fifteen most important brokerage houses in America were represented" at the table, "and they were all displeased with our taking in foreign members. He said they had all spent a great deal of time and money building networks in Europe and now we were diverting some of that business away from them." The president of the PBW replied that "they might represent the fifteen most important firms in the U.S. but [he] had looked up their business on the Philadelphia Exchange and they were not the fifteen most important firms on [his] Exchange." This jibe notwithstanding, none of the fifteen firms gave up their seats on the PBW.[34]

Foreign and institutional membership had an immediate effect on the Philadelphia market. Seat prices rose from a low of $5,000 in 1965 to a high of $33,000 in 1968.[35] Trading volume rose by 25 percent in 1968 and by another 23 percent the next year.[36] The governors were briefly forced to close the trading floor on Wednesdays to allow brokerage firms and the SCCP "to handle the backlog of paperwork created by the sustained high volume of trading."[37] New computers soon solved this problem. By the following year, the PBW counted some thirty institutional members, and institutional trades accounted for 45 percent of its volume.[38]

Despite the arrival of these larger traders, the population of the floor—as well as the upstairs membership—remained dominated by small firms, so the PBW took steps to make its market more secure and thus more attractive to bigger traders. In 1967, the exchange and the SCCP created the Special Trust Fund "to protect public customers of members . . . against financial loss" when a member firm went bankrupt or was otherwise "unable to meet its obligations."[39] The next year, as its market attracted the attention of brokers around the world, the board doubled the number of seats on the exchange. "If we don't create more now," argued Vice Chairman Tom Cameron, "those interested will go to the other regional exchanges."[40]

Out of fairness to existing members, who still constituted a mutual association rather than a corporation, the board split the seats two-for-one. This created a market in which members could sell their extra seats to their clerks or to other brokers wishing to enter the market. With the value of each seat temporarily cut in half, from $33,000 to $16,500, the exchange became accessible to even the smallest brokerage firms. Soon it would begin admitting "market-maker" members who, unlike the dealer-specialists, were not required to handle trading in particular stocks. New membership fees from the extra seats raised enough capital to cover the exchange's next move as well as several rounds of computer upgrades.[41]

The late 1960s and early 1970s were heady days on Sansom Street. Trading volume soared from $1 billion in 1965 to $5.3 billion in 1972, and the exchange's national market share more than doubled, from a tic above 1 percent in 1968 to 2.7 percent in 1972.[42] Although its market still consisted almost entirely of NYSE-listed stocks, the PBW gained a greater measure of independence from the Big Board.

The exchange's newfound prosperity caught the attention of local leaders in Philadelphia, as well. In December 1968, the cash-strapped city government, straining as its industrial tax-base washed away, proposed a stock transfer tax. Wetherill counterattacked in City Council hearings and newspaper editorials, claiming its employees paid $800,000 a year in wage taxes—a quarter of the anticipated revenue from the new tax. The exchange threatened to leave the city, warning that its departure would suck the life out of the recently revived financial district.[43] Mayor James Tate called this

Figure 40. Rendering of Decker Square in Bala Cynwyd, ca. 1967. Jacob Stelman
Collection, Athenaeum of Philadelphia. The stock exchange moved official
transactions into this new office building in early 1969 to avoid and protest
Philadelphia's new stock transfer tax, which was struck down by a local court the
next month.

an "insult" to the firemen and policemen whose salaries depended on the
new tax.[44]

The NYSE could weather its state transfer tax because it was the central
market, with volume that dwarfed all other markets. But for the Philadelphia exchange, the tax represented an incentive for brokers and their customers to take their business elsewhere. As a precaution, the PBW took out
a sixty-day lease in Decker Square, an office building nearing completion in
the suburb of Bala Cynwyd, just across City Line Avenue from Philadelphia
(Figure 40). City Council passed the tax on December 26, making it effective January 1. On New Year's Day, 1969, attentive readers of the *New York
Times* might have found a tiny headline in the corner of the financial sec-

tion reporting "Exchange Moving in Philadelphia." Wetherill informed the *Times* that with new telephone and stock tickers installed over the preceding weekend, the exchange would move all of its taxable operations to the suburbs the next day.[45]

On January 2, some fifty people went to work in the unfinished basement of Decker Square. Sitting around a thirty-foot-long table with a ticker tape running down the middle, representatives of each floor brokerage answered phone calls from their colleagues who remained on Sansom Street. Business went on as usual at Stock Exchange Place, the only change being that the clerks and junior partners in Bala officially executed all trades by filling out the standard three-part transaction tickets.[46] The following month, the Philadelphia Common Pleas Court ruled that the tax was arbitrary and destroyed the very business being taxed. By late winter, the exiles of Decker Square—and the official business of the exchange—were back downtown.[47]

Beyond these defensive measures, the PBW took outward-reaching steps to grow its market. In 1970, Tom Cameron, the chairman of the board, initiated an annual retreat that brought the governors and staff together to strategize. The first such gathering took place in Bermuda. Wives were invited, and not surprisingly the trip helped many gain newfound enthusiasm for their husbands' work.

Soon thereafter, Cameron called a meeting of stock exchange chiefs in Chicago, where he proposed a "central market system" that would report all the exchanges' trades on each other's markets. Robert Haack, the president of the NYSE, objected, claiming, "The federal government would never allow us to do that." Cameron then left the table around which they were gathered, went into the next room, and called his old friend from Harvard, U.S. Attorney General Richard Kleindienst. Returning to the room with the other exchange leaders, he put the attorney general on speakerphone. Without revealing his connection to the chairman of the PBW, Kleindienst told them he thought it was a "great idea" and that the Department of Justice would lend its full support.[48]

Computers proved critical not only for connecting to other markets, but also to the competitive advantages of the PBW itself. In anticipation of the NASDAQ's opening in 1971, the exchange put new staff member Arnie Staloff in charge of installing its new technologies. Staloff arranged with an employee on the NYSE floor to get current electronic quotes, as opposed to waiting for fifteen-minute-old information like the other regionals.[49] The

PBW even tried to trump the NYSE, extending its hours to 4 pm so it could trade for half a hour after Wall Street closed. When the Big Board suspended trading in a particular security, brokers in Philadelphia would keep on trading it, just as H. T. Greenwood had taught their predecessors to do half a century before. When the NYSE temporarily ceased trading Occidental Petroleum in the summer of 1972, the Sansom Street broker John J. Wallace made a killing for himself and the exchange as he drew non-member firms (paying non-member fees) into the Philadelphia market. The board of governors awarded him an official commendation for his "market-making ability."[50]

Also in 1972, the SCCP opened its subsidiary, the Philadelphia Depository Trust Company (PHILADEP). This allowed members of the exchange to maintain their positions in the market on a safekeeping basis, providing them with an automated bookkeeping service that reduced their internal operating costs. The following year, the SCCP and PHILADEP established the securities industry's first automated interface. In 1974 the exchange innovated its own in-house computer system for executing trades—also an industry first. At the same time, the PBW became the primary odd-lot market for Government National Mortgage Association securities and the first exchange with an active odd-lot market in U.S. government bonds.[51]

The exchange's hard work, technological advances, and product innovations enabled it to attract new firms and entrepreneurs from outside the region and even across the class boundaries that characterized the city's old financial sector. It had become an exciting and potentially lucrative place to do business. While Philadelphians left the city in droves as their industrial jobs disappeared, New Yorkers like Jeff Yass moved south in the early 1970s, drawn by the enticing opportunities on Sansom Street.[52] These new arrivals helped further a larger makeover already underway in the culture of the institution.

New Cultures of Exchange

The culture of the exchange changed more slowly than its market. The ninth floor of 1401 Walnut Street remained an antiquated and rather enclosed world. Many members were scions of old Philadelphia families who did little more than manage their relatives' wealth. Only a handful of non-WASPS inhabited the floor, including a few Catholics, Jews, and a Cherokee Indian named John Boone Martin. The decorum of the place was designed to protect the value of members' seats, but it did not necessarily promote an active business.[53]

Richard Hamilton described 1401 Walnut Street as a "gentleman's club."[54] In the separate dining rooms for members and non-members—staff and clerks—waitresses served a formal sit-down lunch. Members and non-members used segregated men's rooms as well. There was no women's room, of course, as there were no women on the trading floor. By some accounts, it often resembled a drinking club. Yet while members, clerks, and staff shared liquor, their social standings in the institution were clearly differentiated. The exchange printed a list of members ranked by seniority, with no apparent practical use beyond marking status. The staff used to call the left column of the page, where the oldest members were listed, "death row."[55] They referred to the top ten people on the list as "in the coffin."[56]

The move to Sansom Street—and the growth of the exchange—changed this culture, although not entirely and not all at once. The environment, recalls Al Brinkman, a former broker, stayed "strictly coat and tie," the atmosphere still "country club."[57] There remained separate lunch parlors for members and non-members. When John F. Wallace applied for membership in 1972, the board still required letters from his minister and banker, and two sponsors who were established members of the exchange.[58]

Old superstitions persisted, too, even in the new computerized market. If he had a winning day on Sansom Street after entering the building through its revolving door, John Showers was sure to use that same door the next day. If he lost, he would use the swinging door and begin a new cycle.[59] Eddie Brylawski always wore the same clothes after a good day—without washing the luck out of them, of course. The broker Michael Belman remembered that other traders knew Eddie was having a good week "if they could smell him." A really long streak of good luck for Brylawski was punishing for his colleagues' noses.[60]

Nor did the new building transform the PBW into a household name. Richard Hamilton remembers standing with fellow brokers at 17th and Sansom, hailing a cab, and saying "take us to Stock Exchange Place"—just for the "fun" of hearing the cabby reply, "What?!"[61]

But despite the persistence of old behaviors, the demographics of the PBW shifted dramatically. Many old WASP firms were taken over by large national brokerage houses that hired new recruits from outside the old-boy networks. More significantly, the seat split in 1968 made many clerks and out-of-towners members of the exchange.[62] Few of them were sons of older brokers. Many came from the Irish and Italian neighborhoods of Kensington, and South and West Philadelphia. When John Egan dropped out of high school in 1961 and went to work as a runner for the exchange at 1401 Walnut, most of his neighbors in Kensington "viewed [it] as a horrible job." John earned fifty dollars a week, compared to his friends making two or three hundred dollars per week in local machine shops and steel mills. Soon, however, the factories would be gone. In 1967 Egan gained a seat on the exchange.

In fact, as the stock exchange expanded rapidly over the next decade, Egan became something of an employment broker as well as a securities broker. He ran the Boys and Girls Club in his old neighborhood, and from its ranks recruited ambitious young people—like the future congressman Bob Borski—to work for his and other PBW firms.[63] The broker Fred Martin, who came from the Irish community of Fishtown, recalled that many members liked hiring Catholic school kids because they perceived them to be disciplined.[64] Sometime in the late 1970s or early 1980s, Egan hired a former bartender named John Roberts, who became one of the first African American members of the exchange.[65]

Bartending may appear an odd steppingstone to membership. But like the older members, most of the new arrivals shared an appreciation for drink. In addition to regular barhopping, Joseph Wagner, a native of South Philadelphia, organized a PBW softball league to play for beer after work. The league held fundraisers for the Children's Hospital of Philadelphia and other charities. The broker Malcolm Pryor remembers that the Miller Lite beer ad of the 1980s—"less filling or tastes great"—was considered a serious question, "debated ad nauseam at rather high decibels."[66]

While the drinking culture persisted, the exclusive male franchise at the exchange finally broke down. The first woman seat holder, Ann Papadais, was an upstairs member and did not set foot on the floor. The staff member Betty Decky ran a Wide Area Telephone Service line to Pittsburgh from downstairs, but she sat behind a partition that segregated her from the official space on the floor, where she was not allowed to tread. There was still no women's restroom near the trading floor, and the closest one to the PBW's eleventh-floor offices was on the thirteenth floor.[67] Behavior hadn't yet caught up with the sexual revolution, either. The broker Bill Terrell remembered that brokers and clerks on the floor would press their faces against the tall glass windows when they spotted a pretty woman walking down Sansom Street.[68]

It took riots in Chicago to admit a woman to the trading floor. In the violent summer of 1968, the broker Walter Devine's two male employees, Fred Martin and Joe France, were called up for National Guard duty during the Democratic Convention in the Windy City. Devine turned to his daughter, Doris, who kept his books and did other back office work, and brought her to work on the floor. Walt Devine was the chairman of the Floor Procedure Committee, so when Doris walked onto the floor, she remembered, "Nobody said a word," but "all eyes were upon me."[69]

Doris Devine stayed on the floor and ultimately bought a seat. Other women soon came to work there, too, including her sister Karen. Men accustomed to cursing on the floor took to shushing one another. Some older members were furious when the building's security guard changed the lock on the non-members' men's room to make it a ladies' room—not only because their male world had been invaded, but also because they now had to mix with non-members in the men's room. Others objected when Doris showed up one day in a pant-suit rather than a dress.

Most of the women who came to work on the floor did not stay—according to Karen Janney—née Devine—because women's perception of themselves as feminine could easily be compromised on the floor. One broker told Walt Devine that he would never allow his own daughter on the floor because of the "animal atmosphere."[70]

Beyond the floor, however, Elkins Wetherill was instrumental in making other changes to the PBW's staff in the 1970s, changes that would ultimately change the culture of the institution. "I just cleaned house," Wetherill recalled, and "brought in all new people." He hired the Russian Jew Arnie Staloff from the SEC, the Italian Nick Giordano from the accounting firm that did the exchange's audit, and George Hender from a local law firm. Staloff applied for membership at the nearby Locust Club in order to have a decent place to eat lunch, but some old German Jewish members of the PBW at the club blackballed him since they had no desire to mix with staff. At the exchange, however, Wetherill allowed these young college graduates the freedom to innovate. They also helped transform the demographics and the culture of the institution.[71]

The increasingly professional management of the exchange had its corollary in the greater pace and pressure of trading on the floor. In 1969, a columnist from the Camden *Courier Post* called the activity on the floor "organized chaos." He was fascinated by the traders' language, reporting that they "speak to each other in a strange verbal shorthand that enables them to trade stock each day valued at several million dollars."[72] The *Philadelphia Inquirer* called them "The Big-Money Wizards of Ulcer Gulch" in a profile in 1971. "Zooming along at the mind-bending pace of up to $124,000 a minute," wrote the reporter Gardiner Cox, "the Philadelphia Stock Exchange is no place to have a hangover. Raw tension is what causes several good men a year to drop out of trading and go back to the retail end of the business. Among those who stick it out, tension-related ailments are common—particularly stomach and digestive problems."[73] John Egan had stomach surgery before he reached the age of thirty.[74]

In a market where a few seconds could make a difference between profit and loss, Cox found that "telephones are used there as they are never used anywhere else, save perhaps at a bookie joint just before the Kentucky Derby. On the pickup stroke, the phone arm moves with the piston-like crispness of a Queen Anne salute; on the return stroke, like a boxer's jab to the face." Richard Hamilton showed Cox "the shiny area on the left shoulder of his jacket, worn smooth by repeated cradling of the phone," which freed his hands to scribble quotes and orders.[75] The frenzy, technologies, and profits on Sansom Street would only grow as the business shifted dramatically in the mid-1970s.

Options

American stock markets got a makeover from the Securities Act of 1975. The new law sanctioned the Central Market System initiated by Tom Cameron and the PBW. This was ultimately embodied in the Intermarket Trading System that gave the nation's exchanges unprecedented access to current information about the best prices offered on each market.[76] The act also threatened the business of regional exchanges by abolishing fixed commissions, easing restrictions on over-the-counter trading, and effectively ending institutional membership. This led to the rise of discount brokerage firms, and the exchange immediately shifted its focus to seek the business of these national brokerages.

Barry Tague, the new chairman, brought in the firm of Raymond James, becoming the head of its Philadelphia office, while Harry Dackerman allied with Laird Bissell and Meade (which later became Dean Witter). The Board of Governors reserved spots on the board for the appointees of big Wall Street firms in an effort to draw and retain their business.

At the same time, the PBW revamped its image, adopting its old name, the Philadelphia Stock Exchange, or the PHLX. The board made this change official at a meeting in the City Tavern, which the National Park Service had recreated for the bicentennial celebration of 1976. The name more accurately reflected the Philadelphia-centered nature of the institution, which had closed its trading floors in Baltimore and Washington.[77] The PHLX also made for a catchier title in the age of the acronym.

Other overhauls were in the offing. To attract discount trades and ensure its ability to offer the most competitive prices on the national market, the exchange refitted its Centramart computer system and renamed it the Philadelphia Stock Exchange Automated Communication and Execution System (PACE). It was the most fully automated trading system in the nation, far superior to the Designated Order Turnaround System soon developed by the NYSE. In its annual report of 1977, the PHLX announced that "a great percentage of the volume coming through PACE is new order flow for the Exchange—orders which would have been diverted to other markets in the past."[78]

One result was that the PHLX succeeded in raising its dollar volume of equity trades from $2.7 billion in 1974 to almost $14 billion a decade later. It did not, however, keep up with the spectacular growth of equities trading in general, as its share of the national equities market declined from 2.25 percent to 1.5 percent in the same period.[79]

Something else was needed, and as it had since the late 1940s, the PHLX responded by remaking itself yet again—once more with the aid of computers. This time, it looked to stock options and other derivative securities. Traded relatively infrequently in the United States before the 1970s, derivatives are securities whose value is determined largely from the value and attributes of other securities. For example, an option is a contract to buy or sell a given amount of stock for a predetermined price by an appointed time in the future; it is a speculation on the anticipated value of that stock.

In 1973, the chairman Barry Tague and the technology whiz Arnie Staloff traveled to the first options exchange, the Chicago Board of Options Exchange (CBOE), to learn about its markets. Staloff then worked with George Hender to design an options trading program, modeled not on the CBOE's hybrid system that mixed futures and securities trading techniques, but on the PHLX's specialist trading system of assigning traders to particular companies' stocks.[80] Tague, Staloff, and Hender negotiated a membership in the national Options Clearing Corporation (OCC) for the PHLX to clear its trades. From an asking price of $10 million, they bargained the

OCC down to $333,000, making it possible for the cash-strapped exchange and its members to afford the new venture.[81]

For many of the newer members, the move to options seemed a sound and exciting idea. Part of the appeal lay in options' ability to help them hedge equities, a form of insurance that protected one's position in a particular stock. But some older PHLX traders opposed the program. Walter Devine, Bob Guarniery, and Dave Warner thought options were a scam, no better than betting, and they did not wish to be tainted with what they assumed was an impending scandal. Others equated the program with Staloff's earlier proposal to trade Scotch whiskey futures, and they threatened to sue the exchange if it tried to raise funds for the program from among the general membership. Addressing their concerns, the PHLX created an options trading privilege whose purchasers financed the undertaking on their own. It also developed training programs that introduced members and non-members alike to the opportunities of options.[82]

Options trading began on Sansom Street on June 27, 1975, on a separate "floor" adapted in the former boardroom adjacent to the equities floor. Philadelphia was the second exchange after Chicago to ask the SEC's permission to trade options, but the federal government allowed the AMEX to launch options before the PHLX. At first, the SEC did not draft rules determining how the nation's four options exchanges—the CBOE, the AMEX, the PHLX, and the Pacific Exchange—should list their options, so the exchanges themselves adopted the practice of exclusive listings, refraining from trading each other's options. This meant that the PHLX, as the third exchange to enter the market, initially had few listings, none of which attracted great interest.

Yet according to Barry Tague, who had been largely responsible for pushing the PHLX to develop options trading, the new program "literally saved the Exchange." In 1974 it had less than $1 million in the bank and was losing $50,000 per month, partly as a result of the oil crisis and market downturn of the previous year. But options brought it roaring back.[83]

The PHLX's biggest option in 1975 resulted from an oversight. Noticing that no other exchange traded options for the paper and wood company Boise Cascade, the exchange listed it. Boise Cascade promptly made a hot market, attracting Merrill Lynch to join the PHLX options program. But the CBOE soon noticed that the company was not qualified to list options since it had not posted five years of continuous profits. The SEC called Wetherill, Staloff, and Giordano down to Washington, and they agreed to make Boise Cascade the first multiple-exchange traded option. The PHLX suggested an SEC-run lottery to assign new listings, which ultimately brought it more attractive options such as Time-Life, the camera maker Konica, and most importantly Dell Computers.[84]

The options floor drew a raft of new members, since it offered a potentially lucrative *primary* market of securities traded nowhere else. Most notorious was "Ivan the Terrible" Boesky, the infamous inside trader of the 1980s, who joined the exchange in 1975. More important was a generation of so-called mathematical traders led by Jeff Yass and Roy Neff. According to Richard Hamilton, they "raised the intelligence level on the floor" and further changed the culture of trading, buying or selling based on a mathematical process called "reverse conversion" they performed on their ever-present slide rules.[85]

The PHLX soon became the place for aspiring options traders to learn the business, long before Wharton or any other business school introduced finance courses on options. "We started inching our way up the Greek alphabet," from beta to delta to theta, recalled John F. Wallace, who watched and learned from Neff and Yass along with many other veteran PHLX members. Neff tried not to read the newspaper, as numbers, not current events, drove his decision-making process. Yass was a former professional poker player who would ultimately build Susquehanna Investments into one of the world's largest programmed trading firms. Susquehanna recruited employees from college mathematics programs and Las Vegas card tables, and by the end of the century it handled close to one out of every seven equity options traded in the world.[86]

Options swelled the wallets of Philadelphia brokers. According to the PHLX member Tom Martinelli, Barry Tague used to say, "you needed $1 million to make $100,000 on the equities floor, but you only need $100,000 to make $1 million on the options floor." Karen Janney remembered that some of her colleagues with newfound wealth were "spending it like drunken sailors," even taking the Concorde to London for lunch. Jeff Yass reportedly carried a suitcase crammed with cash for the racetrack. Michael Belman and John J. Wallace bought racehorses together, frequented the casinos in Atlantic City, and bought the nearly defunct Horn and Hardart luncheonette chain.[87] Some old Philadelphians found this behavior unbecoming, though it paled in comparison to the scandal of the twentieth century's most famous Biddle family member, Sydney Biddle Barrows—the

"Mayflower Madam"—whose upscale escort service was shut down by New York's finest in 1984.

Some options trading at the PHLX and the CBOE was not above board, as the SEC learned when it investigated the two exchanges in 1982, finding brokers making fictitious transactions to establish tax losses that protected their bloated earnings. These infractions notwithstanding, options had positive effects throughout the exchange. Seats rose in value across the board. Even Fred Martin, who never bought or sold an option in his life, garnered benefits in equities business. Since he specialized in stocks of three of the ten original options listings, he gained new business trading stock with the corresponding options specialists, who often had to buy the equities underlying their options when their sales were called in.[88]

The new business demanded new space. By February 1976, the Board of Governors reported that "the options trading floor has been expanded by moving the west wall further west into a portion of the equity trading floor."[89] Two years later, trading volume in options really took off; it grew from $570 million in 1978 to more than $5 billion in 1983. In the same period, the PHLX tripled its share of the national exchange-traded options market, from 3 percent to 9 percent.[90]

Beyond Sansom Street, the exchange and its executives gained prominence nationally and locally. John Egan, the chairman of the board, developed close relationships with members of the House and Senate securities committees in Washington, most notably with Senator John Heinz, whose son clerked at the PHLX. In the late 1970s and early 1980s, Egan brought in public board members, including Thatcher Longstreth, a city councilman, Walter D'Alessio, the chief of the Philadelphia Redevelopment Authority, and Fred DiBona, the chairman of the Chamber of Commerce. The board started the PHLX Charitable Trust and a political action committee. In 1983, Egan resigned as chairman to run for mayor, losing to Wilson Goode, the city's first African American mayor. Before Egan's temporary departure, however, the booming options market would force Egan and the new CEO, Nick Giordano, to move the exchange once again.[91]

Around the Corner, Around the World, and Around the Clock

Space was getting tight on the options floor in the late 1970s, so the PHLX asked the Provident Bank if it could expand into the building's main lobby.

Figure 41. Willard Rouse showing leaders of the exchange a model of the building on Market Street. From *Philadelphia Stock Exchange Journal* (December 1979). Philadelphia Stock Exchange records, Historical Society of Pennsylvania. Rouse's building on Market Street would house the exchange into the twenty-first century.

Since both the landlord and the architect Vincent Kling believed that the "preservation of the building's design" was more important than retaining its lead tenant, in the summer of 1978 the exchange began to look elsewhere. It almost purchased the old Bourse building on Independence Mall, where the U.S. Mint, the Federal Reserve, and other institutions would relocate. In the end, however, the PHLX decided to remain in the corporate downtown, where new office towers had extended the Penn Center district westward to 19th Street.[92]

In 1979, Willard Rouse—an erstwhile shopping mall developer who invested in stock through Tom Cameron—proposed to erect an office building covering the entire 1900 block of Market Street (Figure 41).[93] This location, almost around the corner from 17th and Sansom, would offer the exchange the most up-to-date facility without forcing its local members to move their offices and fragment the city's financial district. An earlier proposal to construct a skyscraper on the site had elicited wild protests from residential neighbors on nearby Chestnut Street. So Rouse and his mall architects, Cope, Linder and Walmsley, proposed a more modest eight-story building, modeled on the Ford Foundation's dramatic new headquarters in Manhattan.[94] Its prime office space would be oriented around an interior atrium filled with plants and light, which its promoters called a "temperature-controlled rain forest."[95]

The exchange again signed a lease with an exit clause in the unpleasant event of a stock transfer tax, and construction began in 1980. Executive offices and the growing staff would occupy the second story. Trading floors for options and equities would be in the basement, with windows facing a sunken patio in the atrium, and room to expand if necessary.[96] Even as the building was under construction, the PHLX reserved more space for options trading.

The new building opened to public acclaim in 1981. Rouse, who would soon become the region's pioneer suburban office park developer and then erect the first skyscraper taller than the statue of William Penn on City Hall, had built a compact office-cum-park in the heart of downtown. His publicist Herb Drill gushed, "It's not a building, it's a super environment for work."[97] On the trading floors, brokers were no longer the tape-watchers they had been for more than a century. Instead, they became screen-watchers, following the visual information that scrolled by on long digital displays of NYSE and AMEX quotes as well as on televisions showing CNN and later CNBC (Figures 42 and 43).[98] If something was lost in the transition, it was what Fred Martin described as the ability to gauge the market with his eyes closed, simply by listening to the ticking of the Trendicator system that tracked trading volume on the electromechanical board on Sansom Street.

The new home on Market Street was state of the art, however, a launching pad for what the PHLX would later describe, in somewhat exaggerated terms, as "the most far-reaching innovation of the twentieth century," options on foreign currency.[99] With this derivative product, the exchange played an important role in the late-twentieth-century shift in the valuation of the American and world economies from real to financial assets.[100] It also aided what the author Gregory Millman called "rebel currency traders" in their quest to "overthrow" the world's central banks.[101]

Perhaps most importantly for world markets, the PHLX's currency options helped stabilize global trade and monetary conditions after the U.S.

Figure 42. The stock exchange floor, 1983. Philadelphia Stock Exchange records, Historical Society of Pennsylvania. In the new building on Market Street, traders became screen-watchers, even as they continued to record trades on paper.

and European governments abandoned the Bretton Woods agreement. That pact had kept currency rates stable through marketplace intervention from World War II to 1973. The new, deregulated climate that followed the end of Bretton Woods raised the risks of international trade, making currency hedging attractive for those seeking security in transactions between countries with potentially volatile exchange rates. It also opened new prospects for speculating in the fluctuation of those rates.[102]

The PHLX seized these opportunities. Arnie Staloff developed the currency options program with John Egan, Michael Bloom, the legal expert Tom Russo, the ex-CBOE chairman Joe Sullivan, and the commodities trader Michael Belman. Because U.S. law treated currency as a commodity, the Commodity Futures Trading Commission (CFTC) and the Chicago Mercantile Exchange challenged the SEC's jurisdiction over the new product. In the Shad-Johnson Accord, named for the chairmen of the two commissions, the PHLX agreed to trade options on cash only—not futures

Figure 43. The stock exchange floor, 1983. Philadelphia Stock Exchange records, Historical Society of Pennsylvania. By the 1980s, the PHLX trading floor had become a busy place.

contracts. (That would come in 1985 when the exchange incorporated a subsidiary Philadelphia Board of Trade to handle commodity futures as well. The board gave the PHLX the capacity to trade a wider array of financial products than any other American exchange.)[103]

As in the case of stock options, PHLX members wishing to trade currency options financed the new program by purchasing stand-alone seats priced initially at $2,500. Trading began on December 10, 1982. As the only exchange-based market for this new product, the program immediately attracted big national and international banks and brokerages, becoming a major source of liquidity for banks and other institutional currency traders. This drove seat prices up to nearly $25,000 in just eight months. The PHLX sponsored seminars around the world; "Our job," according to Nick Giordano, "was to literally educate . . . the world" about this new market.[104]

By 1984, the program had attracted more than four hundred members who traded options on British pounds, German marks, French francs, Canadian dollars, and Japanese yen.[105] The PHLX itself went global, opening an office in London in 1984 and another in Japan soon thereafter. By 1988, its members traded currency options in volumes that reached $4 billion per day in underlying value.

In September 1987, the floor in Philadelphia added an evening trading session to reap trades from the Far East, and in January 1989 it started an early morning session for European currency options trading. It thus became the first U.S. securities exchange to trade around the clock. To promote this twenty-four-hour market, Staloff got Pennsylvania's Jack Frost Ski Resort to truck snow down to Market Street for a snowball fight at 2:30 am that was covered by the national financial news and local radio disk jockeys. This kind of public relations zest was becoming second nature to the exchange. It spiced up the usually dull gala dinner at the annual conference in Florida of the Futures Industry Association, in which the PHLX had become a major player, by flying Dizzy Gillespie in to play against a backdrop depicting the Philadelphia skyline. Leaders of the PHLX relished their ability to show up the other exchanges.[106]

Product innovation continued apace. In 1983, the PHLX began trading options on sector indexes, essentially speculations on the combined value of a group of stocks in a particular industry. It started with two such indexes, one on gold and silver and the other on casino and hotel stocks. The exchange would later develop index options on banks, utilities, semiconductors, and the oil services sector, which made major markets and became leading indicators of financial trends in those sectors. Jeff Yass's Susquehanna Investments would be the dominant specialist in these index options.[107]

In 1988, the PHLX introduced options on the Value Line Composite Index, "an arithmetically averaged and extremely broad-based index composed of approximately 1700 primarily second-tier stocks." This "European-style" option had a fixed date for exercising the contract, as opposed to American-style options that allowed investors to cash in their contracts on any given day. This made the Value Line Composite options a safer way to hedge investment portfolios. The exchange advertised the product as "loaded with all the extras . . . a high-performance vehicle for today's fast track."[108] Still another customized option hit the floor in the early 1990s, a multiple-currency option that allowed customers to combine any two of the exchange-traded foreign currencies into a single option "index" of their own making.[109]

On its two-hundredth birthday, in 1990, the PHLX touted itself as a model for stock exchanges around the world, calling itself "a blueprint for America's free markets." With the fall of the Iron Curtain, it made the high point of its bicentennial celebration an international conference with Eastern European leaders who, the exchange announced, "hope to . . . develop stock exchanges in their newly liberated countries." They came to Philadelphia "in order to learn how it is done."[110] Indeed, the PHLX's leaders were keenly attuned to the changes wrought by the end of the cold war and European economic integration. In 1991, Chairman John J. Wallace organized a trip to Ireland in an attempt to build relationships that would help the exchange gain a foothold in another reemerging economy across the Atlantic.[111]

Prosperity and Its Stumbling Blocks

The 1980s and 1990s were the PHLX's most prosperous years since the nineteenth century—marred only by the crash of 1987. Members reaped the benefits of the exchange's innovative trading technologies and products. Even on the equities floor, Fred Martin claimed he never had a losing month from the early 1980s to the mid-1990s.[112]

But while the dollar value of equity trading rose from $13 billion in 1983 to $80 billion in 2000, the PHLX's market share in exchange-traded equities declined from just over 1.4 percent to below 0.6 percent in the same period, as the NYSE improved its electronic trading system and attracted more small trades. In 1987, some Philadelphia brokers bragged that they had not lost as much as New Yorkers in the crash, but they missed the fact that their inferior equities market gave them less to lose. The PHLX tried to turn this trend around by trading NASDAQ stocks beginning in 1993, but this effort proved unsuccessful and was abandoned in 1996. Moreover, equities traders' profit margins began to shrink as discount brokers pressured specialists to pay them kickbacks for putting their orders on the floor (a legal practice).[113]

The crash of 1987 ruined many options traders, and the nation's options market took a good five years to revive. One reason for this slump carried a name from the past: Ivan Boesky, whose Drexel Burnham bank had failed, causing scandal on Wall Street and inspiring legislation to protect corporations from hostile takeovers. This reduced investors' need to protect their equities with options and limited the market for speculators using options to bet on potential takeover targets.

To rebuild the market, the PHLX convinced the CBOE, the AMEX, and the Pacific Exchange to put up funds proportional to their share of national volume for an industry-wide marketing and training program coordinated by the national Options Clearing Corporation.[114] By 1996, equity options trading had again taken off at the PHLX, and volume rose from just under $5 billion to more than $70 billion by 2000. Significantly, the exchange's share of the nation's exchange-traded equity options market more than doubled, from 7 percent to 15 percent. As a result, by 1998, new members would pay as much as $305,000 for a PHLX seat with options privileges.

The exchange's index options market likewise flowered in this period, growing from below 500 contracts in 1992 to 4,500 in 2001. All of this activity had a downside, though. The explosion in volume was more than the PHLX's dated trading technologies could handle. According to the economist John Caskey, "This hurt the reputation of the exchange and cost it potential business."[115]

Perhaps the most original development at the PHLX in this period—after currency options—was its Cash Index Participations product (CIP). The CIP was based on an index of stocks and paid quarterly dividends based on the dividends of those stocks. In 1988, the SEC approved the product, but soon after it began to trade, the Commodity Futures Trading Commission (CFTC) and Chicago commodities exchanges filed a lawsuit, charging that the CIP was legally a futures contract and could not be traded as a security. A federal court sided with the futures industry, prompting Giordano to retort that the CFTC should stick to things it knows how to do, "like regulating pork bellies."[116]

The PHLX chose not to launch CIPs on its own Board of Trade, however, declining to build a futures market of its own. But the CIP inspired imitators at the CBOE and the AMEX, who learned from the Philadelphia exchange's brush with the CFTC and developed such products as the well-known AMEX "Spiders" index of NASDAQ stocks. The PHLX did innovate other derivatives, such as Primes, Scores, and options with limited stock (OWLS), which separated the elements of a company's stock into its dividends, capital gains, and its more conservative "core value." This allowed investors to choose derivative products according to their levels of risk aversion.[117] But these did not attract the same level of interest that brokers expressed in CIPs.

For the PHLX, the most worrisome development of the early 1990s was the SEC's long-anticipated move to permit multiple listing of options. In particular, the exchange feared the loss of its market in Dell Computers, which accounted for as much as 50 percent of its equity options volume. The SEC began gradually lifting exclusive trading privileges in 1992, beginning with the least actively traded options. Seven years later, the CBOE and the AMEX were trading Dell and immediately took a big chunk out of the PHLX's market. The all-electronic International Securities Exchange, which was about to come online at the same time, threatened to take away even more business.

Fears of multiple listing of options, however, were misguided. In reality, it broadened the market. Yes, the PHLX had enjoyed an exclusive franchise on Dell, but none of the other top one hundred options had been listed on Market Street, and their business more than compensated for the loss of that exclusive franchise. By 2003, Al Brinkman, a PHLX marketing representative and former trader, could assert, "Multiple listing is the best thing that happened to this exchange."[118]

The exchange was not so fortunate in its market for currency options, although it had proved a marvelous success for more than a decade. Other exchanges in America and Europe tried and failed to make inroads into this market. The CBOE started trading currency options in late 1985 but stopped just two years later. The London International Financial Futures and Options Exchange and the Marché à Terme International de France found themselves equally incapable of breaking into what was unquestionably a PHLX market. Yet the volume of foreign currency options contracts in Philadelphia fell from more than thirteen thousand in 1993 to fewer than one thousand in 2000, becoming an insignificant line of the exchange's business. Partly, this was the result of European monetary unification with the euro, and of tough times for the Japanese yen. The larger cause, however, was that the big international banks, which had sustained the PHLX currency program, developed their own over-the-counter market—and simply no longer needed to trade on the exchange.[119]

Apprehension about the future of its markets led the PHLX to explore a variety of mergers in the 1980s and 1990s. As early as 1981, Egan and Giordano raised the prospect of a merger over dinner with AMEX chief Arthur Levitt. Negotiations never got under way, as Levitt refused to entertain the idea of keeping the Philadelphia trading floor open. The PHLX held more serious merger talks with the AMEX in 1989, the NYSE in 1990, and with the CBOE in 1993.[120] All three exchanges coveted the Philadelphia options and currency options businesses.

Then in 1997, Levitt, by then the chairman of the SEC, took the unprecedented step of restructuring the exchange's board, requiring that more than half of its members come from outside of the membership. He effectively directed the new board to merge into the AMEX. Levitt's ire had been roused principally by the behavior of the Stock Clearing Corporation and PHILADEP, where the SEC and the Federal Reserve had uncovered serious violations of oversight and clearing requirements. Conflicts of interest in the exchange's purchases of floor equipment gave the SEC further reason to consider the PHLX a corrupt institution that merited closure. Sandy Frucher, a new member of the board, termed it "an incestuous little club."[121]

The SEC forced the exchange to sell PHILADEP to its New York counterpart, the Depository Trust Company. Promoting a vision of consolidated national markets—in Manhattan, of course—Levitt then pushed the new PHLX board to sell out to the AMEX. After a century of struggling with (and sometimes transcending) its position as a regional market, it appeared that the Philadelphia stock exchange's end had finally been mandated by powers in Washington.

8

Remapping Financial Capitalism:
The PHLX's Long Ending

Regardless of his immediate motives, Arthur Levitt's decree to merge the PHLX anticipated one of the defining dynamics of early twenty-first-century financial markets. While the turn of the twentieth century witnessed a wave of mergers that created mega-corporations, the dawn of the present century has seen the world's securities exchanges jockeying to engineer mergers that would build dominant global financial institutions. In 1998, the AMEX was bought by the NASDAQ, which the following year became the world's largest stock market by dollar volume.[1] It would be the NASDAQ that ultimately acquired the PHLX a full decade later. By that time, the PHLX had once again remade itself as an institution, and in the process played a significant part in the latest restructuring of financial capitalism.

Initially, the obstacle to merger lay in the refusal of old-time members of the exchange to cede power over their membership association. Yet as the new century loomed, the exchange, its finances, its trading technology, and its reputation were in dire conditions. It would require more than an entrenched membership to keep the exchange alive another decade.

At the end of the twentieth century, the PHLX and its leaders took the approach of flirting with other exchanges while investing in their own capacity to compete. In the early twenty-first century, they used that renewed technological capacity to jolt what had become a reactive, narrowly focused operation into expansive mode. Its relationship with the city around it remained limited, and its market became increasingly digital. Yet by becoming a more liquid and more valuable asset itself, the PHLX gained greater influence over its own future.

Survival and Beyond

The leaders of the PHLX were unwilling simply to sell out to the AMEX, which they had only recently aspired to take over themselves. On the eve of the SEC's restructuring of the PHLX in 1997, the outgoing board had hired Leopold Korins, the former leader of the Pacific Exchange, as its new chairman and CEO. He lasted only a few months, and John F. Wallace then became the acting chairman. This gave the board just what the SEC did not want—a chief executive from the PHLX floor.

As his main survival strategy, Wallace concentrated on protecting what was arguably the exchange's most important business, its options on Dell, just at the moment the technology on the floor was failing to meet the needs of this market. Specialists on the floor in Philadelphia had lost confidence in the PHLX and demanded that he sell to the CBOE. But when he traveled to Chicago, its leaders offered nothing substantial. Wallace took the next plane to New York and worked out an arrangement with the AMEX that allowed Dell to trade on AMEX technology under the PHLX banner. This temporarily saved this vital line of business.[2] But Wallace soon relinquished his position to an old friend of Arthur Levitt, Meyer "Sandy" Frucher (Figure 44).

The Board of Governors informed Frucher that the PHLX had no more than six months to live and that his mandate as CEO was simply to negotiate a good deal in the sale to the AMEX. In June 1998, the board tentatively agreed to a merger proposal, but two problems stood in the way.[3] First, the PHLX remained a mutual association, as it had been for more than two centuries. Technically, its members owned it, and they were loath to give up their position as an independent exchange. Second, the leaders of the AMEX, assuming that the PHLX was moribund, were not offering anything of consequence in the deal. Why should they buy it if they could presumably take it for free?

Sandy Frucher thus found himself confronting the prospect of running a stock exchange that the SEC thought should close—with technology that might very well doom it anyway. Like Elkins Wetherill before him, he had little experience in the securities industry and was not part of its culture. Instead, he had worked in government for decades, for the likes of New York's John Lindsay, Mario Cuomo, and David Dinkins. This was, in fact, a body of experience that would prove valuable. Frucher knew how to build consensus and cut deals. He and the board developed what he described

Figure 44. Sandy Frucher in front of the Merchants Exchange, 2008. Photo from
Philadelphia Stock Exchange. Two centuries after the optical telegraph connected
Philadelphia's financial district to New York, the exchange merged with the
NASDAQ's global trading space.

as a "stealth strategy"—to rebuild the PHLX's trading technology while appearing to negotiate with the AMEX.[4] With Frucher and John F. Wallace, exchange staffers including Bill Morgan, Tom Wittman, and Bill Briggs developed new systems that could compete with even their biggest competitors.

The big challenge lay in how to pay for the upgrades. Frucher and Wallace approached Philadelphia mayor Ed Rendell, who helped assemble a consortium of banks, as well as the city's own development agency, the PIDC, to lend the exchange the capital necessary to build a competitive trading infrastructure. As collateral, the PHLX created a sort of seat-backed security in the form of a $1,500 monthly technology fee paid by each of its 504 members. Though unpopular with the members, this cash flow helped give the exchange a future.[5]

On the day the PHLX broke off negotiations with the AMEX in 1999, Frucher made its new technology public. The next day, the headline in the *Wall Street Journal* did not announce the death of the merger deal and the consequent death of the Philadelphia exchange. Instead, it announced that the PHLX would be restructured.[6]

Before the exchange could enjoy any rebirth, however, it had to confront the CBOE. Perceiving an opportunity to steal the market in Dell options, the CBOE announced it would list Dell options two weeks before the PHLX's new technology was scheduled to come on line. Yet the exchange's tech staff was ahead of schedule. The PHLX accelerated the return of Dell trading from the AMEX, which by that time was left with inferior technology, and headed off the threat from the CBOE.

In the wake of the failed merger and the PHLX's new technology rollout, the NASDAQ tried to hire away the designers of the exchange's computer systems. The New York–based exchange sent a limo to one programmer's house to take him and his wife to see mansions in suburban Connecticut that the NASDAQ offered to buy for them. But Frucher succeeded in keeping his entire tech team intact by raising salaries and asserting their central place in the functioning of the institution. He also pointed out the advantages of the comfortable life of affordable houses in Philadelphia and vacations at the Jersey shore. Wall Street firms made similar raiding forays, all apparently thwarted.

Warmer relations prevailed in the wake of September 11, 2001, when the AMEX building in lower Manhattan sustained considerable damage in the attacks on the World Trade Center. By that time, the AMEX had merged with the NASDAQ, but the two markets retained their own facilities, as they operated separate specialist and market maker systems. On Wednesday evening, September 12, the PHLX offered to share its technology and trading floor with the AMEX. The SEC passed an emergency rule allowing this temporary move. Over the weekend, Bill Terrell, the chief of floor operations, and his staff installed new telephone and connectivity lines, while technicians input all of the AMEX securities into the PHLX computer system. They did not sleep until the following Monday, when 690 traders from the AMEX arrived on Market Street.[7] Ironically, it was this crisis at the AMEX that, in the words of Norman Steisel, the PHLX's chief operating officer, provided a "real world validation of what for many was a theoretical belief that our systems could be expandable" and still sustain quick, reliable trading.[8]

But new technology and the death of the merger plan did not in themselves ensure a bright future for the PHLX. The exchange still had to offer competitive prices and products to trade, especially after exclusive options listings were phased out entirely in 1999. To boost liquidity on the Philadelphia floor, Frucher offered specialist privileges in newly multiple-listed options for free to large national firms, mandating that the specialists in the top one hundred options had to capture at least 10 percent of the national market. With this incentive, the PHLX became the only floor-based exchange to increase its market share in the wake of multiple listing, from 8 percent in 1999 to around 14 percent in late 2003.[9] On the last day of the year—admittedly a slow trading day for everyone—the exchange even led the industry in market share for equity options, topping 29 percent.[10] Over the next three years, it more than doubled the number of equity options it traded, from 1,100 to 2,327.[11]

However, the good news about the PHLX's technology and its options market was tempered by changes in its equities market. Most damaging to its equities specialists was the shift mandated by the SEC in February 2001 from minimum spreads of one-sixteenth of one dollar—or 6 cents—to a decimal system in which spreads often ended up being just a penny. This drove many specialist units off the floor and dropped seat prices for equities trading to as little as $12,500.[12] With traders pressured to increase their volume to offset the loss of their spread, the exchange reintroduced NASDAQ stocks to provide a wider range of tradable products. Between the beginning of 2004 and the end of 2006, the number of stocks traded on the PHLX rose from two thousand to seven thousand.[13] It also began a remote trading system that enabled lower operating costs for specialists located outside Philadelphia. Reaching beyond the Delaware Valley would be one of the key factors in determining the PHLX's ability to grow—as it had been for the entire history of the exchange.

The Sixth Borough: From Demutualization to Merger

Yet the institution's ownership structure, a legacy of the eighteenth century, remained a bulwark against radical change. It had prevented the sale to the AMEX, but it also impeded new strategies to make the PHLX competitive. In 2003, therefore, Frucher led a campaign to make the exchange a different corporate animal altogether. After 213 years as a member-owned mutual association, the membership voted 330 to 59 to become a stockholder corporation. The exchange's 504 members received 100 shares of stock each in lieu of their seats, creating a far more liquid market in this stock than the previous market for seats. The vote made the PHLX the first of the old floor-based exchanges to demutualize, although the all-electronic NASDAQ, the International Securities Exchange, and the Pacific Exchange had done so previously.

The new organizational structure gave the PHLX more flexibility to develop relationships with other exchanges and companies, along with the ability to raise capital outside the old membership base.[14] The move away from seats also opened the doors to greater access for trading firms by establishing trading permits to traders who wanted to access the PHLX. Continued investment in technology also kept it competitive. The exchange's new electronic options trading platform, launched in February 2005, made it the first floor-based exchange to trade all of its options and sectors indexes both on and off the floor—a fully electronic "hybrid market" accessible to traders virtually anywhere.[15] Together, demutualization and this technology enabled a new connection to the vast capital of Wall Street.

In September 2005, the *New York Times* dubbed Philadelphia "the sixth borough" of New York. Everyone from office workers to artists was finding cheaper housing, friendly neighborhoods, and a lively arts and cultural scene in what *National Geographic* called the "next great American city"—all within commuting distance of Manhattan. One might say that Philadelphia was an outer borough of New York in a financial sense, too, as the PHLX had been a secondary market to Wall Street for close to a century.

But in the digital age the "financial sixth borough" gained a new and more explicit meaning, as well. Two events in particular tied the exchange to New York.

First, in the summer of 2005, the PHLX announced that six of the largest firms in the equities and derivatives markets would acquire major stakes in the exchange. The investments included warrants that gave the firms incentives to nearly double their respective stakes by attaining a certain volume of order flow on the Philadelphia options market. All six met these goals, giving Morgan Stanley, Merrill Lynch, and Citadel Investment Group each 19.97 percent of the PHLX, while Citigroup, UBS, and Credit Suisse First Boston each held 9.97 percent—totaling a combined 89.4 percent of the exchange's ownership. Other regional exchanges soon followed this model. For example, Deutsche Bank, E*Trade, and seven other firms purchased 49 percent of the International Securities Exchange, while Susquehanna and three other brokerages together bought 45 percent of the Chicago Board Stock Exchange, the CBOE's demutualized equities market.[16]

The six firms, who represented some of the largest order flow and liquidity providers in the options market, were attracted by the PHLX's superior technology, including its new electronic trading platform connecting specialists and market makers on the floor to off-floor traders, as well as its wide range of trading products. "Our clients want quality executions delivered quickly and economically from a range of trading venues," explained Rohit D'Souza, the managing director of Merrill Lynch. Citadel's Matthew Andresen added, "Our investment in the PHLX reflects our belief that electronic markets are inherently faster, more efficient and fairer."[17] Industry analysts focused on the logic of big options trading firms effectively owning their own (not so little) market. Their orders on Philadelphia not only brought more option contracts—they also helped grow the overall market share and, by extension, the value of PHLX shares themselves. The benefits to the exchange were immediate. As U.S. options trading reached record levels, the volume of equity and index options traded at the PHLX increased 71 percent in the year following the deal with the big six. As of September 2006, the exchange was on track to record pretax year-end earnings of at least $30 million, a stark contrast with the pretax loss of almost $15 million in 2005, although that loss was driven mainly by the expense associated with the strategic investment warrants. In September 2006, spurred partly by SEC regulation, the PHLX closed its equities trading floor, shifting to an electronic platform where its equities trading volume has increased. In October it re-launched the Philadelphia Board of Trade as a "greenhouse" for new trading products that could complement its other lines of business.

These internal changes helped reposition the PHLX within a fast-changing financial sector. In 2006, it overtook the AMEX as the third most active U.S. options exchange. With close to 13 percent market share in 2006, it was still well behind the CBOE (34 percent) and the International Securities Exchange (30 percent). Nonetheless, in the words of Bill Cline, the managing director of the capital markets group of the consulting firm Accenture, the PHLX had earned a "seat at the table" as securities exchanges transformed the institutional landscape of twenty-first-century finance.[18]

For the first time since the go-go days of currency options, the alliance with the six big brokerages revived the exchange's position as a place for global firms to do business. "Our long-term objective—to offer multiple product classes traded in one venue, at a competitive cost," a sort of one-stop-shop, Frucher affirmed in August 2005, "will ensure that the investing public is not captive to the forces of market center convergence."[19] Like other leaders of the PHLX before him, he asserted the continuing value of regional exchanges in international markets. Moreover, the exchange's growing share of the options market, together with its technology and multiple trading platforms, also made it attractive to buyers.

And the early twenty-first century certainly witnessed a lot of buying, in a context of increasingly open, digital securities trading and demutualized exchanges. Mergers and alliances gave birth to a new set of transatlantic and transpacific "exchange spaces." The NYSE outbid the German Deutsche Boerse for Euronext, which itself was a conglomerate of exchanges in Paris, Amsterdam, Brussels, and Lisbon. Deutsche Boerse consoled itself by purchasing the New York–based International Securities Exchange. The NASDAQ expanded its stake in the London Stock Exchange, though it ultimately abandoned this "unrequited effort."[20] The NASDAQ did acquire the Nordic exchange group OMX with Bourse Dubai, and formed alliances with exchanges in China, Korea, and Japan. Exchanges in Singapore, India, and eastern Europe also established transcontinental connections.

Consolidation remade the landscape of U.S. markets, too. In October 2006, the Chicago Mercantile Exchange bought the Chicago Board of Trade.[21] A year later, the NASDAQ purchased the Boston Stock Exchange. On November 7, 2007, the NASDAQ announced it would acquire the

PHLX.[22] Its price tag of $652 million brought the worldwide total of mergers and joint ventures completed or announced thus far in 2007 to some $39 billion.[23]

The sale had been rumored since April, though for a time, the OMX merger drew the NASDAQ away from talks with Philadelphia.[24] Frucher and his colleagues had been working to establish the value of the PHLX, especially its options business. In late summer, the exchange hired the investment bank Greenhill and Co. to assess alternatives, including an initial public offering of PHLX stock, a sale, or merger of equals. Out of a number of interested parties, the exchange invited three formal offers—reportedly from NYSE Euronext, the NASDAQ, and a consortium led by Goldman Sachs and Susquehanna. The NASDAQ submitted the highest bid.[25]

The logic of the deal could be found in the underlying dynamics of the world's securities markets. The PHLX represented diversification for the NASDAQ, whose deeper pockets and global trading space might be able to leverage the Philadelphia Board of Trade and other underutilized assets of the PHLX. Most importantly, the PHLX would provide what was already the largest electronic stock market in the world with what Ben Craig, a vice president of the PHLX, termed "an instant credible foothold in the options markets." At the time of closing in July 2008, the NASDAQ would become the third largest options market, with roughly 15 percent of the U.S. market share. When the NASDAQ introduced its own new "price/time order book" options trading platform in March 2008, the consolidation with the PHLX's hybrid model made it the only exchange offering this range of trading possibilities. With the volume of equity options trading on the PHLX up 59 percent over the year prior to the deal, the NASDAQ even announced an intention to maintain and grow the Philadelphia options trading floor. (As of April 2008, there were nearly 250 options traders and personnel on the floor, down from nearly 1,000 nine years earlier.)[26]

The sale of the PHLX again raised the question of whether it would or should remain in its native city. The *Wall Street Journal* reported that one interested investor group led by Goldman Sachs and Susquehanna "was considering keeping a presence in Philadelphia if it bought the exchange," though it was unclear what the NASDAQ might maintain in the city.[27] When the deal was announced, 380 people worked for the PHLX, approximately 200 of them in the technology division. Although the two exchanges' boards of directors unanimously approved the transaction, for some it offered proof that demutualization had enabled yet another local institution to forfeit Philadelphia's control over its own economy.[28] But that was an old story.

The PHLX and the City It Made

A century earlier, the Philadelphia Stock Exchange had ceased being a significant engine of urban economic development. Its uneven though often remarkable successes in the last half-century belied its disconnection with the city around it. Other sorts of institutions—public sector agencies, universities, medical systems, communications and real estate firms—became the main shapers and drivers of the urban economy. While it may be the next great American city because of its livable neighborhoods and vibrant downtown, most of its skyscrapers remain inhabited by branch offices of companies headquartered elsewhere. The great majority of students at the region's seventy-some colleges and universities still leave upon graduation.[29] Finally, in perhaps the most salient indication of the limited economic opportunities in Philadelphia, in 2006 the Census Bureau revealed that it had become the poorest big city in the United States, with one quarter of residents living below the dismally low federal poverty level.[30]

The exchange itself bucked these trends and in some ways amplified its impact on the region in the late twentieth century. It attracted skilled professionals to the city in an era when most high-paying jobs had left for the suburbs or the Sun Belt. From the 1970s to the 1990s, the exchange was one of the fastest growing establishments in the Delaware Valley, enlarging its staff by some 500 percent; at the same time, the numbers of employees of its members and related concerns increased as well.[31] Still, as the region lost its industrial economy and failed to replace it with a robust service economy, the PHLX had little to capitalize or leverage in the city and region around it. The NYSE, the NASDAQ, and the CBOE, by contrast, have logical, symbiotic relationships with local institutions and global firms in New York and Chicago.

With the notable exception of the loan that rebuilt its technology, at the dawn of the twenty-first century the PHLX remained largely disconnected from other institutions in the region. Unlike the eighteenth and nineteenth centuries, when the Board of Brokers was an important part of a larger complex of firms and institutions shaping the region and its economy, in the twentieth and twenty-first centuries the exchange operated in relative isolation. The region today has no locally based national banks of note, and its insurance companies have merged into international conglomerates. It is no accident that the six big firms that bought a 90 percent stake in the PHLX are headquartered in New York, Chicago, and Zurich. Nor has Philadelphia itself shown much passion for supporting the exchange. According to Malcolm Pryor, a former member, the "institutions of Philadelphia don't seem to care about Philadelphia being a financial center."[32] In this, it is like most American cities, which have made a greater effort to hold onto their major league sports teams than their exchanges, most of which closed or merged into regional conglomerates or went digital with no apparent loss to civic life.

Why should a city like Philadelphia have a stock exchange anyway? There are no especially good answers to this question in an era of "virtual" markets. Even before demutualization, already the vast majority of the capital that flowed in and out of the PHLX neither originated nor ended up in Philadelphia. The exchange had forfeited its role as an institution mediating regional economic development by the early twentieth century. Since then, the job of fostering regional economic development has largely fallen to state and city departments, industrial redevelopment authorities, workforce agencies, and other intermediaries between the public, private, and third sectors. In recent years, these have included technology transfer centers, enterprise incubators, business improvement districts, and community development financial institutions like the Reinvestment Fund. Of course, the usual cast of boosters continues to push flashy marketing campaigns through chambers of commerce and other groups that promote the region to firms in sectors like biotechnology—especially biotechnology—but not so much finance.

As of the writing of this book, the NASDAQ-OMX still maintains an operation in downtown Philadelphia, with offices for staff, executives, computers, and a trading floor, though one week after the merger it cut one-quarter of the old PHLX staff.[33] Beyond this, it is a "sixth borough" institution. While the label is new, the pattern is old by now. For the last decade, the PHLX's CEO has commuted from Manhattan. For a little more than a century, New York capital has dominated Philadelphia firms and financial institutions.

Of course, in the preceding century, the Philadelphia Board of Brokers helped float the nation, underwrite industrial revolutions, and make its city a vital node in the world economy. The very different roles the exchange played in different eras of economic development reveal some of the tectonic shifts in the institutional arrangement of cities and their economies. The institution's decline in the late nineteenth century and the early twentieth offers a sobering lesson about the consequences of stagnant capital and weak networks for the fortunes of a region. Its various revivals over the past half-century, as well as its sale, point up the challenges and opportunities of making and remaking markets in post-industrial cities.

In the most general sense, the history of the Philadelphia Stock Exchange reminds us that institutions can play various, evolving roles in shaping metropolitan economies. Their abilities to adapt in response to change help make cities resilient. Their failures sometimes have harsh consequences for the place of their cities in the larger world. However, when urban institutions build strong relationships with one another and with the world around them, they can help mediate the wholesale restructuring of local and global economies.

As we grapple with the economic prospects of cities in the twenty-first century, institutions remain vital to our capacity to leverage human, social, and financial capital to promote urban prosperity. Today, finance transcends geography, leaving cities looking to institutions other than stock exchanges to shape their economic development. Yet the PHLX and other bygone exchanges leave a legacy of metropolitan networks of transportation, communication, and trade that still make cities run and connect them to the world economy. In that sense, though the story of America's first stock exchange has come to an end, Philadelphia remains the city it made.

Appendix

Table A.1. Value of All Securities (Stocks and Bonds) Listed on the PHLX in 1892, by Category

Category	Range of Valuation	Median Value	Total Value	% of PHLX
Railroads	$120,650–234,647,558	$2,595,050	$1,270,547,906	55.4
Public	445,000–650,065,362	4,548,319	758,141,100	33.0
Trusts, R.E.	208,000–40,000,000	1,000,000	61,133,000[a]	2.7
Mining	175,000–32,823,650	1,500,000	54,576,650	2.4
Pass. RW	500,000–6,000,000	1,000,000	31,501,362	1.4
Banks	100,000–2,000,000	500,000	26,103,900	1.1
Misc.	277,000–6,770,400	1,350,000	25,749,800	1.1
Canals	640,900–10,000,000	4,659,700	25,001,800	1.0
Manufactng.	577,587–6,000,000	3,224,875	18,624,637	0.8
Utilities	187,550–7,000,000	1,000,000	12,617,550	0.6
Insurance	200,000–3,000,000	601,438	10,702,875	0.5
Total	100,000–650,065,362	1,078,275	2,294,700,579	100.0

Sources: The directory of securities listed on the PHLX and individual company profiles by sector in the *Philadelphia Securities* statistical manual for 1892; Philadelphia Stock Exchange, Daily Quotations and Stock Sales, January 2–December 30, 1893 (PHLX Archival Collection); and PHLX, Securities Admitted to the List—Bonds, 1886–1911, and Stocks, 1891–1937 (PHLX Archival Collection).

[a] The North American Company accounts for $40,000,000, nearly two-thirds of the securities traded in the category of financial trust and real estate companies.

Table A.2. Value of Stock Listed on the PHLX in 1892, by Category

Category	% Trading Stock	Range of Stock Valuation (Common & Preferred)	Median Value (Common)[a]	Total Value	% of PHLX
Railroads	51	$120,650–126,771,200	$1,900,000	$526,942,947	72.5
Trusts, R.E.	90	250,000–40,000,000	1,000,000	59,750,000[b]	8.2
Pass. RWs	100	500,000–6,000,000	1,000,000	29,552,862	4.1
Banks	100	100,000–2,000,000	500,000	26,103,900	3.6
Mining	73	175,000–14,358,650	965,000	20,703,650	2.8
Canals	100	146,900–10,000,000	2,056,750	18,904,850	2.6
Manufactng.	100	577,587–5,000,000	1,645,575	16,124,637	2.2
Misc.	54	277,000–3,000,000	1,750,000	13,947,400	1.9
Insurance	100	200,000–3,000,000	601,438	10,702,875	1.5
Utilities	86	187,500–2,000,000	737,500	5,628,550	0.8
Total		100,000–126,771,200		728,361,671	100.0

Sources: The directory of securities listed on PHLX and individual company profiles by sector in the *Philadelphia Securities* statistical manual for 1892; Philadelphia Stock Exchange, Daily Quotations and Stock Sales, January 2–December 30, 1893 (PHLX Archival Collection); and PHLX, Securities Admitted to the List—Bonds, 1886–1911, and Stocks, 1891–1937 (PHLX Archival Collection).

[a] Mean value of common stock only; does not include preferred stock.

[b] The North American Company accounts for $40,000,000, over two-thirds of the stock traded in the category of financial trust and real estate companies.

Table A.3. Top Twenty-five Securities Listed on the Philadelphia Stock Exchange in 1892, by Combined Value of All Stocks and Bonds

Company	Category	Value	% of PHLX
1) U.S. bonds	Public	$650,065,362	28.3
2) Philadelphia & Reading RR Co.†	RR	234,647,558	10.2†
3) Northern Pacific RR Co.	RR	206,393,612	9.0
4) Pennsylvania RR Co.*	RR	153,071,200ª	6.7*
5) Texas & Pacific RR Co.	RR	86,766,700	3.8
6) Norfolk & Western RR Co.*	RR	66,808,000	2.9*
7) Philadelphia City	Public	54,389,600	2.4
8) West Shore RR Co.*	RR	50,000,000	2.2*
9) Western NY & PA RR Co.*	RR	48,950,000	2.1*
10) North American Co.	Trust	40,000,000	1.7
11) Lehigh Coal & Navigation. Co.†	Mine/canal	32,823,650	1.4†
12) United New Jersey RR Co.*	RR	31,574,400	1.4*
13) Denver & Rio Grande RR Co.	RR	28,957,500	1.3
14) Philadelphia & Erie RR Co.*	RR	26,473,000	1.2*
15) Allegheny Valley RR Co.*	RR	26,166,500	1.1*
16) Central Pacific RR Co.	RR	25,883,000	1.1
17) Chicago, St. Louis, & Pittsburgh RR Co.	RR	22,000,000	1.0
18) Philadelphia, Wilmington, & Baltimore RR Co.*	RR	21,733,350	0.9*
19) Northern Central RR Co.*	RR	20,029,000	0.9*
20) Central RR of New Jersey†	RR	18,563,200	0.8†
21) Pennsylvania Co.*	RR	15,249,000	0.7*
22) District of Columbia	Public	14,577,000	0.6
23) Cincinnati City	Public	13,962,000	0.6
24) Philadelphia & Reading Coal/ Mining. Co.†	Mining	12,338,000	0.5†
25) North Pennsylvania RR Co.†	RR	11,610,050	0.5†
Mean		76,521,267	
Total		1,913,031,6828	3.4

Sources: The directory of securities listed on the PHLX and individual company profiles by sector in the *Philadelphia Securities* statistical manual for 1892; Philadelphia Stock Exchange, Daily Quotations and Stock Sales, January 2–December 30, 1893 (PHLX Archival Collection); and PHLX, Securities Admitted to the List—Bonds, 1886–1911, and Stocks, 1891–1937 (PHLX Archival Collection).

ª In addition, the Pennsylvania Railroad Company listed £10,231,400 (British pounds) worth of bonds on the Philadelphia Stock Exchange in 1892.

* Companies controlled by the Pennsylvania Railroad.

† Companies controlled by the Philadelphia and Reading Railroad.

Table A.4. Top Twenty-five Stocks Listed on the Philadelphia Stock Exchange in 1892, by Combined Value of Common and Preferred Stock

Company	Category	Stock	% of PHLX
1) Pennsylvania RR Co.*	RR	$126,771,200	17.4*
2) Northern Pacific RR Co.	RR	85,658,612	11.8
3) Norfolk & Western RR Co.*	RR	49,500,000	6.8*
4) Lehigh Valley RR Co.†	RR	40,441,300	5.6†
5) North American Co.	Trust	40,000,000	5.5
6) Philadelphia & Reading RR Co.†	RR	39,560,500	5.4†
7) Texas & Pacific RR Co.	RR	38,706,700	5.3
8) United New Jersey RR Co.*	RR	21,240,400	2.9*
9) Western NY & PA RR Co.*	RR	20,000,000	2.7*
10) Central RR of New Jersey†	RR	18,563,200	2.5†
11) Lehigh Coal & Navigation Co.†	Mining	14,358,650	2.0†
12) Philadelphia, Wilmington, & Baltimore RR Co.*	RR	11,818,350	1.6*
13) Atlantic & Gulf Coast Canal & Okechobee Land Co.	Canal	10,000,000	1.4
14) St. Paul & Duluth RR Co.	RR	9,432,377	1.3
15) Philadelphia & Erie RR Co.*	RR	7,975,000	1.1*
16) Northern Central RR Co.*	RR	7,150,000	1.0*
17) Delaware & New England Trust Certificates.	Misc.	6,770,400	0.9
18) Newark, NJ Passenger RW Co.	Pass. RW	6,000,000	0.8
19) Cambria Iron Co.	Manuf.	5,000,000	0.7
Pennsylvania Steel Co.*	Manuf.	5,000,000	0.7*
Philadelphia Traction Co.	Pass. RW	5,000,000	0.7
Finance Co. of Pennsylvania	Trust	5,000,000	0.7
23) North Pennsylvania RR Co.†	RR	4,556,550	0.6†
24) Pennsylvania Canal Co.	Canal	4,501,200	0.6
25) Minehill & Schuylkill Haven RR†	RR	4,081,900	0.6†
Total		587,086,3398	0.6

Sources: The directory of securities listed on the PHLX and individual company profiles by sector in the *Philadelphia Securities* statistical manual for 1892; Philadelphia Stock Exchange, Daily Quotations and Stock Sales, January 2–December 30, 1893 (PHLX Archival Collection); and PHLX, Securities Admitted to the List—Bonds, 1886–1911, and Stocks, 1891–1937 (PHLX Archival Collection).

* Companies controlled by the Pennsylvania Railroad.

† Companies controlled by the Philadelphia and Reading Railroad.

Table A.5. Securities Controlled by the Pennsylvania Railroad on the PHLX, 1892

Company	Stock (Common and Preferred)	Stock & Bonds
Pennsylvania RR Co.	$126,771,200	$153,071,200[a]
Norfolk & Western RR Co.	49,500,000	66,808,000
West Shore RR Co.		50,000,000
Western NY & PA RR Co.	20,000,000	48,950,000
United New Jersey RR Co.	21,240,400	31,574,400
Philadelphia & Erie RR Co.	7,975,000	26,473,000
Allegheny Valley RR Co.	2,166,500	26,166,500
Chicago, St. Louis, & Pittsburgh RR Co.		22,000,000
Philadelphia, Wilmington, & Baltimore RR Co.	11,818,350	21,733,350
Northern Central RR Co.	7,150,000	20,029,000
Pennsylvania Co.		15,249,000
Pittsburgh, Cincinnati, & St. Louis RR Co.		6,863,000
Pennsylvania Steel Co.	5,000,000	6,000,000
Richmond & Danville RR Co.		6,000,000
Huntingdon & Broad Top Mountain. RR & Coal Co.	3,362,300	5,642,800
West Jersey RR Co.	2,134,850	4,883,350
NY, Philadelphia, & Norfolk RR Co.	1,715,000	4,563,000
Baltimore & Potomac RR Co. Main Line		4,500,000
Western Pennsylvania RR Co.		4,268,000
Pennsylvania & Northwestern RR Co.	2,000,000	4,000,000
Grand Rapids & Indiana RR Co.		3,715,000
Ashtabula and Pittsburgh RR Co.	1,658,592	3,158,592
Erie & Western Transportation Co.	3,000,000	3,000,000
Steubenville & Indiana RR Co.		3,000,000
Camden & Atlantic RR Co.	1,258,050	2,595,050
Elmira & Williamsport RR Co.	1,000,000	2,570,000
Sunbury, Hazelton, & Wilkes-Barre RR Co.		2,350,000
Susquehanna Coal Co.		2,000,000
19 Other Companies	7,612,487	19,977,487
Total Parr-Controlled (47 firms)	275,362,729	571,140,729
Total Philadelphia Stock Exchange	728,361,672	2,294,700,579
% of PHLX Total Capital	37.81	24.89

Sources: The directory of securities listed on the PHLX and individual company profiles by sector in the *Philadelphia Securities* statistical manual for 1892; Philadelphia Stock Exchange, Daily Quotations and Stock Sales, January 2–December 30, 1893 (PHLX Archival Collection); and PHLX, Securities Admitted to the List—Bonds, 1886–1911, and Stocks, 1891–1937 (PHLX Archival Collection). H. W. Schotter, *The Growth and Development of the Pennsylvania Railroad Company* (Philadelphia, 1927), provided information on which companies with securities listed on the Philadelphia Stock Exchange were owned or effectively controlled by the Pennsylvania Railroad by 1892.

[a] In addition, the Pennsylvania Railroad Company listed £10,231,400 (British pounds) worth of bonds on the Philadelphia Stock Exchange in 1892.

Table A.6. Securities Controlled by the Philadelphia and Reading Railroads on the PHLX, 1892

Name	Stock (Common and Preferred)	Stock & Bonds
Philadelphia & Reading RR Co.	$39,560,500	$234,647,558
Central RR of New Jersey	18,563,200	18,563,200
Philadelphia & Reading Coal & Mining Co.		12,338,000
North Pennsylvania RR Co.	4,556,550	11,610,050
East Pennsylvania RR Co.	1,714,900	6,000,000
Catawissa RR Co.	4,359,500	5,890,000
Minehill & Schuylkill Haven RR Co.	4,081,900	4,081,900
Delaware & Bound Brook RR Co.	1,800,000	3,300,000
Little Schuylkill Navigation, RR & Coal Co.	2,487,850	2,487,850
Perkiomen RR Co.		2,250,000
Philadelphia, Germantown, & Norristown RR Co.	2,246,900	2,246,900
Atlantic City RR Co.		2,200,000
Shamokin, Sunbury, & Lewisburg RR Co.		2,000,000
Philadelphia, Newtown, & New York RR Co.	1,200,000	1,900,000
People's Passenger RW Co.	1,500,000	1,500,000
Wilmington & Northern RR Co.		516,000
Delaware River Ferry Co. of New Jersey		489,000
Allentown Terminal RR Co.		450,000
Stony Creek RR Co.		350,000
Gettysburg & Harrisburg RW		215,000
Chestnut Hill RR Co.	120,650	120,650
Total P&R RR-Controlled (21 Firms)	78,991,950	313,156,108
Total Philadelphia Stock Exchange	728,361,672	2,294,700,579
% of PHLX Total Capital	10.85	13.65

Sources: The directory of securities listed on the PHLX and individual company profiles by sector in the *Philadelphia Securities* statistical manual for 1892; Philadelphia Stock Exchange, Daily Quotations and Stock Sales, January 2–December 30, 1893 (PHLX Archival Collection); and PHLX, Securities Admitted to the List—Bonds, 1886–1911, and Stocks, 1891–1937 (PHLX Archival Collection). James L. Holton, *The Reading Railroad: History of a Coal Age Empire*, vol. 1, *The Nineteenth Century* (Laury's Station, Pa., 1989), 247–93, provided information on which companies with securities listed on the Philadelphia Stock Exchange were owned or effectively controlled by the Philadelphia and Reading Railroad by 1892.

Notes

Preface

1. All of the exchange's own records were examined at the exchange before their transfer to the Historical Society of Pennsylvania (HSP). Therefore, all records cited as part of the PHLX Archival Collections are either at the HSP or, in rare cases, remained at the PHLX offices. Images from this collection were selected at the HSP, thus credits for figures reflect their location as of February 2008.

Introduction

1. Elkins Wetherill, fax (October 13, 2003); the incident is also recounted in Marshall E. Blume, Jeremy J. Siegel, and Dan Rottenberg, *Revolution on Wall Street: The Rise and Decline of the New York Stock Exchange* (New York: Norton, 1993), 161. The broader history of the Philadelphia Stock Exchange is also chronicled in George Shore, "The Philadelphia Stock Exchange: A Study in Tradition, Adaptation, and Survival" (Ph.D. diss., Temple University, 2003). Its mid- and late twentieth-century history is examined by John Caskey in two articles: "The Philadelphia Stock Exchange: Adapting to Survive in Changing Markets," *Business History Review* 78, no. 3 (2004): 451–87; and "The Evolution of the Philadelphia Stock Exchange, 1964–2002," Federal Reserve Bank of Philadelphia Working Paper No. 03–21 (August 2003).

2. Many urban and planning historians have focused on the economic development of cities. See, for example, Anthony Sutcliffe, *Towards the Planned City: Germany, Britain, the United States, and France, 1780–1914* (New York: St. Martin's Press, 1981); Marc Weiss, *The Rise of the Community Builders: The American Real Estate Industry and Urban Land Planning* (New York: Columbia University Press, 1989); Greg Hise, *Magnetic Los Angeles: Planning the Twentieth-Century Metropolis* (Baltimore: Johns Hopkins University Press, 1999); Robert Lewis, ed., *Manufacturing Suburbs: Building Work and Home on the Metropolitan Fringe* (Philadelphia: Temple University Press, 2004); Paul Bairoch, *Cities and Economic Development: From the Dawn of History to the Present*, trans. Christopher Braider (Chicago: University of Chicago Press, 1988). Yet few have taken financial institutions as their subject. Exceptions include Youssef Cassis, *Capitals of Capital: A History of International Financial Centres, 1780–2005*, trans. Jacqueline Collier (New York: Cambridge University Press, 2007); and William Cronon, *Nature's Metropolis: Chicago and the Great West* (New York: W. W. Norton,

1991). Geographers and sociologists have paid more explicit attention to the impacts of finance capital on urbanization, for example, Philip Abrams and E. A. Wrigley, eds., *Towns in Societies: Essays in Economic History and Historical Sociology* (New York: Cambridge University Press, 1978); Rondo Cameron and Leo Schnore, *Cities and Markets: Studies in the Organization of Human Space* (Lanham, Md.: University Press of America, 1997); David Harvey, *Spaces of Capital: Towards a Critical Geography* (New York: Routledge, 2002); Allen J. Scott, *Regions and the World Economy* (New York: Oxford University Press, 2000), and *Geography and Economy* (New York: Oxford University Press, 2007); Jane Jacobs, *Cities and the Wealth of Nations* (New York: Vintage, 1985), and *The Economy of Cities* (New York: Vintage, 1970); and especially Saskia Sassen, *The Global City: New York, London, Tokyo* (Princeton, N.J.: Princeton University Press, 1991), and *Cities in a World Economy* (Thousand Oaks, Calif.: Pine Forge Press, 1994).

3. In placing institutions at the center of the history of economic development, this study follows the "new institutional economics" that has dominated recent economic history. For overviews of this literature and its theoretical bases, see Richard N. Langlois, ed., *Economics as a Process: Essays in the New Institutional Economics* (New York: Cambridge University Press, 1986); Douglass C. North, *Institutions, Institutional Change, and Economic Performance* (New York: Cambridge University Press, 1990); John N. Drobak and John V. C. Nye, eds., *The Frontiers of the New Institutional Economics* (San Diego: Academic, 1997). Urban scholars who have highlighted the roles of institutions in shaping metropolitan economies include Hise, Cronon, Harvey, Scott, and Sassen, all cited in note 2.

4. For a more academic discussion of networks of economic development, see Domenic Vitiello, "Engineering the Metropolis: The Sellers Family and Industrial Philadelphia" (Ph.D. diss., University of Pennsylvania, 2004).

5. Though written by an urban historian (Vitiello) with the assistance of an architectural historian (Thomas), this book draws heavily on the work of economic and financial historians. In particular, the first five chapters owe much to the "new financial history" pioneered in recent decades by such scholars as Richard Sylla, John Wallis, and Robert Wright, who together with their colleagues have shown how the development of public and private financial institutions, services, and markets enabled industrialization and the integration of national and global markets from the colonial era through the Gilded Age. Beyond this explanation of economic growth, the financial sector is equally important for understanding the twentieth-century deindustrialization of Philadelphia and other manufacturing centers, as well as those cities' efforts to cope with the transition to a consumer- and service-based economy. Significant works in the "new financial history" include Richard Sylla, "Financial Systems and Economic Modernization," *Journal of Economic History* 62 (2002): 277–92; Richard Sylla and Peter L. Rousseau, "Emerging Financial Markets and Early U.S. Growth," National Bureau of Economic Research Working Paper No. 7448 (December 1999); Robert Wright, *The Wealth of Nations Rediscovered: Integration and Expansion in American*

Financial Markets, 1780–1850 (New York: Cambridge University Press, 2002), *Hamilton Unbound: Finance and the Creation of the American Republic* (Westport, Conn.: Greenwood, 2002), *The First Wall Street: Chestnut Street, Philadelphia, and the Birth of American Finance* (Chicago: University of Chicago Press, 2005), and Robert Wright, ed., *The History of Corporate Finance: Development of Anglo-American Securities Markets, Financial Practices, Theories, and Laws* (London: Pickering and Chatto, 2003); Richard Sylla, John B. Legler, and John J. Wallis, "Banks and State Public Finance in the New Republic: The United States, 1790–1860," *Journal of Economic History* 47 (1987): 391–403; Richard Sylla, *The American Capital Market, 1846–1914: A Study of the Effects of Public Policy on Economic Development* (New York: Arno, 1975).

6. Sassen, *The Global City*, and *Cities in a World Economy*; also Saskia Sassen, ed., *Global Networks, Linked Cities* (New York: Routledge, 2002).

Chapter 1

1. Minutes of Common Council, October 7, 1746, cited in *Souvenir History: Philadelphia Stock Exchange* (Philadelphia, 1903), n.p.

2. Andrew W. Barnes, ed., *History of the Philadelphia Stock Exchange, Banks, and Banking Interests* (Philadelphia: Cornelius Baker, 1901), 3.

3. Mary Maples Dunn and Richard S. Dunn, eds., *The Papers of William Penn, 1644–1679* (Philadelphia: University of Pennsylvania Press, 1981), especially 381–421; Gary Nash, *Quakers and Politics: Pennsylvania, 1682–1726* (Princeton, N.J.: Princeton University Press, 1968), 3–28. The Free Society of Traders' charter is reprinted in Samuel Hazard, ed., *Annals of Pennsylvania, from the Discovery of the Delaware, 1609–1682* (Philadelphia: Hazard and Mitchell, 1850), 541–50. See also *The Articles Settlement and Offices of the Free Society of Traders in Pennsilvania . . .* (London, 1682), reprinted in *Pennsylvania Magazine of History and Biography* (hereafter *PMHB*) 5 (1881): 37–50; Simeon E. Baldwin, "American Business Corporations before 1786," *American Historical Review* 8 (1902–3), 453–56; Nash, *Quakers and Politics*, 19–28.

4. John William Wallace, *Colonel William Bradford, the Patriot Printer of 1776: Sketches of His Life* (Philadelphia: Sherman, 1884), 337–40. For a discussion of early private enterprise in the city, see Sam Bass Warner, *The Private City: Philadelphia in Three Periods of Its Growth*, rev. ed. (Philadelphia: University of Pennsylvania Press, 1987), 3–21.

5. James M. Davis Jr., "The Colonial Coffee House," *Early American Life* 9, no. 1 (February 1978): 26–29, 86; Peter John Thompson, "A Social History of Philadelphia's Taverns, 1683–1800" (Ph.D. diss., University of Pennsylvania, 1989); David S. Shields, *Civil Tongues and Polite Letters in British America* (Chapel Hill: University of North Carolina Press, 1997), 55–98.

6. Jacob M. Price, "The Great Quaker Business Families of Eighteenth-Century London: The Rise and Fall of a Sectarian Patriciate" and "English Quaker Merchants and the War at Sea, 1689–1783," in Jacob M. Price, *Overseas Trade and Traders: Essays on Some Commercial, Financial, and Political Challenges Facing British Atlantic Mer-*

chants, 1660–1775 (Brookfield, Vt.: Varorium, 1998), chapters 3 and 4; Peter Mathias, "Risk, Credit, and Kinship in Early Modern Enterprise," in *The Early Modern Atlantic Economy*, ed. John J. McCusker and Kenneth Morgan (New York: Cambridge University Press, 2000), 15–35; Larry Neal, *The Rise of Financial Capitalism: International Capital Markets in the Age of Reason* (New York: Cambridge University Press, 1990); Sam A. Mustafa, *Merchants and Migrations: Germans and Americans in Connection, 1776–1835* (Burlington, VT: Ashgate, 2001).

7. Neal, *The Rise of Financial Capitalism*, 4; John J. McCusker and Russell R. Menard, *The Economy of British America, 1607–1789* (Chapel Hill: University of North Carolina Press, 1985), 98, 347–48.

8. Neal, *The Rise of Financial Capitalism*, 5–20.

9. John J. McCusker, "Sources of Investment Capital in the Colonial Philadelphia Shipping Industry," in McCusker, *Essays in the Economic History of the Atlantic World* (New York: Routledge, 1997), 248; see also John J. McCusker, "The Pennsylvania Shipping Industry in the Eighteenth Century" (1973), unpublished study, Historical Society of Pennsylvania (hereafter HSP); Joseph A. Goldenberg, *Shipbuilding in Colonial America* (Charlottesville: University of Virginia Press, 1976).

10. Nash, *Quakers and Politics*, 320–21.

11. See, for example, "Petition to Richard Penn for the opening of a road from Middle Ferry on the Schuylkill River to the tavern at the Sign of the Ship on the Conestoga Road and thence to the Village of Strasbourgh, Lancaster County, PA. Signed November 10, 1770 by John Morton, Robert Morris, Clement Biddle and others," Petitions, HSP.

12. Economic historians have concluded that "the substantial continuing immigration of indentured servants as well as free workers generally held the cost of labor below levels that prevailed in the regions to the south of Pennsylvania, and consequently below a level at which the large-scale importation of slaves would have been profitable." Social historians, however, point out that by 1790 one in seven city residents was a slave. David W. Galenson, "The Settlement and Growth of the Colonies: Population, Labor, and Economic Development," in *The Cambridge Economic History of the United States*, vol. 1, *The Colonial Era*, ed. Stanley L. Engerman and Robert E. Gallman (New York: Cambridge University Press, 1996), 176; Billy G. Smith, "Philadelphia: The Athens of America," in *Life in Early Philadelphia: Documents from the Revolutionary and Early National Periods*, ed. Billy G. Smith (University Park: Penn State Press, 1995), 5–7.

13. The volume of trade in bills of exchange saw a marked rise between the 1740s and the 1770s. See, for example, William Fisher, Receipts, 1753–1761, Society Miscellaneous Collection; Joseph Richardson, Letter Book, 1747–1757, and Day Book, 1732–1734; Joseph Richardson, Account Book, 1742–1752, Coates and Reynell Papers, #140; Clement Biddle and Co., Letter Book, 1769–1770; and Letters and Papers of Willing and Morris, Levis Collection, all HSP. For detailed treatment of Willing and

Morris, see Eugene R. Slaski, "Thomas Willing: Moderation During the American Revolution" (Ph.D. diss., Florida State University, 1971).

14. Daniel Vickers, "The Northern Colonies: Economy and Society, 1600–1775," in *Cambridge Economic History of the United States*, vol. 1, *The Colonial Era*, ed. Engerman and Gallman, 214; McCusker and Menard, *The Economy of British America*, 195–205; James G. Lydon, "Philadelphia's Commercial Expansion, 1720–1739," *PMHB* 91, no. 4 (October 1967): 401–18; Arthur L. Jensen, *The Maritime Commerce of Colonial Philadelphia* (Madison: University of Wisconsin Department of History, 1963); Thomas M. Doerflinger, *A Vigorous Spirit of Enterprise: Merchants and Economic Development in Revolutionary Philadelphia* (Chapel Hill: University of North Carolina Press, 1986); Kenneth Morgan, "Business Networks in the British Export Trade to North America, 1750–1800," in *The Early Modern Atlantic Economy*, ed. McCusker and Morgan, 36–62; Marc Egnal, "The Changing Structure of Philadelphia's Trade with the British West Indies, 1750–1775," *PMHB* 99, no. 2 (April 1975): 156–79.

15. William Bradford papers, MS vol. 2, Wallace Collection, HSP, *Pennsylvania Gazette*, April 11, 1754, p. 2, col. 3.

16. "Lease of messuage and lot of ground on the sw corner of Front and Market by John Pemberton and Wm. Bradford, et al. for 3 years," William Bradford Papers, Wallace Collection, HSP, May 27, 1754.

17. Cited in *Souvenir History*, n.p.

18. William Bradford Papers, Wallace Collection, HSP; Davis, "The Colonial Coffee House."

19. For a contemporary overview of market history, see John McMillan, *Reinventing the Bazaar: A Natural History of Markets* (New York: W. W. Norton and Company, 2002). See also Joseph Jackson, *Market Street: America's Most Historic Highway* (Philadelphia: Joseph Jackson, 1918).

20. John Watson, *Annals of Philadelphia and Pennsylvania, in the Olden Time*, vol. 1 (Philadelphia: Stuart, 1890), 394.

21. *Pennsylvania Journal and Weekly Advertiser*, April 8, 1762, p. 3, col. 2.

22. Robert E. Wright, *Origins of Commercial Banking in America, 1750–1800* (New York: Madison House, 2001), 49–50; Vickers, "The Northern Colonies," 237; Jacob Price, "Economic Function and the Growth of American Port Towns," in Price, *The Atlantic Frontier of the Thirteen American Colonies and States* (Burlington, Vt.: Ashgate, 1996), 153.

23. Thomas Willing to David Barclay (April 2, 1755), Charles Willing and Son Letter Book, 1754; Thomas Willing to Thomas Willing (November 22, 1755), Charles Willing and Son Letter Book; William Allen Letter Book; Isaac Norris Letter Book, all HSP; Wright, *Origins of Commercial Banking in America*, 23.

24. Wright, *Origins of Commercial Banking in America*, 51.

25. Ibid., 51–52.

26. Receipts, Certificates, Cash Book, and Account Book of the Commissioners

for Indian Affairs for the Province of Pennsylvania, 1756–1766, HSP, Coates and Rey-nell Collection; Wright, *Origins of Commercial Banking in America*, 24.

27. McCusker, "Sources of Investment Capital in the Colonial Philadelphia Ship-ping Industry," 252–57; McCusker and Menard, *The Economy of British America*, 190.

28. Quoted in Wright, *Origins of Commercial Banking in America*, 61; Joseph Albert Ernst, *Money and Politics in America, 1755–1775: A Study in the Currency Act of 1764 and the Political Economy of Revolution* (Chapel Hill: University of North Caro-lina Press, 1973), 43, 357–61.

29. "Anecdote of the Late William Bradford," *Pennsylvania Mercury* (October 1791).

30. *Pennsylvania Journal*, December 31, 1773, Independence National Historic Park (hereafter INHP) files.

31. Diary of J. Hiltzheimer, May 3, 1774, p. 30, INHP files.

32. Colonial Record, X Minutes of the Council of Safety, 526, Special Meeting of the Committee of Safety at the Coffee House (March 27, 1776). The account of the king's coat of arms being burned is reported by Thompson Westcott, *The Historic Mansions and Buildings of Philadelphia* (Philadelphia: Porter and Coates, 1877), 76.

33. Demolished in the mid-nineteenth century, the City Tavern was reconstructed in the 1970s for the bicentennial celebration, so that visitors could experience historic foods and drink in spaces that recreated the rooms where the founders debated issues of the Revolution. Clear written documentation and William Birch's engraving of the building in 1800 provided strong evidence of the original appearance. See Philadelphia Contributionship Survey 1767–69 (November 2, 1773), 34, n. 62.

34. *Pennsylvania Packet and Daily Advertiser*, August 27, 1785.

35. "Extract from the Deed describing the rules agreed upon by the Proprietors of the City Tavern" (October 9, 1776), HSP, Cadwalader Collection; City Tavern lease (July 7, 1778), HSP, Society Collection; John D. R. Platt, *Historic Resource Survey: The City Tavern* (1973), Independence National Historic Park.

36. Most were members of the Mount Regale Fishing Company of Philadelphia. Platt, *Historic Resource Survey: The City Tavern*, 16 and Appendix C, 83–84; Carl Briden-baugh, *Rebels and Gentlemen* (New York, 1942).

37. Richard Sylla, "Shaping the U.S. Financial System, 1690–1913: The Dominant Role of Public Finance," in *The State, the Financial System, and Economic Moderniza-tion*, ed. Richard Sylla, Richard Tilley, and Gabriel Tortella (New York: Cambridge University Press, 1999), 254; Wright, *Origins of Commercial Banking in America*, 62–77.

38. McCusker, "Sources of Investment Capital in the Colonial Philadelphia Ship-ping Industry," 257.

39. Quoted in Platt, *Historic Resource Survey: The City Tavern*, 114.

40. Instructions from the Committee of Secret Correspondence (June 3, 1776), Gratz Collection; Robert Morris to William Bingham (September 24, 1776), Gratz

Collection; Robert Morris to William Bingham (October 4, 1776), Gratz Collection, all HSP. See also Doerflinger, *A Vigorous Spirit of Enterprise*, 237–42.

41. Quoted in Anne Bezanson, *Prices and Inflation During the American Revolution: Pennsylvania, 1770–1790* (Philadelphia: University of Pennsylvania Press, 1951), 18.

42. Warner, *The Private City*, 34–44; Cathy Matson, "The Revolution, the Constitution, and the New Nation," in *Cambridge Economic History of the United States*, vol. 1, *The Colonial Era*, ed. Engerman and Gallman, 370.

43. *Journals of the Continental Congress* (November 16, 1780), 1060.

44. Quoted in Belden L. Daniels, *Pennsylvania: Birthplace of Banking in America* (Harrisburg: Pennsylvania Bankers Association, 1976), 9–12. See also Burton Alva Konkle, *Thomas Willing and the First American Financial System* (Philadelphia: University of Pennsylvania Press, 1937).

45. Minutes of Congress (February 7 and March 20, 1781), Franklin Papers, vol. 1, p. 225, HSP.

46. Ibid.

47. Stock Transfer Book and Stock Ledgers, Bank of North America Papers, HSP. Morris's tenure as superintendent of finance is treated in William Graham Sumner, *The Financier and the Finances of the American Revolution* (New York: Burt Franklin, 1891); Clarence L. Ver Steeg, *Robert Morris: Revolutionary Financier* (New York: Octagon, 1976).

48. For a recent discussion of the American economy after the Revolution, see Bruce H. Mann, *Republic of Debtors: Bankruptcy in the Age of American Independence* (Cambridge, Mass.: Harvard University Press, 2002), especially chapter 6, "The Politics of Insolvency."

49. Platt, *Historic Resource Survey: The City Tavern*, 190; *The Pennsylvania Packet and Daily Advertiser*, August 27, 1785.

50. Wright, *Origins of Commercial Banking in America*, 66.

51. "Report on Public Credit" (July 29, 1782), in *The Papers of Robert Morris, 1781–1784*, ed. John Catanzariti et al. (Pittsburgh: University of Pittsburgh Press, 1973–), 7: 561.

52. Wright, *Origins of Commercial Banking in America*, 6.

53. Daniels, *Pennsylvania: Birthplace of Banking in America*, 31–37.

54. Wright, *Origins of Commercial Banking in America*, 93.

55. Edwin Wolf 2nd and Maxwell Whiteman, *The History of the Jews of Philadelphia from Colonial Times to the Age of Jackson* (Philadelphia: Jewish Publication Society of America, 1957), 168. For discussion of other brokers' advertisements, see Jerry W. Markham, *A Financial History of the United States*, vol. 1, *From Christopher Columbus to the Robber Barons (1492–1900)* (Armonk, N.Y.: M. E. Sharpe, 2001), 115.

56. Joseph Stancliffe Davis, *Essays in the Earlier History of American Corporations* (Cambridge, Mass.: Harvard University Press, 1917), 1: 197–98.

57. Stuart Banner, *Anglo-American Securities Regulation: Cultural and Political*

Roots, 1690–1860 (New York: Cambridge University Press, 1998), 130; Edwin J. Perkins, *American Public Finance and Financial Services, 1700–1815* (Columbus: Ohio State University Press, 1994), 311.

58. Quoted in Banner, *Anglo-American Securities Regulation*, 130.

59. Doerflinger, *A Vigorous Spirit of Enterprise*, 310.

60. Clement Biddle and Co. Journal, 1789–1795, Thomas A. Biddle Co. Business Books, vol. 19, HSP.

61. Banner, *Anglo-American Securities Regulation*, 131.

62. For discussion of land markets, see, for example, Alan Taylor, *William Cooper's Town: Power and Persuasion on the Frontier of the Early American Republic* (New York: Vintage, 1996). The importance of small cities for early American interior economic development is highlighted in Diane Shaw, *City Building on the Eastern Frontier: Sorting the New Nineteenth-Century City* (Baltimore: Johns Hopkins University Press, 2004).

63. Matson, "The Revolution, the Constitution, and the New Nation," 390–91; Cathy Matson, "Public Vices, Private Benefit: William Duer and His Circle, 1776–1792," in *New York and the Rise of American Capitalism*, ed. William Pencak and Conrad Edick Wright (New York: New York Historical Society, 1989), 96; Sylla, "Shaping the U.S. Financial System," 257–60; E. James Ferguson, "Speculation in the Revolutionary Debt: The Ownership of Public Securities in Maryland, 1790," *Journal of Economic History* 14, no. 1 (Winter 1954): 35–45; Whitney K. Bates, "Northern Speculators and Southern State Debts: 1790," *William and Mary Quarterly*, 3rd ser., 19 (1962): 30–48.

64. Quoted in Banner, *Anglo-American Securities Regulation*, 138.

Chapter 2

1. See, for example, Robert E. Wright and David J. Cowen, *Financial Founding Fathers: The Men Who Made America Rich* (Chicago: University of Chicago Press, 2006).

2. Matthew McConnell, *An Essay on the Domestic Debts of the United States of America* (Philadelphia: Robert Aitken, 1787), HSP. Other merchants of this period published similar treatises, all aimed at lobbying the new federal and state governments to establish favorable laws and systems of finance. In his *Seventh Essay on Free Trade and Finance* (1785), for example, the Philadelphian Peletiah Webster stressed "the expediency of funding the public securities [and] striking further sums of paper money."

3. Richard Sylla, "Shaping the U.S. Financial System, 1690–1913: The Dominant Role of Public Finance," in *The State, the Financial System, and Economic Modernization*, ed. Richard Sylla, Richard Tilley, and Gabriel Tortella (New York: Cambridge University Press, 1999), 249.

4. *Souvenir History: Philadelphia Stock Exchange* (Philadelphia, 1903), n.p.

5. McConnell to Coxe (August 19, 1790), HSP.

6. City of Philadelphia, *An Ordinance Providing for the Raising of a Sum of Money for Supplying the City of Philadelphia with Wholesome Water* (Philadelphia: Poulson, 1799), Library Company of Philadelphia; *Philadelphia Death Records*, HSP, microfilm XR 696.

7. Lawrence Lewis Jr., *A History of the Bank of North America, the First Bank Chartered in the United States* (Philadelphia: Lippincott, 1882), 133–47.

8. John Donaldson succeeded Whelen as the board's fourth president. J. Thomas Scharf and Thompson Westcott, *History of Philadelphia, 1609–1884* (Philadelphia: Everts, 1884), 2086–87; see also Lewis, *A History of the Bank of North America*, 138; *Souvenir History*.

9. Henry Simpson, *The Lives of Eminent Philadelphians Now Deceased* (Philadelphia: William Brotherhood, 1859), 81–83.

10. Clement Biddle, *Philadelphia Directory and Register* (Philadelphia, 1793–94), HSP.

11. Sylla, "Shaping the U.S. Financial System," 260; Edwin J. Perkins, *American Public Finance and Financial Services, 1700–1815* (Columbus: Ohio State University Press, 1994), 201.

12. Jerry W. Markham, *A Financial History of the United States*, vol. 1, *From Christopher Columbus to the Robber Barons (1492–1900)* (Armonk, N.Y.: M. E. Sharpe, 2001), 116.

13. "PHLX at 200: 'A Blueprint for America's Free Markets,'" *PACEsetter* 6 (May 30, 1990), 1.

14. For an account of the issues that shaped the earliest exchanges, see John McMillan, *Reinventing the Bazaar: A Natural History of Markets* (New York: Norton, 2001), 22–23.

15. Robert Wright, *The Wealth of Nations Rediscovered: Integration and Expansion in American Financial Markets, 1780–1850* (New York: Cambridge University Press, 2002), 137.

16. Andrew W. Barnes, ed., *History of the Philadelphia Stock Exchange, Banks, and Banking Interests* (Philadelphia: Cornelius Baker, 1901), 4. Similar guild-like organizations controlled many of the markets of the city. The Carpenters' Company, for example, published a *Rule Book* that listed prices for typical building projects and elements, thereby setting prices in the construction industry.

17. Sylla, "Shaping the U.S. Financial System," 1690–1913: The Dominant Role of Public Finance," in *The State, the Financial System and Economic Modernization*, ed. Richard Sylla, Richard Tilly, and Gabriel Tortella (New York: Cambridge University Press, 1999), 250.

18. Jefferson to Edward Pendleton (July 24, 1791), Washburn Papers, vol. 2, fol. 6.

19. Sylla, "Shaping the U.S. Financial System," 260.

20. Ibid., 258.

21. Burton Alva Konkle, *Thomas Willing and the First American Financial System* (Philadelphia: University of Pennsylvania Press, 1937), 145; Edward S. Kaplan, *The*

Bank of the United States and the American Economy (Westport, Conn.: Greenwood, 1999); Scharf and Westcott, *History of Philadelphia*, 2093.

22. In the early nineteenth century, the mint would later move west to 13th and Market Streets. In the 1890s, it made way for John Wanamaker's department store and moved to 16th and Spring Garden Streets, in what was then the region's premier district of machine makers. The building on Spring Garden Street was later occupied by the Community College of Philadelphia, when a new building for the mint was erected on Independence Mall in time for the bicentennial of 1976.

23. John Thom Holdsworth, *Financing an Empire: History of Banking in Pennsylvania* (Philadelphia: Clarke, 1928), 85–86.

24. *New World*, July 26, 1797, p. 3, col. 1. The final cost of the building and ground was $480,000; Gallatin Secretary of Treasury, report March 2, 1809, American State Papers, Finance, II, 352.

25. Mark Prager Letter Book (1794–98), HSP, Amb. 6955.

26. Wright, *The Wealth of Nations Rediscovered*, 137.

27. Perkins, *American Public Finance and Financial Services*, 310.

28. Wright, *The Wealth of Nations Rediscovered*, 127.

29. Robert E. Wright, *Origins of Commercial Banking in America, 1750–1800* (New York: Madison House, 2001), 134.

30. Robert E. Wright, *Hamilton Unbound: Finance and the Creation of the American Republic* (Westport, Conn.: Greenwood, 2002), 111–12.

31. Wright, *The Wealth of Nations Rediscovered*, 141.

32. Ibid., 139.

33. Barnes, *A History of the Philadelphia Stock Exchange*, 7. See also E. S. Gibbons, "The Building of the Schuylkill Navigation System, 1815–1828," *Pennsylvania History* 57 (1990): 13–43.

34. Wright, *The Wealth of Nations Rediscovered*, 143.

35. Barnes, *A History of the Philadelphia Stock Exchange*, 4.

36. Ibid., 9.

37. For discussion of early collaboration between investors in Philadelphia and New York, see Ranald C. Michie, *The London and New York Stock Exchanges, 1850–1914* (Boston: Allen and Unwin, 1987), 171–72.

38. Some debate exists regarding the geographic spread of the panic. In his work of 1994, Perkins argued that no evidence suggests that markets outside New York shared in the panic. More recently, however, price data collected by Richard Sylla, Jack Wilson, and Robert Wright suggest that market integration among New York, Philadelphia, and Boston rendered the panic similar in these centers. Perkins, *American Public Finance and Financial Services*, 315; Richard Sylla, Jack Wilson, and Robert Wright, *Price Quotations in Early U.S. Securities Markets* (database housed at Inter-University Consortium for Political and Social Research, www.icpsr.org).

39. David R. Brigham, *Public Culture in the Early Republic: Peale's Museum and Its Audience* (Washington, D.C.: Smithsonian Institution Press, 1995), 157–60. Clem-

ent Biddle reported a taxable wealth of £127, placing him in the middle of the taxed citizens, while William W. Biddle was in the bottom 10 percent in terms of taxable wealth. Another broker, Thomas Biddle, also had a negligible net worth. It is noteworthy that most wealth was concentrated in the bankers and in federal agents. David Rittenhouse, the astronomer and director of the U.S. Mint, was in the top 20 percent.

40. *Philadelphia General Advertiser* (August 12, 1791), 3, quoted in Stuart Banner, *Anglo-American Securities Regulation: Cultural and Political Roots, 1690–1860* (New York: Cambridge University Press, 1998), 151.

41. *Philadelphia General Advertiser*, March 27, 1792, 2.

42. *National Gazette* (Philadelphia), June 4, 1792, quoted in Banner, *Anglo-American Securities Regulation*, 155.

43. Matthew McConnell to Benjamin Rush (October 26, 1793), Rush Papers, HSP.

44. J. Bennett Nolan, ed., *Southeastern Pennsylvania: A History of the Counties of Berks, Bucks, Chester, Delaware, Montgomery, Philadelphia, and Schuylkill* (Philadelphia: Lewis, 1943), 513.

45. Lewis, *A History of the Bank of North America*, 82, 152–53.

46. Scharf and Westcott, *History of Philadelphia*, 2091.

47. Marquis James, *Biography of a Business, 1792–1942: Insurance Company of North America* (New York: Bobbs-Merrill, 1942), 17.

48. Wright, *Origins of Commercial Banking in America*, 149–51.

49. Wright, *Hamilton Unbound*, 108.

50. For a discussion of the concentration of power among early national Philadelphia capitalists, see Andrew Schocket, *Founding Corporate Power in Early National Philadelphia* (DeKalb: Northern Illinois Press, 2007).

51. Howard Bodenhorn, *A History of Banking in Antebellum America: Financial Markets and Economic Development in an Era of Nation-Building* (New York: Cambridge University Press, 2000), 35. With this charter, Pennsylvania's government discovered that state-chartered banks could be useful sources of revenue. By charging fees, requiring loans, and reserving shares of bank stock for the state, the legislature could effectively buy down the property taxes that sustained much of the state budget. When the commonwealth renewed the charters of the Bank of North America in 1799 and 1814 and the Bank of Pennsylvania in 1810, it perpetuated this pattern. For its charter renewal of 1814, the Bank of North America was obliged to pay a bonus of $120,000 to the commonwealth. Sylla, "Shaping the U.S. Financial System," 263; Scharf and Westcott, *History of Philadelphia*, 2095.

52. Wright, *The Wealth of Nations Rediscovered*, 129.

53. Wright, *Origins of Commercial Banking in America*, 134.

54. McEuen, Hale, and Davidson Lands in Bradford and Tioga Counties, 1799–1830, HSP, Am. 0494.

55. As quoted in John Lauritz Larson, *Internal Improvement: National Public*

Works and the Promise of Popular Government in the Early United States (Chapel Hill: University of North Carolina Press, 2001), 25.

56. As quoted in Raymond Walters, Jr., *Albert Gallatin: Jeffersonian Financier and Diplomat* (New York: Macmillan, 1957), 47.

57. *An act to enable the president, managers and company of the Philadelphia and Lancaster Turnpike Road to increase the width of the said road in certain cases* (1795), Van Pelt Library, University of Pennsylvania, Early American imprints, first series, no. 47551; *An Act to Enable the Governor of this Commonwealth to Incorporate a Company for Making an Artificial or Turnpike Road* (1804), Van Pelt Library, Early American imprints, second series, no. 7006; Scharf and Westcott, *History of Philadelphia*, 2087; Matthias Slough, *To the Stockholders of the Philadelphia and Lancaster Turnpike Road* (1794), HSP, Am. 26710; Charles Israel Landis, *History of the Philadelphia and Lancaster Turnpike: The First Long Turnpike in the United States* (Philadelphia, 1919), HSP.

58. Wright, *The Wealth of Nations Rediscovered*, 134.

59. Schuylkill and Susquehanna Navigation, *An Historical Account of the Rise, Progress, and Present State of the Canal Navigation in Pennsylvania* (Philadelphia: Poulson, 1795), Van Pelt Library, University of Pennsylvania, Special Collections, Forrest Collection.

60. Alan Taylor, *William Cooper's Town: Power and Persuasion on the Frontier of the Early American Republic* (New York: Vintage, 1995).

61. Daniel M. Friedenberg, "The Strange Case of Robert Morris," in *Life, Liberty, and the Pursuit of Land: The Plunder of Early America* (Buffalo, N.Y.: Prometheus, 1992), 338–47. Federalists, Jeffersonian Republicans, and later Jacksonian Democrats all agreed, though for different reasons, that westward expansion and affordable land on the frontier were among the foremost requirements for a healthy nation. As speculation and the market for family farms both swelled, by the 1830s the government in Washington derived more revenue from the sale of land than it did from customs revenue—nearly $25 million in 1836 alone. For discussion of the early American land market, see Charles Sellers, *The Market Revolution: Jacksonian America, 1815–1846* (New York: Oxford University Press, 1991), 149; Louis Ray Wells, *Industrial History of the United States* (New York: Macmillan, 1922), 206.

62. Quoted in Emily T. Cooperman, "William Russell Birch (1755–1834) and the Beginnings of the American Picturesque" (Ph.D. diss., University of Pennsylvania, 1999), 144.

63. Quoted in ibid., 143.

64. Elkins Wetherill, *The Story of the Philadelphia Stock Exchange* (Downingtown, Pa.: Newcomen Society, 1976), 11. Wetherill's account is largely based on Barnes, *A History of the Philadelphia Stock Exchange*, 9.

65. Markham, *A Financial History of the United States*, 1: 163.

66. Nicholas Wainwright, *History of the Philadelphia National Bank* (Philadelphia: Ayer, 1976), 5. In addition, since the customers of the Bank of the United States were largely importers while those of the Bank of Pennsylvania were primarily retailers, by

1802 the latter institution had become indebted to the former "at the rate of $100,000 a week." Konkle, *Thomas Willing and the First American Financial System*, 180.

67. For a profile of the Bank of North America's customers in this period, see Wright, *Origins of Commercial Banking in America*, 152.

68. Wainwright, *History of the Philadelphia National Bank*, 12.

69. Ibid., 13.

70. Wright, *Hamilton Unbound*, 107.

71. Bodenhorn, *A History of Banking in Antebellum America*, 36.

72. Wright, *Origins of Commercial Banking in America*, 167.

73. "The very earliest policies on lives were offshoots of marine underwriting. In addition to insuring vessels and cargoes, underwriters sometimes assumed risks on ship passengers—frequently a wealthy merchant accompanying his goods overseas or perhaps a close relative in transit." Perkins, *American Public Finance and Financial Services*, 299–302. See also *One Hundred and Twenty-Fifth Anniversary* (Philadelphia: Pennsylvania Company for Insurances on Lives and Granting Annuities, 1937).

74. Barnes, *A History of the Philadelphia Stock Exchange*, 7–9.

75. James, *Biography of a Business*, 86–87.

76. Wright, *Origins of Commercial Banking in America*, 149–51.

Chapter 3

1. Domenic Vitiello, "Reading the Corps of Discovery Backwards: The Metropolitan Context of Lewis and Clark's Expedition," in *The Shortest and Most Convenient Route: Lewis and Clark in Context*, ed. Robert Cox (Philadelphia: American Philosophical Society, 2004).

2. Papers of James Madison, March 6, 1796, vol. 19, fol. 37, Library of Congress, in INHP files.

3. Donald R. Adams Jr., *Finance and Enterprise in Early America: A Study of Stephen Girard's Bank, 1812–1831* (Philadelphia: University of Pennsylvania Press, 1978), 15.

4. Ibid., 140.

5. Burton Alva Konkle, *Thomas Willing and the First American Financial System* (Philadelphia: University of Pennsylvania Press, 1937), 199.

6. Andrew W. Barnes, ed., *History of the Philadelphia Stock Exchange, Banks, and Banking Interests* (Philadelphia: Cornelius Baker, 1901), 9; J. Thomas Scharf and Thompson Westcott, *History of Philadelphia, 1609–1884* (Philadelphia: Everts, 1884), 2092.

7. J. G. Leach, *History of the Girard National Bank* (Philadelphia, 1902), 71.

8. Charles B. Trego, *A Geography of Pennsylvania* (Philadelphia: Biddle, 1843), 139.

9. Elkins Wetherill, *The Story of the Philadelphia Stock Exchange* (Downingtown, Pa.: Newcomen Society, 1976), 10; John R. Dos Passos, *A Treatise on the Law of Stock-Brokers and Stock-Exchanges* (New York: Banks Law Publishing Co., 1905), 11.

10. Charles F. Mumford, Esquire, *The Doctrine of Constructive Larceny Considered; as Developed in the Recent Case of George Tyson, the Stock and Exchange Broker, Who Was Tried at the Mayor's Court, for the City of Philadelphia, at the March Session, in 1825* (Philadelphia: Small, 1825), 10, Historical Society of Pennsylvania (hereafter HSP), WK*.225 v. 2.

11. Alexander Lardner Journal (1832–34), HSP, 1493, v. 3; see also Nalbro Frazier Cash Book (1805–11), HSP, Am. 9841; Thomas Biddle and Co., Stock Book (1817), HSP, accession 50; John P. Hutchinson Account Book (1809–37), HSP, Am. 9154.

12. When nineteenth-century courts were called upon to clarify the legal status of this association, they concluded:

The Philadelphia Board of Brokers is not a corporation. It is not a joint-stock company, in the sense in which such companies are regarded by the English law, although it has a large amount of property which belongs to it in its joint or aggregate capacity. Such private associations are said not to be partnerships as between themselves, whatever may be their relation to third persons.

The Board of Brokers is a voluntary association of persons who, for convenience in the transaction of business with each other, have associated themselves to provide a common place for the transaction of their individual business, agreeing among themselves to pay the expenses incident to the support of the objects of the association, in which each for himself, at stated hours of the day, and for his individual profit, may prosecute his own business, and enter into separate engagements with his fellow-members. The association does not share in the losses of the individual associates; each member takes his own gains, and individually sustains the losses incident to his engagements.

Quoted in Dos Passos, *A Treatise on the Law of Stock-Brokers and Stock-Exchanges*, 21.

13. Arthur and George Biddle, *A Treatise on the Law of Stock Brokers* (Philadelphia: Lippincott, 1882), 39–50.

14. Ranald C. Michie, *The London Stock Exchange: A History* (New York: Oxford University Press, 1999), 35.

15. Figures for the New York Board of Brokers are found in Jerry W. Markham, *A Financial History of the United States*, vol. 1, *From Christopher Columbus to the Robber Barons (1492–1900)* (Armonk, N.Y.: M. E. Sharpe, 2001), 123.

16. Musgrave was succeeded by William M. Walmsley and, in the 1830s, William F. Emlen. *Souvenir History*, n.p.; United States Army, *Rules and Regulations for the Officers, Non-Commissioned Officers, and Privates Belonging to the Regiment of Artillery, under Command of Lieut. Col. A. M. Prevost* (Philadelphia, 1814), Library Company of Philadelphia, Th*.9, v. 6.

17. Robert Wright, *The Wealth of Nations Rediscovered: Integration and Expansion in American Financial Markets, 1780–1850* (New York: Cambridge University Press, 2002), 153–54.

18. Scharf and Westcott, *History of Philadelphia*, 2094.

19. Walter Licht, *Getting Work: Philadelphia, 1840–1950* (Cambridge, Mass.: Harvard University Press, 1992), 10.

20. Edward S. Kaplan, *The Bank of the United States and the American Economy* (Westport, Conn.: Greenwood, 1999), 67–68.

21. Ibid., x.

22. "Biographical Dictionary of Philadelphia Financiers," *New York Herald* (1837), HSP, Wo*.99, v. 6.

23. Front and rear images of the first mint are published in *Official Souvenir History: Philadelphia; Its Founding and Development, 1683–1908* (Philadelphia, 1908), 88, 89.

24. Charles Sellers, *The Market Revolution: Jacksonian America, 1815–1846* (New York: Oxford University Press, 1991), 149.

25. Wright, *The Wealth of Nations Rediscovered*, 161; and Robert E. Wright, *Hamilton Unbound: Finance and the Creation of the American Republic* (Westport, Conn.: Greenwood, 2002), 120.

26. *Biographies of Successful Philadelphia Merchants* (Philadelphia: James K. Simon, 1864), 181–85; Eliza Cope Harrison, *Philadelphia Merchant: The Diary of Thomas Pym Cope 1800–1851* (South Bend, Ind.: Gateway Editions, 1978), vii–xii.

27. "Fulton" [Matthew Carey], "Canal Policy—No. III," *United State Gazette*, January 26, 1825; see also *A Connected View of the Whole Internal Navigation of the United States, Natural and Artificial, Present and Prospective* (Philadelphia: Carey and Lea, 1826).

28. John Lauritz Larson, *Internal Improvement: National Public Works and the Promise of Popular Government in the Early United States* (Chapel Hill: University of North Carolina Press, 2001), 82–84.

29. Randall Miller, "Transportation," in *Pennsylvania: A History of the Commonwealth*, ed. Randall Miller and William Pencak (University Park: Pennsylvania State University Press, 2002), 235–36; Robert McCullough and Walter Leuba, *The Pennsylvania Main Line Canal*, 4th printing (York, Pa.: American Canal and Transportation Center, 1976), 22.

30. For analysis of internal improvements' impacts on rural economies, see, for example, David Meyer, *The Roots of American Industrialization* (Baltimore: Johns Hopkins University Press, 2003).

31. John Thom Holdsworth, *Financing an Empire: History of Banking in Pennsylvania* (Philadelphia: Clarke, 1928), 147.

32. Marquis James, *Biography of a Business, 1792–1942: Insurance Company of North America* (New York: Bobbs-Merrill, 1942), 96.

33. Wright, *The Wealth of Nations Rediscovered*, 155–57.

34. Pennsylvania had a small number of banks relative to the less populous states of Massachusetts and Rhode Island, which had sixty-six and forty-seven, respectively. The rest of New England also had more banks per capita than Pennsylvania. Banking

capital was most concentrated in the South. Virginia had four banks—two with a total of $4.74 million, the other two with $831,100 between them. Louisiana was home to three banks: the Orleans Bank, which presumably served the artisan class of that region, was capitalized at $424,700; the Louisiana State Bank at $1.2 million; and the Bank of Louisiana at $4 million. Finally, Manhattan resembled Philadelphia in its overwhelming dominance of New York State banking. Albert Gallatin, *Considerations on the Currency and Banking System of the United States* (Philadelphia: Carey and Lea, 1831), 97–100.

35. Quoted in Patricia Cline Cohen, *A Calculating People: The Spread of Numeracy in Early America* (Chicago: University of Chicago Press, 1982), 3.

36. "Minutes of the Subscribers to the Private Room at the Merchants' Coffee House," MS. HSP Am. 308.

37. Jeffrey A. Cohen and Charles E. Brownell, *The Architectural Drawings of Benjamin Latrobe* (New Haven, Conn.: Yale University Press, 1994), 2: 645.

38. Sandra Tatman and Roger Moss, *Biographical Dictionary of Philadelphia Architects, 1700–1930* (Boston: G. K. Hall, 1985), 468.

39. A brief history of the Chamber of Commerce is in James Mease, *The Picture of Philadelphia* (Philadelphia: Kite, 1811), 67.

40. *National Gazette and Literary Register*, May 1, 1821.

41. *National Gazette and Literary Register*, November 28, 1826; Thomas Cope Letters (January 3, 1827), Quaker Collection, Haverford College.

42. "Prospectus of a Plan" (1831), Library Company of Philadelphia.

43. Ibid.

44. "An application was made for a subscription to the proposed Merchants Exchange on Third, Dock, and Walnut Streets, whereupon it was agreed to subscribe five shares of $500.00 each"; T. A. Alexander to William D. Lewis (1831), Merchants Exchange folder, Dreer Collection, HSP.

45. These plans reside in the Stephen Girard Papers of the American Philosophical Society.

46. William Strickland, Order Book (1831), Independence Seaport Museum, J. Welles Henderson Collection.

47. *Hazard's Register*, February 22, 1832; see also Scharf and Westcott, *History of Philadelphia*, 634–35.

48. *National Gazette*, November 5, 1833.

49. *Hazard's Register* 12, November 29, 1833.

50. Contributionship Board Minutes (March 5, 1834), HSP. The ultimate expenditures were calculated at $98,000 for the land and $184,000 for the building. Jane A. Hyde, "The Past—1754–1924," *Investment Dealers' Digest* (January 30, 1967): 42.

51. "Fire Damage to Merchant's Coffee House in City Tavern," March 22, 1834, *Hazard's Register* 13 (January-July 1834): 208; the same story was carried in the *Pennsylvanian*, March 24, 1834, p. 2 under the heading of "Fires": "On Saturday afternoon, between 3 and 4 o'clock, the roof of the Merchant's Coffee house, South Second Street,

was discovered on fire. The firemen repaired to the ground with their accustomed promptness, and succeeded in quenching the flames after nearly two hours. The upper part of the building was destroyed. — probably from sparks from a nearby chimney." The *Pennsylvanian* followed by noting that "in consequence of the fire at the Coffee house, Mr. Sanderson opened the Exchange [Merchants' Exchange] yesterday [Sunday] which was crowded all day by admiring citizens."

52. *The National Gazette*: "The Public is informed that this establishment is now completed, and will be open for exhibition on Tuesday and Wednesday next, the 25th and 26th inst. J. F. Fenimore, Secretary."

53. R. A. Smith, *Philadelphia as It Is in 1852* (Philadelphia: Lindsay and Blakiston, 1852), 384.

54. Ibid., 118.

55. The Atlantic, Union, and American Insurance Companies took offices in the building—the *National Gazette* reported on June 6, 1833, that the building would be ready for occupancy by the end of winter, and that the board had secured Joseph M. Saunders at $1,500 per year as agent. The post office was located in the west end of the building with a ten-year lease, rents engaged were $9,800, with $1,500 in unrented rooms and with the reading room worth an additional $3,000 more.

56. "Minutes of the Green Room, 1818–1853." See also Stephen Winslow, "Joseph Evans," in *Biographies of Successful Philadelphia Merchants*, 107–11.

57. Agnes Addison Gilchrist, *William Strickland: Architect and Engineer 1788–1854* (Philadelphia: University of Pennsylvania Press, 1950), 86.

58. While the Board of Brokers departed in 1876, most of these groups remained in the Merchants Exchange into the 1890s. Fragmentary records of the Green Room and the Commercial Room are in the collections of the HSP. Those of the Green Room contain its rules of 1818 establishing a limited membership, regular elections of directors, and the principal that "sigars would not be allowed until $1/2$ after 7'o'clock."

59. *Commercial Herald*, republished in *Hazard's Register* 13 (April 5, 1834): 238.

60. See, for example, *Atkinson's Saturday Evening Post*, March 19, 1834.

61. *Report of a Committee of Directors of the Bank of the United States* (ca. November 1833), 1.

62. Varying historical interpretations of the bank war may be found in Schlesinger, *Age of Jackson* (New York: Book Find Club, 1946); Bray Hammond, *Banks and Politics in America from the Revolution to the Civil War* (Princeton, N.J.: Princeton University Press, 1957); Robert Remini, *Andrew Jackson and the Bank War: A Study in the Growth of Presidential Power* (New York: Norton, 1967); Jean Alexander Wilburn, *Biddle's Bank: The Crucial Years* (New York: Columbia University Press, 1967); Peter Temin, *The Jacksonian Economy* (New York: Norton, 1969); Sidney Ratner, James Soltow, and Richard Sylla, *The Evolution of the American Economy: Growth, Welfare, and Decision Making* (New York: Basic Books, 1979); Sean Wilentz, *The Rise of American Democracy: Jefferson to Lincoln* (New York: Norton, 2005). For primary sources on the bank war, see Reginald McGrane, *The Correspondence of Nicholas Biddle* (New York:

Houghton Mifflin, 1919); George Rogers Taylor, ed., *Jackson Versus Biddle: The Struggle over the Second Bank of the United States* (Boston: Heath, 1949).

63. E. James Ferguson, ed., *Selected Writings of Albert Gallatin* (Indianapolis: Bobbs-Merrill, 1967), 359–60; Howard Bodenhorn, *A History of Banking in Antebellum America: Financial Markets and Economic Development in an Era of Nation-Building* (New York: Cambridge University Press, 2000), 169.

64. Scharf and Westcott, *History of Philadelphia*, 2094.

65. *The Bank of the United States* (Boston: Lewis, 1931), 44.

66. *Report of a Committee of Directors of the Bank of the United States* (ca. November 1833), 1, 16.

67. Kaplan, *The Bank of the United States and the American Economy*, 141.

68. *Report of the Committee of Investigation Appointed at the Meeting of the Stockholders of the Bank of the United States* (Philadelphia, 1841), 59.

69. Kaplan, *The Bank of the United States and the American Economy*, 154.

70. Trego, *A Geography of Pennsylvania*, 149–50.

71. Pennsylvania's increased spending is documented in J. W. Hammond, *A Tabular View of the Financial Affairs of Pennsylvania* (Philadelphia: Biddle, 1844). See also John J. Wallis, "What Caused the Crisis of 1839?" NBER Working Paper no. h0133 (April 2001).

72. Arthur Grinath, III, John J. Wallis, and Richard Sylla, "Debt, Default, and Revenue Structure: The American State Debt Crisis in the Early 1840s," NBER Working Paper no. h0097 (March 1997).

73. Trego, *A Geography of Pennsylvania*, 107.

74. Quoted in Stuart Banner, *Anglo-American Securities Regulation: Cultural and Political Roots, 1690–1860* (New York: Cambridge University Press, 1998), 222–23.

75. Green Board records, HSP, Am. 308 (1835–57).

76. Wright, *The Wealth of Nations Rediscovered*, 158, and *Hamilton Unbound*, 109.

77. Walter Werner and Stephen T. Smith, *Wall Street* (New York: Columbia University Press, 1991), 184.

78. *Report of a Committee Appointed to Investigate the Evils of Lotteries in the Commonwealth of Pennsylvania, and to Suggest a Remedy for the Same* (Philadelphia: Shrieves, 1831).

Chapter 4

1. Vincent P. Carosso, *Investment Banking in America: A History* (Cambridge, Mass.: Harvard University Press, 1970), 8.

2. See, for example, Thomas Biddle and Co. to Gen. George Cadwalader (September 21 and 24, 1857), Historical Society of Pennsylvania (hereafter HSP), Cadwalader Collection.

3. R. W. Hiddy, "The Organization and Functions of Anglo-American Merchant Bankers, 1815–1860," in *The Development of London as a Financial Centre*, vol. 1, *1700–1850*, ed. R. C. Michie (New York: Tauris, 2000), 237–47.

4. For discussion of the remarkable amount of regulation in the American economy and society in the nineteenth century, see William Novak, *The People's Welfare: Law and Regulation in Nineteenth-Century America* (Chapel Hill: University of North Carolina Press, 1996).

5. Quoted in Norris Hansel, *Josiah White, Quaker Entrepreneur* (Easton, Pa.: Canal History and Technology Press, 1992), 33.

6. Solomon W. Roberts, *Report to the Board of Managers of the Schuylkill Navigation Company, on the Improvement of the Schuylkill Navigation, January 2nd, 1845* (Philadelphia: Kite, 1845), 4.

7. Charles B. Trego, *A Geography of Pennsylvania* (Philadelphia: Biddle, 1843), 156; Stuart William Wells, "The Schuylkill Navigation and the Girard Canal" (Master's thesis, University of Pennsylvania, 1989), 14–25.

8. See, for example, Thomas Biddle and Co. to James Dundas (March 29, 1859), HSP, Arthur C. Bining Collection.

9. Edwin Freedley, *Philadelphia and Its Manufactures* (Philadelphia: Young, 1857), 79–80.

10. Trego, *A Geography of Pennsylvania*, 116.

11. Ranald C. Michie, *The London and New York Stock Exchanges, 1850–1914* (Boston: Allen and Unwin, 1987), 171; *The Financial Register of the United States: Devoted Chiefly to Finance and Currency, and to Banking and Commercial Statistics*, vol. 1 (Philadelphia: Wirtz and Tatem, 1838).

12. Philadelphia Board of Brokers Account Book of Henry Ewing (1844), HSP.

13. Whereas New York's growth in this period was driven largely by extra-regional forces, Philadelphia's early industrialization was shaped by intra-regional supply and demand. Diane Lindstrom, *Economic Development in the Philadelphia Region, 1810–1850* (New York: Columbia University Press, 1978).

14. Burton W. Folsom Jr., *Urban Capitalists: Entrepreneurs and City Growth in Pennsylvania's Lackawanna and Lehigh Regions, 1800–1920* (Baltimore: Johns Hopkins University Press, 1981), 156.

15. Howard Bodenhorn, *A History of Banking in Antebellum America: Financial Markets and Economic Development in an Era of Nation-Building* (New York: Cambridge University Press, 2000), 178–79.

16. Ibid., 182; Andrew W. Barnes, ed., *History of the Philadelphia Stock Exchange, Banks, and Banking Interests* (Philadelphia: Cornelius Baker, 1911), 25.

17. Bodenhorn, *A History of Banking in Antebellum America*, 181.

18. Dan Rottenberg, *The Man Who Made Wall Street: Anthony J. Drexel and the Rise of Modern Finance* (Philadelphia: University of Pennsylvania Press, 2002), 29.

19. Ibid., 35.

20. *Digest of the Rules and Regulations of the Philadelphia Board of Brokers* (Philadelphia: Clark, 1850), 6. This passage appears to have been written on May 15, 1840.

21. *Rules and Regulations of the Philadelphia Stock and Exchange Board* (Philadelphia: Elliott, 1837), 6.

22. Ibid., 3.

23. Ibid., 6.

24. Ibid., 4.

25. Ibid.

26. Ibid., 6.

27. Record Book of the Commercial Room Association, Merchants Exchange (1841–68), HSP.

28. Philadelphia Stock Exchange, *Souvenir History, Album of Members, Gallery of Men of Affairs* (Philadelphia, 1903); 3.

29. Ibid.

30. Philadelphia Stock Exchange Brokerage Transaction Book (1859–61), HSP.

31. Barnes, *History of the Philadelphia Stock Exchange*, 9, 11.

32. Ibid., 11.

33. *Digest of the Rules and Regulations of the Philadelphia Board of Brokers*, 16.

34. Ibid., 15.

35. Alfred D. Chandler Jr., *The Visible Hand: The Managerial Revolution in American Business* (Cambridge, Mass.: Harvard University Press, 1977); Walter Licht, *Working for the Railroad: The Organization of Work in the Nineteenth Century* (Princeton, N.J.: Princeton University Press, 1983).

36. William Cronon, *Nature's Metropolis: Chicago and the Great West* (New York: Norton, 1991), 81.

37. *Digest of the Rules and Regulations of the Philadelphia Board of Brokers*. The nineteenth-century evolution of the New York Stock Exchange is recounted in Robert Sobel, *The Big Board* (New York: Free Press, 1965); Charles Geisst, *Wall Street: A History, From Its Beginnings to the Fall of Enron*, 2nd ed. (New York: Oxford University Press, 2004).

38. Covenant between Nicholas Biddle and the Philadelphia, Wilmington and Baltimore Rail Road Company (December 7, 1840), HSP, Biddle Family Papers.

39. Thomas Biddle and Co. Ledger Books, Biddle Family Papers, HSP.

40. At the same time, they held stock in a wide variety of transportation concerns, including turnpikes, canals, railroads, bridges, and steamboat companies, exerting their influence over complementary—and sometimes competing—modes and routes. See Stock Certificates and Transfers of Biddle, Whelen and Co. and Thomas Biddle and Co., 1804–66, HSP.

41. Freedley, *Philadelphia and Its Manufactures*, 86.

42. "Philadelphia Stock Exchange Sales, April 25th, 1855," HSP, Society Collection; William Z. Ripley, *Railroads: Finance and Organization* (New York: Longmans, Green, 1920), 537.

43. Ripley, *Railroads*, 478.

44. "By 1871 Britain contained 170,000 'persons of rank and property' without visible occupation—almost all of them women, or rather 'ladies'; a surprising number of them unmarried ladies. Stocks and shares . . . were a convenient way of providing

for widows, daughters and other relatives who could not—and no longer needed to be—associated with the management of property and enterprise." Eric Hobsbawm, *Industry and Empire: From 1750 to the Present Day*, revised with Chris Wrigley (New York: New Press, 1999), 97–98.

45. M. C. Reed, "Railways and the Growth of the Capital Market," in *The Development of London as a Financial Centre*, vol. 1, *1700–1850*, ed. R. C. Michie (New York: Tauris, 2000), 266–85.

46. R. C. Michie, *Money, Mania, and Markets: Investment, Company Formation, and the Stock Exchange in Nineteenth-Century Scotland* (Edinburgh: John Donald, 1981).

47. Michie, *The London and New York Stock Exchanges*, 167.

48. This characterization of different stock exchanges is perceptible in the distribution of concerns listing and/or trading their securities on these exchanges, as detailed in *The Manual of Statistics, Stock Exchange Hand-Book* (New York, 1900), 453–520.

49. For a macroeconomic treatment of this economic geography, see Douglass North, *The Economic Growth of the United States, 1790–1860* (New York: Norton, 1966). For a picture of British investment in nineteenth-century America, see Robert Lucas Nash, *Fenn's Compendium of the English and Foreign Funds, Debts, and Revenues of All Nations; Banks, Railways, Mines, and the Principal Joint Stock Companies: Forming an Epitome of the Various Objects of Investment and Speculation Negotiable in London* (London: Effingham Wilson, Royal Exchange, 1867).

50. Sven Beckert, *The Monied Metropolis: New York City and the Consolidation of the American Bourgeoisie, 1850–1896* (New York: Cambridge University Press, 2001), 22.

51. Cronon, *Nature's Metropolis*.

52. Quoted in Walter Johnson, *Soul by Soul: Life Inside the Antebellum Slave Market* (Cambridge, Mass.: Harvard University Press, 1999), 83.

53. In nineteenth-century North America, primary production was financed principally through partnerships or the "insider lending" of banks founded and controlled by industrialists—"lending clubs" that financed their directors' own firms. This latter phenomenon was particularly widespread in antebellum New England, where bank directors allied with manufacturers kept interest rates low. Naomi R. Lamoreaux, *Insider Lending: Banks, Personal Connections, and Economic Development in Industrial New England* (New York: Cambridge University Press and National Bureau of Economic Research, 1996); Joshua L. Rosenbloom, "The Challenges of Economic Maturity: New England, 1880–1940," in *Engines of Enterprise: An Economic History of New England*, ed. Peter Temin (Cambridge, Mass.: Harvard University Press, 2000), 153–99. By contrast, Philadelphia's leading manufacturers became directors of prominent banks only after the Civil War, capitalizing their enterprises typically through mortgages on property and sometimes on capital equipment. Philip S. Benjamin, *The Philadelphia Quakers in the Industrial Age, 1865–1920* (Philadelphia: Temple University

Press, 1976); Nicholas B. Wainwright, *History of the Philadelphia National Bank: A Century and a Half of Philadelphia Banking, 1803–1953* (Philadelphia: PNB, 1953), 235–43; Lemuel C. Simon, *A Century of the National Bank of the Northern Liberties of Philadelphia, Pennsylvania* (Philadelphia: National Bank of the Northern Liberties, 1910), 8, 52.

54. Barnes, *History of the Philadelphia Stock Exchange*, 9–10.

55. Wainwright, *History of the Philadelphia National Bank*, 92.

56. Joseph Edward Hedges, *Commercial Banking and the Stock Market before 1863* (Baltimore: Johns Hopkins University Press, 1938), 39.

57. *Public Ledger*, April 10, 1847, 2.

58. Rottenberg, *The Man Who Made Wall Street*, 46–47.

59. Ibid., 48–55. For profiles of the city's capitalists around mid-century, see R. A. Smith, *Philadelphia As It Is in 1852* (Philadelphia: Lindsay and Blakiston, 1852); Henry Simpson, *The Lives of Eminent Philadelphians* (Philadelphia: Brotherhead, 1859); Stephen Noyes Winslow, *Biographies of Successful Philadelphia Merchants* (Philadelphia: Simon, 1864).

60. Carosso, *Investment Banking in America*, 11; Barnes, *History of the Philadelphia Stock Exchange*, 23; J. Thomas Scharf and Thompson Westcott, *History of Philadelphia, 1609–1884* (Philadelphia: Everts, 1884), 2100.

61. See, for example, Henry D. Cooke to Jay Cooke (January 13 and 20, 1857), Pitt Cooke to Jay Cooke (January 17, 1857), both HSP, Jay Cooke Collection.

62. See, for example, W. J. Barney and Co. to Jay Cooke (February 18, 1857), HSP, Jay Cooke Collection.

63. Herman LeRoy Collins, *Philadelphia: A Story of Progress* (Philadelphia: Lewis Historical Publishing, 1941), 1: 266.

64. Walter Licht, *Industrializing America: The Nineteenth Century* (Baltimore: Johns Hopkins University Press, 1995), 86.

65. Wainwright, *History of the Philadelphia National Bank*, 97, 105.

66. See, for example, *An Act to Incorporate the Baltimore and Port Deposit Rail Road Company* (Baltimore: Lucas and Deaver, 1832), HSP, Biddle Family Papers. For discussion and some debate over states' roles in early- and mid-nineteenth-century economic development, see L. Ray Gunn, *The Decline of Authority: Public Economic Policy and Political Development in New York State 1800–1860* (Ithaca, N.Y.: Cornell University Press, 1998); Oscar and Mary Handlin, *Commonwealth: A Study of the Role of Government in the American Economy; Massachusetts, 1774–1861* (Cambridge, Mass.: Belknap Press, 1947); Louis Hartz, *Economic Policy and Democratic Thought: Pennsylvania 1776–1860* (New York: Quandrangle Books, 1948); Richard Sylla, J. B. Legler, and John Wallis, "Banks and State Public Finance in the New Republic: The United States, 1790–1860," *Journal of Economic History* 47 (1987): 391–403.

67. *An Act Relating to Brokers and Private Bankers, Passed April 30, 1861* (Philadelphia: King and Baird, 1861), HSP.

68. James Schott et al. to John Sergeant and George W. Toland (December 7, 1840), HSP, Society Collection.

69. Thomas Biddle and Co. to Eli K. Price (January 17, 1855), HSP, Eli Kirk Price, Incoming Correspondence.

70. For example, a week after Thomas Biddle and Co. wrote Eli K. Price to propose new legislation, the firm implored Price to oppose a proposed law that would impose weekly reporting requirements on the state's private banks. Thomas Biddle and Co. to Eli K. Price (January 22, 1855), HSP Eli Kirk Price, Incoming Correspondence.

71. HSP, Jay Cooke Collection.

Chapter 5

1. J. Matthew Gallman, *Mastering Wartime: A Social History of Philadelphia during the Civil War* (New York: Cambridge University Press, 1990), 268.

2. Maxwell Whiteman, *Gentlemen in Crisis: The First Century of the Union League of Philadelphia, 1862–1962* (Philadelphia: Union League, 1975); Wallace Triplett, "History of LaMott" (Philadelphia, 1949); Recruiting Pamphlet and Appeal for Contributions (June 27, 1863), Barker Collection, Historical Society of Pennsylvania (hereafter HSP); Free Military School for Command of Colored Regiments, Register and Scrapbook (1863–64), HSP.

3. *The Treason Bill, Approved April 18, 1861* (Philadelphia: King and Baird, 1861), HSP.

4. J. Thomas Scharf and Thompson Westcott, *History of Philadelphia, 1609–1884* (Philadelphia: Everts, 1884), 2101.

5. Quoted in Dan Rottenberg, *The Man Who Made Wall Street: Anthony J. Drexel and the Rise of Modern Finance* (Philadelphia: University of Pennsylvania Press, 2002), 65.

6. See, for example, Andrew G. Curtin to Drexel and Co. (May 28, 1861); Jasper Jones to A. J. Drexel (June 7, 1861); Morris, Tasker and Co. to A. J. Drexel (June 8, 1861); Andrew G. Curtin to A. J. Drexel (June 14, 1861), all HSP, Jay Cooke Collection. See also Vincent P. Carosso, *Investment Banking in America: A History* (Cambridge, Mass.: Harvard University Press, 1970), 15.

7. Gallman, *Mastering Wartime*, 277.

8. *America, Money, and War: Financing the Civil War* (New York: Museum of American Financial History, 1994), 19.

9. Quoted in Rottenberg, *The Man Who Made Wall Street*, 65.

10. *America, Money, and War*, 12; Carosso, *Investment Banking in America*, 15–16; "Letter of Mr. Jay Cooke on the Payment in Gold of the U.S. Five-Twenty Bonds," to the Editor of the *Philadelphia Inquirer*, HSP.

11. Louis Ray Wells, *Industrial History of the United States* (New York: Macmillan, 1922), 447; Lance Davis, Larry Neal, and Eugene White, "The Effect of Deflation on the First Global Capital Market: The Financial Crises of the 1890s and the Reponses

of the Stock Exchanges in London, New York, Paris, and Berlin," National Bureau of Economic Research (June 2002): 2.

12. Quoted in Rottenberg, *The Man Who Made Wall Street*, 71.

13. Nicholas B. Wainwright, *History of the Philadelphia National Bank: A Century and a Half of Philadelphia Banking, 1803–1953* (Philadelphia: PNB, 1953), 120.

14. Gallman, *Mastering Wartime.*

15. Wainwright, *History of the Philadelphia National Bank*, 116.

16. Richard Sylla, *The American Capital Market, 1846–1914: A Study of the Effects of Public Policy on Economic Development* (New York: Arno, 1975).

17. Hugh Rockoff, "Banking and Finance, 1789–1914," in *The Cambridge Economic History of the United States*, vol. 2, *The Long Nineteenth Century*, ed. Stanley L. Engerman and Robert E. Gallman (New York: Cambridge University Press, 2000), 643–84.

18. "To the Philadelphia Board of Brokers, Christmas 1865," "To the Philadelphia Board of Brokers, January 1866," and "Philadelphia Board of Brokers' Annual Dinner, January 22d, 1866," all HSP.

19. "Philadelphia Brokers Dinner, Bill of Fare, January 22nd, 1866," HSP.

20. Of course, the longevity of individual wells fluctuated widely. This was reflected in considerable price fluctuation of their securities, as illustrated in Philadelphia Public Stock Exchange Stock Book, 1865–66; and *Highest and Lowest Quotations of Philadelphia Securities and Petroleum, Monthly for 1886* (Philadelphia: Charles Keen), both HSP.

21. See, for example, *Philadelphia Stock Exchange Sales, 1870–1871* (Philadelphia: Drexel and Co. and McLaughlin Bros., 1871); *Daily Quotations and Stock Sales, Philadelphia Stock Exchange, 1876* (Philadelphia: McLaughlin Bros., 1876); *Highest and Lowest Quotations, Philadelphia Securities, September-December 1886*; Reports of the List Committee, Philadelphia Stock Exchange (November 21, 1881–August 19, 1887), Philadelphia Stock Exchange Archives (hereafter PHLX Archives).

22. Among the many brokers who joined the Board of Brokers between the Civil War and the depression of 1893, roughly half traded under their own names, while slightly more than half traded as members of firms. Firm profiles as well as the Philadelphia Stock Exchange membership roster are found in Andrew W. Barnes, ed., *History of the Philadelphia Stock Exchange, Banks, and Banking Interests* (Philadelphia: Cornelius Baker, 1901).

23. Wallace Rice, *The Chicago Stock Exchange* (Chicago: Chicago Stock Exchange, 1928), 20, 29. Yerkes's life is the basis of Theodore Dreiser's "Titan trilogy," beginning with *The Financier* (New York: Harper, 1912).

24. Rottenberg, *The Man Who Made Wall Street*, 80.

25. Quoted in ibid., 104.

26. Arthur and George Biddle, *A Treatise on the Law of Stock Brokers* (Philadelphia: Lippincott, 1882), 56. Clearing houses had been used by consortiums of banks, including in Philadelphia, since mid-century, while the first stock exchange clearing

house appears to have been started in 1867 at the exchange in Frankfurt, Germany. Richard Lewis Dole, *Historical Development of the Philadelphia Stock Exchange* (ca. 1931; reproduced for the PHLX Bicentennial, 1990), 13.

27. Philadelphia Stock Exchange, *Souvenir History, Album of Members, Gallery of Men of Affairs* (Philadelphia, 1903), n.p.

28. Louis H. Sullivan, *Autobiography of an Idea* (New York: P. Smith, 1956), 192.

29. Barnes, *History of the Philadelphia Stock Exchange*, 11.

30. Walter Licht, *Industrializing America: The Nineteenth Century* (Baltimore: Johns Hopkins University Press, 1995), 146; Barnes, *History of the Philadelphia Stock Exchange*, 33.

31. Sandra Tatman and Roger Moss, *Biographical Dictionary of Philadelphia Architects, 1700–1930* (Boston: G. K. Hall, 1985), 871.

32. "Sherry Marks 50th Year on Exchange," clipping from the *Philadelphia Evening Bulletin* (1930), PHLX Archives.

33. The governance of the exchange is described in Philadelphia Stock Exchange, *Souvenir History, Album of Members, Gallery of Men of Affairs* (Philadelphia, 1903), n.p.; Dole, *Historical Development of the Philadelphia Stock Exchange*, 15; Scharf and Westcott, *History of Philadelphia*, 2109.

34. "War on the Bucket Shops: The Philadelphia Stock Exchange Resolved to Crush Them," *New York Times*, January 8, 1886, p. 4; Jane A. Hyde, "The Past—1754–1924," *Investment Dealers' Digest* (January 30, 1967): 41–43.

35. Hyde, "The Past—1754–1924," 43.

36. Reports of the List Committee, PHLX Archives; *Daily Quotations and Stock Sales, Philadelphia Stock Exchange, Jan. 1st to Dec. 31st, 1885*, PHLX Archives.

37. Hyde, "The Past—1754–1924," 43.

38. For discussion of the Republican machine, its "contractor bosses," and the political activities of the "utility monopolists" Widener, Elkins, and Kemble, see Peter McCaffery, *When Bosses Ruled Philadelphia: The Emergence of the Republican Machine, 1867–1933* (University Park: Pennsylvania State University Press, 1993).

39. Charles Cheape, *Moving the Masses: Urban Public Transit in New York, Boston, and Philadelphia, 1880–1912* (Cambridge, Mass.: Harvard University Press, 1980), 172.

40. Clarence Stedman, ed., *The New York Stock Exchange* (New York: Stock Exchange Historical Company, 1905), 327.

41. Report of the List Committee, PHLX Archives.

42. Nicholas B. Wainwright, *History of the Philadelphia Electric Company, 1881–1961* (Philadelphia: PECO, 1961), 12.

43. J. P. Crittenden and Charles B. Helffrich, *Philadelphia Securities: A Descriptive Manual of the Corporations of Philadelphia* (Philadelphia: Burk and McFetridge, 1891), 265–72; *Highest and Lowest Quotations of Philadelphia Securities, Monthly for 1882*; Reports of the List Committee, PHLX Archives.

44. For discussion of political machines, growth machines, and metropolitan development in the United States, see John Logan and Harvey Molotch, *Urban For-*

tunes: The Political Economy of Place (Berkeley: University of California Press, 1988); Clarence Stone, *Regime Politics: Governing Atlanta, 1946–1988* (Lawrence: University of Kansas Press, 1989); Bruce Stave, *Urban Bosses, Machines and Progressive Reformers* (New York: Krieger, 1984); Robert Lewis, ed., *Manufacturing Suburbs: Building Work and Home on the Metropolitan Fringe* (Philadelphia: Temple University Press, 2004).

45. A certificate for Horticultural Hall hung in the boardroom of the exchange as recently as February 2004.

46. Reports of the List Committee; *Daily Quotations and Stock Sales, Philadelphia Stock Exchange, Jan. 2nd to Dec. 31st, 1889* (Philadelphia: McLaughlin Bros., 1890); Crittenden and Helffrich, *Philadelphia Securities*, 265–72.

47. Reports of the List Committee, PHLX Archives; *Daily Quotations and Stock Exchange Sales, Philadelphia Board of Brokers, 1873* (Philadelphia: McLaughlin Bros., 1874); *The Financiers of Philadelphia: A Practical Directory of Directors; A Gallery of Men of Affairs* (Philadelphia: Financial Publishing Company, 1900), HSP.

48. Barnes, *History of the Philadelphia Stock Exchange*, 54; Crittenden and Helffrich, *Philadelphia Securities*, 265–72.

49. Eric Hobsbawm, *Industry and Empire: From 1750 to the Present Day*, revised with Chris Wrigley (New York: New Press, 1999), 145.

50. Domenic Vitiello, "Engineering the Metropolis: William Sellers, the Wilson Brothers, and Industrial Philadelphia," *Pennsylvania Magazine of History and Biography* 126, no. 2 (April 2002): 297; "In Their New Quarters," *New York Times*, October 27, 1888.

51. Elkins Wetherill, *The Story of the Philadelphia Stock Exchange* (Downingtown, Pa.: Newcomen Society, 1976), 12.

52. "Sherry Marks 50th Year on Exchange."

53. Quoted in Wainwright, *History of the Philadelphia National Bank*, 143.

Chapter 6

1. Press coverage of the turn of the century in Philadelphia is surveyed in George E. Thomas, *William L. Price: Arts and Crafts to Modern Design* (New York: Princeton Architectural Press, 2000), 18–20.

2. James Maher, *The Twilight of Splendor* (Boston: Little, Brown and Co., 1975), n.p.

3. John A. Wright, *An Open Letter to Mr. William Brockie, Chairman Committee on Decadence of the Commerce of Philadelphia* (Philadelphia: Buchanan, 1889), 6–8, Historical Society of Pennsylvania (hereafter HSP).

4. Matthew Frye Jacobson, *Barbarian Virtues: The United States Encounters Foreign People at Home and Abroad, 1876–1917* (New York: Hill and Wang, 2001).

5. George Engelhardt, *Philadelphia, Pa.: The Book of the Bourse* (Philadelphia: The Bourse, 1899), 108.

6. Lincoln Steffens, *The Shame of the Cities* (New York, 1904).

7. Late nineteenth-century Philadelphia did, however, receive a larger proportion

than most other cities of highly skilled immigrants from Northern Europe who typically worked in specialized metalworking firms.

8. Kevin O'Rourke and Jeffrey Williamson, *Globalization and History: The Evolution of a Nineteenth-Century Atlantic Economy* (Cambridge: MIT Press, 1999).

9. Wright, *An Open Letter to Mr. William Brockie*, 5–6.

10. Minnie Throop England, "On Speculation in Relation to the World's Prosperity, 1897–1902," *University Studies* (Lincoln, Neb.) 6, no. 1 (January 1906): 23. See also Jonathan Barron Baskin and Paul J. Miranti Jr., *A History of Corporate Finance* (New York: Cambridge University Press, 1997); Lance E. Davis and Robert E. Gallman, *Evolving Financial Markets and International Capital Flows: Britain, the Americas, and Australia, 1865–1914* (New York: Cambridge University Press, 2001).

11. Richard Bensel, *Yankee Leviathan: The Origins of Central State Authority in America, 1859–1877* (New York: Cambridge University Press, 1991), 316.

12. Jean Strouse, *Morgan: American Financier* (New York: Perennial, 1999); Dan Rottenberg, *The Man Who Made Wall Street: Anthony J. Drexel and the Rise of Modern Finance* (Philadelphia: University of Pennsylvania Press, 2001).

13. Herman LeRoy Collins, *Philadelphia: A Story of Progress*, vol. 1 (Philadelphia: Lewis Historical Publishing), 343; Naomi R. Lamoreaux, *The Great Merger Movement in American Business, 1895–1904* (New York: Cambridge University Press, 1985); Ralph L. Nelson, *Merger Movements in American Industry, 1895–1956* (Princeton, N.J.: Princeton University Press, 1959); Lance Davis, "The Capital Markets and Industrial Concentration: The U.S. and U.K., a Comparative Study," *Economic History Review*, 2nd ser., 19 (August 1966): 255–72; Martin J. Sklar, *The Corporate Reconstruction of American Capitalism, 1890–1916* (New York: Cambridge University Press, 1988); Walter Licht, *Industrializing America: The Nineteenth Century* (Baltimore: Johns Hopkins University Press, 1995), 133–65.

14. In her study of banking in the coastal cities of nineteenth-century New England, the economic historian Naomi Lamoreaux traces the migration at the end of the century of both investment capital and bankers from cities such as Boston and Providence to Manhattan, where they increasingly collaborated with New York banking houses and invested their clients' money on Wall Street. Naomi Lamoreaux, *Insider Lending: Banks, Personal Connections, and Economic Development in Industrial New England* (New York: Cambridge University Press, 1994), 133–56; see also Lamoreaux, *The Great Merger Movement in American Business*.

15. Vincent Carosso, *Investment Banking in America* (Cambridge, Mass.: Harvard University Press, 1970); Sven Beckert, *The Monied Metropolis: New York City and the Consolidation of the American Bourgeoisie, 1850–1896* (New York: Cambridge University Press, 2001), especially 237–72.

16. See, for example, Jefferson Cowie, *Capital Moves: RCA's Seventy-Year Quest for Cheap Labor* (Ithaca, N.Y.: Cornell University Press, 1999); William Lazonick and Mary O'Sullivan, "Finance and Industrial Development: Part I; The United States and the United Kingdom," *Financial History Review* 4, part 1 (April 1997): 7–30.

17. Lance Davis, Larry Neal, and Eugene White, "The Effect of Deflation on the First Global Capital Market: The Financial Crises of the 1890s and the Reponses of the Stock Exchanges in London, New York, Paris, and Berlin," National Bureau of Economic Research (June 2002), 2–12; see also Kenneth Warren, *Big Steel: The First Century of the United States Steel Corporation, 1901–2001* (Pittsburgh: University of Pittsburgh Press, 2001).

18. Donald L. Kemmerer, "American Financial Institutions: The Marketing of Securities, 1930–1952," *Journal of Economic History* 12, no. 4 (Autumn 1952): 454–68 (quote is from 455).

19. Throop England, "On Speculation in Relation to the World's Prosperity, 1897–1902," 25–26.

20. Thomas R. Navin and Marian V. Sears, "The Rise of a Market for Industrial Securities, 1887–1902," *Business History Review* 28 (June 1955); Strouse, *Morgan*, 301–24; Mira Wilkins, *The History of Foreign Investment in the United States to 1914* (Cambridge, Mass.: Harvard University Press, 1989).

21. This argument runs counter to the inherited wisdom of financial historians, who have largely written off Philadelphia as a financial center due to the relative decline of its port in the early nineteenth century and New York's more advantageous position in national and international telegraph networks beginning in the 1840s. See, for example, Robert Sobel, *The Big Board: A History of the New York Stock Market* (New York: Free Press, 1965), 52; Robert Sobel, *Panic on Wall Street: A History of America's Financial Disasters* (New York: Macmillan, 1968); Sonali Garg, "Innovations in Communications Technology and the Structure of Securities Markets: A Case Study of the Telegraph and the Rise of the NYSE to Preeminence, 1830–1860" (Ph.D. diss., Ohio State University, 2000).

22. In the new global hierarchy of stock exchanges, by 1900 New York had come to occupy a dominant position, with London close behind; Boston, Philadelphia, Chicago, and Liverpool made up a second tier of markets, while smaller exchanges existed in Cincinnati, Pittsburgh, Montreal, Toronto, St. Louis, Glasgow, and elsewhere. This categorization is based on the portrait of exchanges in *The Manual of Statistics, Stock Exchange Hand-Book* (New York: Goodsell, 1900), 453–520.

23. Davis, Neal, and White, "The Effect of Deflation on the First Global Capital Market," 14.

24. Carosso, *Investment Banking in America*, 24–25, 32.

25. H. W. Schotter, *The Growth and Development of the Pennsylvania Railroad Company* (Philadelphia: Allen, Lane, and Scott, 1927), 265. See also George H. Burgess and Miles C. Kennedy, *Centennial History of the Pennsylvania Railroad Company, 1846–1946* (Philadelphia: Pennsylvania Railroad, 1949), 504–12.

26. "Pennsylvania Office Here," *New York Times*, October 11, 1900, p. 8, cols. 4–5 (my emphasis).

27. Similar concerns were evident in the 1906 obituary of former stock exchange president Nicholas Brice, "one of the venerable figures of Third Street." The marriage

ceremony of his daughter at his deathbed and his membership in the Philadelphia Club, the Society of the Colonial Wars, and the Philadelphia Country Club were of more significance to the papers than his long career in finance. "Nicholas Brice Dies of Paralysis, Venerable Figure of Third Street, Daughter Married at His Bedside" (1906), HSP; "New Officials Named by the Pennsylvania Directors; Listing Stock in New York," *Record*, October 11, 1900, p. 10, col. 1; "Railroad Men Are Promoted; Pennsylvania Directors Create Two New Positions and Appoint to Them Veteran Employees," *North American*, October 11, 1900, p. 15, col. 2; E. Digby Baltzell, *Philadelphia Gentlemen: The Making of a National Upper Class* (New York: Free Press, 1958), and *Puritan Boston and Quaker Philadelphia: Two Protestant Ethics and the Spirit of Class Authority and Leadership* (Boston: Beacon, 1979).

28. Steffens, *The Shame of the Cities*. The terms "contractor bosses" and "utility monopolists" are from Peter McCaffery, *When Bosses Ruled Philadelphia: The Emergence of the Republican Machine, 1867–1933* (University Park: Pennsylvania State University Press, 1993).

29. For discussion of the politics of its construction, see Howard Gillette, "Philadelphia's City Hall: Monument to a New Political Machine," *Pennsylvania Magazine of History and Biography* 97 (April 1973): 233–49.

30. "Philadelphia Stock Exchange Expansion," *Wall Street Journal*, January 13, 1927, p. 8.

31. Philadelphia Stock Exchange (hereafter PHLX), Securities Admitted to the List—Stocks, 1891–1937 (PHLX Archives), 171, 257, 260

32. Ibid., 52–88.

33. Clarence Stedman, ed., *The New York Stock Exchange* (New York: Stock Exchange Historical Company, 1905), 473; Davis, Neal, and White, "The Effect of Deflation on the First Global Capital Market," 15.

34. Henry Crosby Emery, *Speculation on the Stock and Produce Exchanges of the United States* (New York: Columbia Studies in History, Economics, and Public Law, 1896), 24.

35. *Souvenir History: Philadelphia Stock Exchange*, n.p.

36. H. L. Bennet, *A Glimpse at Wall Street and Its Markets* (1904; repr., New York: Greenwood, 1968) (emphasis in original).

37. Horace H. Lee to Theodore Dreiser (August 12, 1912), Van Pelt Library, University of Pennsylvania, Special Collections, Ms. Coll. 30, Folder 4869.

38. "Stock Exchange in 1847 and Now," unidentified newspaper clipping (1897), Philadelphia Stock Exchange Collection, HSP.

39. See, for example, In the Court of Common Pleas No. 3, for the County of Philadelphia, September Term, 1897 (no. 346), *Evans R. Dick, Frank M. Dick, and William A. Dick, Trading as Dick Brothers and Company, vs. The Philadelphia Stock Exchange*, in J. Rodman Paul, *Select Cases*, HSP.

40. Jane A. Hyde, "The Past—1754–1924," *Investment Dealers' Digest* (January 30, 1967): 43.

41. Nicholas B. Wainwright, *History of the Philadelphia National Bank: A Century and a Half of Philadelphia Banking, 1803–1953* (Philadelphia: PNB, 1953), 142–43.

42. *Souvenir History: Philadelphia Stock Exchange*, n.p.

43. Hickman's drawings survive in the Philadelphia Contributionship collection (Policy # 11807; Work # 92; roll C-3) at HSP.

44. Philadelphia Stock Exchange, *Souvenir History, Album of Members, Gallery of Men of Affairs* (Philadelphia, 1903), n.p.

45. The second floor plan containing the exchange was published in the 1900–1901 *Journal of the T-Square Club.*

46. Philadelphia Stock Exchange, *Souvenir History, Album of Members, Gallery of Men of Affairs* (Philadelphia, 1903), n.p.

47. Ibid.

48. Andrew W. Barnes, ed., *History of the Philadelphia Stock Exchange, Banks, and Banking Interests* (Philadelphia: Cornelius Baker, 1911), 6–7.

49. Philadelphia Stock Exchange, weekly bulletin (January 13 and February 10, 1912), PHLX Archives.

50. *Philadelphia Real Estate Record and Builders' Guide* 26, no. 37 (September 13, 1911). Deakyne is listed on p. 308 of the 1913 *Philadelphia Business Directory*, under Real Estate.

51. For the role of architecture in describing the social hierarchy of Philadelphia, see George E. Thomas, "Architectural Patronage and Social Stratification in Philadelphia, 1840–1920," in *The Divided Metropolis: Social and Spatial Dimensions of Philadelphia, 1800–1975*, ed. William Cutler and Howard Gillette (Westport, Conn.: Greenwood, 1980), 85–123.

52. *Philadelphia Real Estate Record and Builders' Guide* 30, no. 47 (November 27, 1915).

53. Program commemorating opening of the PHLX building at Bellevue Stratford Hotel and Philadelphia Stock Exchange Punch certificate (both 1913), PHLX Archives.

54. This trend is also documented in weekly stock exchange bulletins from the 1910s. Philadelphia Stock Exchange, weekly bulletins (1910–29), PHLX Archives; *Tri-State Business Directory of Philadelphia and More Than 100 Surrounding Cities and Towns* (Philadelphia: Business Directory Company, 1913), 41–42.

55. Philadelphia Stock Exchange, *Souvenir History, Album of Members, Gallery of Men of Affairs* (Philadelphia, 1903), n.p.

56. *The Financiers of Philadelphia: A Practical Directory of Directors; A Gallery of Men of Affairs* (Philadelphia: Financial Publishing Company, 1900), HSP.

57. Philip Scranton, *Figured Tapestry: Production, Markets, and Power in Philadelphia Textiles, 1885–1941* (New York: Cambridge University Press, 1989). Following Scranton, the labor historian Walter Licht argues that the "growth of a standardized marketplace proved to be the critical blow to Philadelphia's production system." Walter Licht, *Getting Work: Philadelphia, 1840–1950* (Cambridge, Mass.: Harvard University Press, 1992), 269, n. 30.

58. Thomas Heinrich, *Ships for the Seven Seas: Philadelphia Shipbuilding in the Age of Industrial Capitalism* (Baltimore: Johns Hopkins University Press, 1997), 154.

59. PHLX, Securities Admitted to the List—Stocks, 1891–1937 (PHLX Archives), 394.

60. John K. Brown, *The Baldwin Locomotive Works, 1831–1915* (Baltimore: Johns Hopkins University Press, 1995), 216, 223.

61. PHLX, Securities Admitted to the List—Stocks, 1891–1937 (PHLX Archives), 355, 360.

62. Ibid.; Securities Admitted to the List—Bonds, 1911–1937 (PHLX Archives); Philip Scranton, "Large Firms and Industrial Restructuring: The Philadelphia Region, 1900–1980," *Pennsylvania Magazine of History and Biography* 116, no. 4 (October 1992): 419–65; Howell John Harris, *Bloodless Victories: The Rise and Fall of the Open Shop in the Philadelphia Metal Trades, 1890–1940* (New York: Cambridge University Press, 2000), 275; Collins, *Philadelphia: A Story of Progress*, 97.

63. Collins, *Philadelphia: A Story of Progress*, 372–78.

64. Philadelphia Stock Exchange, weekly bulletin (February 8, 1913), PHLX.

65. Ibid. (May 15, 1915).

66. Ibid. (February 27, April 3, and April 10, 1915)

67. Christopher Morley, *Travels in Philadelphia* (Philadelphia: McKay, 1920), 4–5. See also Baltzell, *Philadelphia Gentlemen*; Nathaniel Burt, *The Perennial Philadelphians: The Anatomy of an American Aristocracy* (Boston: Little Brown, 1963).

68. Collins, *Philadelphia: A Story of Progress*, 391–92.

69. Although the Philadelphia Stock Exchange recorded more than 27 million shares of stock and almost $10 million in bonds traded in 1930, its overall trading volume declined from the beginning of the century through World War II. Sales of Stock and Bonds, 1920–30; *The Philadelphia Stock Exchange Directory* (Philadelphia: McLaughlin, 1912); *The Philadelphia Stock Exchange Directory* (Philadelphia: Priestley, 1921); *The Philadelphia Stock Exchange Directory* (Philadelphia: Budenz, 1931); *Philadelphia Stock Exchange, 1942–1943* (Philadelphia: Exchange, 1943); Philadelphia Stock Exchange, weekly bulletin (October 8, 1921), all PHLX Archives; Richard Lewis Dole, *Historical Development of the Philadelphia Stock Exchange* (ca. 1931; reproduced for the PHLX Bicentennial, 1990), 14.

70. Nick Giordano, video interviews with Eddie Brylawski (June 24, 1986) and George Snyder (June 25, 1986), videotape in the collection of Nick Giordano.

71. Elkins Wetherill, *The Story of the Philadelphia Stock Exchange* (Downingtown, Pa.: Newcomen Society, 1976), 12–13.

72. Philadelphia Stock Exchange, weekly bulletin (September 3, 1927), PHLX Archives.

73. Economists explain this trend as a result of declining communications costs and changes in securities regulation that followed the crash of 1929, particularly the higher listing standards that bolstered the NYSE's status as the favored market for big firms. Tom Arnold, Philip Hersch, J. Harold Mulherin, and Jeffry Netter, "Merging

Markets," *Journal of Finance* 54, no. 3 (June 1999): 1083–1107 (the quote is from 1086).

74. Giordano, video interviews with Eddie Brylawski, Robert Y. Guarniery (June 24, 1986), and Morris Waber (June 24, 1986).

75. Giordano, video interview with Morris Waber; *The Philadelphia-Baltimore Stock Exchange* (1951), PHLX Archives; Wetherill, "The Story of the Philadelphia Stock Exchange," 14; "Phila. Stock Exchange Expansion," *Wall Street Journal*, January 13, 1927.

76. Wetherill, "The Story of the Philadelphia Stock Exchange," 13–14; "Philadelphia Broadens Trading," *Wall Street Journal*, November 4, 1931. For subsequent expansion of unlisted trading, see "Philadelphia Exchange Unlisted Trade Need Cited at SEC Hearing," *Wall Street Journal*, March 17, 1937; "Stocks for Exchanges," *New York Times*, August 4, 1944.

77. Securities admitted to unlisted trading privileges, 1932, PHLX Archives.

78. Giordano, video interviews with Robert Y. Guarniery, George Snyder, and Frank Newburger (June 25, 1986).

79. Griffith and Company, *Stock Clearing Corporation: Report on Examination of the Financial Records, December 31, 1931*; Griffith and Company, *Stock Clearing Corporation of Philadelphia: Report on Audit of Accounts and Financial Records for the Year Ended December 30, 1933*; Griffith and Company, *Stock Clearing Corporation of Philadelphia: Report on Audit of Accounts and Financial Records for the Year Ended December 31, 1934*, all PHLX Archives.

80. Interview with Barry Tague (December 1, 2003). All interviews were conducted by the author unless noted otherwise.

81. Giordano, video interview with George Snyder.

82. Herbert T. Webster, ed., *1850–1950: A Century of Service; Spring Garden Institute* (Philadelphia: Spring Garden Institute, 1950), 161.

83. Further analysis of the dismantling of regional networks of industrial research and economic development may be found in Domenic Vitiello, "Engineering the Metropolis: The Sellers Family and Industrial Philadelphia" (Ph.D. diss., University of Pennsylvania, 2004), chapter 8.

84. Giordano, video interviews with George Snyder and Morris Waber; Arnold et al., "Merging Markets," 1086; "Philadelphia-Baltimore Stock Exchange and Insurance Company of North America Share Common Heritage and Modern, Progressive Viewpoints," *INA Fieldman* (October 1960) and *The Philadelphia-Baltimore Stock Exchange* (1951), PHLX Archives; William W. Uchimoto, "Evolution of Best Execution in the National Market System," *Transaction Performance* (Spring 2002): 95–97; Wetherill, "The Story of the Philadelphia Stock Exchange," 14.

85. *50 Years of the U.S. Securities and Exchange Commission* (Washington, D.C.: SEC, 1984), 27.

86. Ibid., 27–28.

87. Scranton, "Large Firms and Industrial Restructuring," 446.

88. These large-scale changes in the economic geography of the United States are treated in Ann R. Markusen, Peter Hall, Scott Campbell, and Sabrina District, *The Rise of the Gunbelt: The Military Remapping of Industrial America* (New York: Oxford University Press, 1991); Roger Lotchin, *Fortress California, 1910–1961: From Warfare to Welfare* (New York: Oxford University Press, 1992); Bruce Schulman, *From Cotton Belt to Sunbelt: Federal Policy, Economic Development, and the Transformation of the South, 1938–1980* (New York: Oxford University Press, 1991).

89. For discussion of deindustrialization, see Carolyn Adams et al., *Philadelphia: Neighborhoods, Division, and Conflict in a Postindustrial City* (Philadelphia: Temple University Press, 1991); Scranton, "Large Firms and Industrial Restructuring"; Philip Scranton and Walter Licht, *Work Sights: Industrial Philadelphia, 1890–1950* (Philadelphia: Temple University Press, 1986); Barry Bluestone and Bennett Harrison, *The Deindustrialization of America* (New York: Basic Books, 1982); Thomas J. Sugrue, *The Origins of the Urban Crisis: Race and Inequality in Postwar Detroit* (Princeton, N.J.: Princeton University Press, 1996); John T. Cumbler, *A Social History of Economic Decline: Business, Politics, and Work in Trenton* (New Brunswick: Rutgers University Press, 1989); Cowie, *Capital Moves*.

90. For the first half of the century, see Bruce Allen Hardy, "American Privatism and the Urban Fiscal Crisis of the Interwar Years: A Financial Study of the Cities of New York, Chicago, Philadelphia, Detroit, and Boston, 1915–1945" (Ph.D. diss., Wayne State University, 1977), 220.

Chapter 7

1. Interview with Paul Cerecino, a former computer technician for the Philadelphia-Baltimore-Washington Stock Exchange (March 29, 2003). All interviews were conducted by the author unless noted otherwise.

2. Interview with Arnold Staloff (October 29, 2003).

3. Donald L. Kemmerer, "American Financial Institutions: The Marketing of Securities, 1930–1952," *Journal of Economic History* 12, no. 4 (Autumn 1952): 454–68; "Philadelphia Stock Exchange Sales Up 28% for Four Months," *Wall Street Journal*, May 16, 1946.

4. For examples of rule changes that facilitated inter-market trading, see Board of Governors minutes (May 16, 1951 and February 3, 1954); see also "Philadelphia Stock Exchange Names Group to Seek More Business," *Wall Street Journal*, September 7, 1948.

5. "Merger of Baltimore, Philadelphia Stock Exchanges Is Planned," *Wall Street Journal*, December 20, 1948.

6. "Philadelphia-Baltimore Stock Exchange," special issue of *Investment Dealers' Digest* (March 10, 1952). This perception of the industrial market persisted throughout the 1950s. See, for example, Philadelphia-Baltimore Stock Exchange, *Let's Look at the Record* (Philadelphia: Philadelphia-Baltimore Stock Exchange, 1959).

7. Interview with Tom Cameron (February 3, 2004).

8. Philadelphia-Baltimore Stock Exchange, "The Oldest Stock Exchange in the United States Now Provides the Newest and Most Modern Facilities . . ." (1951), PHLX Archives; Board of Governors minutes (November 21, 1951 and May 1965); "Oldest Exchange Makes Its Seventh Move in 161 Years," *Wall Street Journal*, March 27, 1951. The original term of the lease was from July 20, 1950, through 1965. Extra space was leased in 1958 and 1961 to accommodate the exchange's new computers.

9. Pittsburgh's financial and manufacturing sectors had suffered following the panic of 1907, making its stock exchange ripe for takeover by the post–World War II period. For an account of the development of Pittsburgh's financial sector and its relationship to industry, see Mark David Samber, "Networks of Capital: Creating and Maintaining a Regional Industrial Economy in Pittsburgh, 1865–1919" (Ph.D. diss., Carnegie Mellon University, 1995).

10. "Two Stock Exchanges in Pennsylvania Set Formal Merger Pact," *Wall Street Journal*, January 30, 1969; "SEC Approves Merger of Pittsburgh Board, Philadelphia Exchange," *Wall Street Journal*, December 31, 1969.

11. See, for example, Board of Governors minutes (November 5, 1952; October 3, 1956; and December 19, 1962).

12. Philadelphia-Baltimore Stock Exchange, *Let's Look at the Record*. Stock exchange directories from this period also show considerable growth among the staffs of member firms. Compare, for example, Philadelphia-Baltimore Stock Exchange, *Directory* (1952–53) and Philadelphia-Baltimore Stock Exchange, *Directory* (1962).

13. Interview with Paul Cerecino; "History and Progress Intertwined," reprinted from INA Feldman (October 1960), PHLX Archives. For subsequent investments, see "Philadelphia Exchange to Lease a 'Full Line' of Electronic Equipment," *Wall Street Journal*, December 16, 1965.

14. Board of Governors minutes (May 27, 1952).

15. The newly merged regionals had negative effects on one another, as well. For example, the Philadelphia and Boston exchanges "suffered large seat-price declines in the period surrounding the announcement and execution of the Midwest merger (a greater than 62 percent decline on the Philadelphia-Baltimore Exchange, the largest seat-price decline of any exchange, and a 58 percent decline on the Boston Exchange)." Tom Arnold, Philip Hersch, J. Harold Mulherin, and Jeffry Netter, "Merging Markets," *Journal of Finance* 54, no. 3 (June 1999): 1083–1107 (the quote is from 1099).

16. Philadelphia-Baltimore Stock Exchange, *Let's Look at the Record*; Board of Governors minutes (October 17, 1951; November 21, 1951; and November 21, 1956).

17. Philadelphia-Baltimore-Washington Stock Exchange, *Securities Traded* (May 1966): 5–8.

18. Interviews with Barry Tague (December 1, 2003) and Thomas Martinelli (February 11, 2004).

19. Board of Governors minutes (November 16, 1955; January 18, February 1, and March 1, 1956).

20. John Caskey, "The Evolution of the Philadelphia Stock Exchange, 1964–

2002," Federal Reserve Bank of Philadelphia Working Paper No. 03–21 (August 2003), 8–9. See also, Caskey, "The Philadelphia Stock Exchange: Adapting to Survive in Changing Markets," *Business History Review* 78, no. 3 (2004): 451–87.

21. Joseph Daughen and Peter Binzen, *The Wreck of the Penn Central* (Boston: Little, Brown, 1971), 12.

22. Board of Governors minutes (January 17, 1962; see also April 1 and December 16, 1964; January 6, February 17, and May 11, 1965).

23. Interview with Elkins Wetherill (February 2, 2004).

24. Ibid.

25. Ibid; also, interview with Barry Tague; Kelly Associates, "A Public Relations and Promotion Proposal," in Board of Governors minutes (November 17, 1965).

26. Board of Governors minutes (February 17 and May 2, 1965).

27. Board of Governors minutes (May 6, 1965).

28. *Philadelphia Evening Bulletin*, May 2, 1966; Gardiner Cox, "Philadelphia's Stock Exchange— Working Inside a Pressure Cooker," *Philadelphia Inquirer*, May 30, 1971. .

29. Cox, "Philadelphia's Stock Exchange."

30. Interviews with Elkins Wetherill (February 2, 2004) and Don Stanton (October 29, 2003).

31. Quoted in Marshall E. Blume, Jeremy J. Siegel, and Dan Rottenberg, *Revolution on Wall Street: The Rise and Decline of the New York Stock Exchange* (New York: Norton, 1993), 164.

32. Elkins Wetherill, fax (October 13, 2003); see also "Philadelphia Exchange Joins Protest Against Proposals by Big Board," *Wall Street Journal*, June 13, 1969.

33. For a time, the PBW also found ways to compete on commission costs. Beginning in 1964, it allowed member firms to share commissions with members of other exchanges as they split large orders between regional markets. Two years later, the board raised the amount of commission that brokers could give up in these deals. All of the regional exchanges adopted basically the same rules, but the NYSE opposed them and the SEC eventually put a stop to these give-ups in December 1968. Board of Governors minutes (April 20, 1966; April 1 and June 6, 1968); Caskey, "The Evolution of the Philadelphia Stock Exchange," 17–19.

34. Elkins Wetherill, fax (October 13, 2003); see also "Philadelphia Board Reaffirms Stand on Institutions," *Wall Street Journal*, February 10, 1972.

35. Certificates of Philadelphia-Baltimore Stock Exchange membership, 1958–69, PHLX Archives.

36. Caskey, "The Evolution of the Philadelphia Stock Exchange," 16.

37. Board of Governors minutes (June 26, 1968).

38. Joel Seligman, *The Transformation of Wall Street: A History of the Securities and Exchange Commission and Modern Corporate Finance* (Boston: Houghton Mifflin, 1982), 396.

39. Board of Governors minutes (November 15, 1967).

40. Ibid. (August 15, 1968).

41. Ibid. (October 31, 1968; January 7 and 10, 1969); interview with Tom Cameron (October 16, 2003).

42. Caskey, "The Evolution of the Philadelphia Stock Exchange," 16–17.

43. Lawrence Campbell, "Stock Market Pays Little in Taxes but Sees Its Loss as Costly to City," *Philadelphia Evening Bulletin*, December 22, 1968 sec. 1, 3, Temple University Urban Archives, *Bulletin*, morgue, "Philadelphia Stock Exchange."

44. *Philadelphia Evening Bulletin*, December 14, 1968, Temple University Urban Archives, *Bulletin* morgue, "Philadelphia Stock Exchange."

45. Vartanig G. Vartan, "Exchange Moving in Philadelphia," *New York Times*, January 1, 1969, 31. See also *Philadelphia Evening Bulletin*, January 3, 1969, Temple University Urban Archives, *Bulletin* morgue; Board of Governors minutes (December 23 and 30, 1968, and February 19 and May 21, 1969); "Philadelphia Exchange Opens Its New Office with Brisk Trading; Most of Volume Switches to Bala-Cynwyd; Possibility of Stool Tax Review Hinted," *Wall Street Journal*, January 3, 1969.

46. Interviews with Doris Elwell, nee Devine (December 3, 2003), and Barry Tague.

47. The exchange would fight off another city tax four years later. Board of Governors minutes (May 16, 1973).

48. The Department of Justice would also side with the PBW in a suit of 1972 against the SEC to preserve institutional membership. Interviews with Thomas Cameron (October 16, 2003 and February 3, 2004); Seligman, *The Transformation of Wall Street*, 471–72.

49. Interview with Arnold Staloff.

50. Board of Governors minutes (July 19, 1972); interview with John Wallace (April 11, 2008).

51. Philadelphia Stock Exchange, *A Profile of America's First Exchange* (Philadelphia: Philadelphia Stock Exchange, 1976).

52. Vincent J. Casella, speech at the PHLX memorial service for John J. Wallace (February 26, 2003).

53. Interview with John F. Wallace (February 26, 2003).

54. Interview with Richard Hamilton (December 1, 2003).

55. Group interview at Bill O'Shea's party for retired staff (March 29, 2003); also, interviews with Joseph Wagner and Bill Terrell (December 3, 2003).

56. Interview with Richard Hamilton and Bill Terrell (April 13, 2007).

57. Interview with Al Brinkman (March 27, 2003).

58. Interview with John F. Wallace.

59. Interview with Joseph Wagner.

60. Interview with Michael Belman (December 2, 2003).

61. Interview with Richard Hamilton.

62. Interviews with Richard Hamilton and John F. Wallace. The staffs of member firms continued to grow rapidly in this period, as the industry and its personnel

expanded and became more diverse. See, for example, Philadelphia-Baltimore-Washington Stock Exchange, *Directory* (May 8, 1972).

63. Interview with John Egan (February 19, 2004).

64. Interview with Fred Martin (May 6, 2003).

65. Interview with Joseph Wagner.

66. Ibid.; interview with Malcolm Pryor (March 16, 2004).

67. Board of Governors minutes (July 1, 1965).

68. Interview with Bill Terrell (December 3, 2003).

69. Interview with Doris Elwell.

70. Interviews with Doris Elwell and Karen Janney (December 3, 2003).

71. Interviews with Arnold Staloff, Nick Giordano (December 11, 2003), and Elkins Wetherill (February 2, 2004).

72. Larry Williams, "Philly's Exchange: Money in Motion," *Courier Post*, February 22, 1969.

73. Cox, "Philadelphia's Stock Exchange."

74. Interview with John Egan.

75. Cox, "Philadelphia's Stock Exchange."

76. Seligman, *The Transformation of Wall Street*, 523.

77. Board of Governors minutes (June 27, 1974, and April 21 and May 10, 1976).

78. Philadelphia Stock Exchange, *Annual Report* (1977).

79. Caskey, "The Evolution of the Philadelphia Stock Exchange," 21–25.

80. Jerry W. Markham, *A Financial History of the United States* (Armonk, N.Y.: M. E. Sharpe, 2002), 3: 53.

81. Interviews with Arnold Staloff and Barry Tague; Board of Governors minutes (February 20 and October 23, 1974).

82. Interviews with Barry Tague and John F. Wallace; Board of Governors minutes (August 7, 1974).

83. Interview with Barry Tague; Board of Governors minutes (October 18, 1972).

84. Interviews with Arnold Staloff and Nick Giordano; Caskey, "The Evolution of the Philadelphia Stock Exchange," 27–29.

85. Interview with Richard Hamilton.

86. Interviews with William Uchimoto (March 21, 2003), Barry Tague, Richard Hamilton, and John F. Wallace; Sarah Jordan, "76 Revolutionary Minds," *Philadelphia Magazine* (November 2001).

87. Interviews with Barry Tague, Michael Belman, Karen Janney, Joseph Wagner, and Thomas Martinelli; Loren Feldman, "They're in the Money," *Philadelphia Magazine* (December 1983): 189–218; Markham, *A Financial History of the United States*, 83.

88. Interview with Fred Martin.

89. Board of Governors minutes (February 18, 1976).

90. Caskey, "The Evolution of the Philadelphia Stock Exchange," 67.

91. Interviews with William Uchimoto, Nick Giordano, and John Egan.

92. Board of Governors minutes (June 5 and October 18, 1978); interview with Tom Cameron.

93. Raymond E. Berens, "34.1 Million Office Building Slated in Center City Philadelphia," *Evening Bulletin*, May 30, 1979.

94. Interview with Nick Giordano.

95. Raymond Berens, "Why Atrium Limit Was Eight Floors," *Philadelphia Bulletin*, June 9, 1979.

96. Board of Governors minutes (May 1 and 2, 1980).

97. Herb Drill, "The Atrium: It's Not a Building, It's a Super Environment for Work," *Philadelphia Bulletin*, June 4, 1981.

98. Interview with Fred Martin.

99. PHLX, "A Blueprint for America's Free Markets: The History of the Philadelphia Stock Exchange" (1990), 14.

100. Interview with Malcolm Pryor.

101. Gregory J. Millman, *The Vandals' Crown: How Rebel Currency Traders Overthrew the World's Central Banks* (New York: Free Press, 1995).

102. Philadelphia Stock Exchange, *Understanding Foreign Currency Options: The Third Dimension to Foreign Exchange* (Philadelphia: Philadelphia Stock Exchange, ca. 1983).

103. Interviews with William Uchimoto, Arnold Staloff, Michael Belman, and Nick Giordano.

104. Interviews with William Uchimoto, Arnold Staloff, and Nick Giordano.

105. Philadelphia Stock Exchange, *The Philadelphia Stock Exchange* (Philadelphia: Philadelphia Stock Exchange, ca. 1984).

106. Interviews with Arnold Staloff and Nick Giordano; Arthur Howe, "Philadelphia Exchange Is Taking a Place in the Big Leagues," *Philadelphia Inquirer*, January 2, 1985, C2; PHLX, "A Blueprint for America's Free Markets," 14.

107. Interviews with Al Brinkman and Arnold Staloff.

108. Philadelphia Stock Exchange, "European-Style Value Line Index Options at the PHLX" (ca. 1988), PHLX Archives; see also PHLX, "Now Available: European-*Style* Makes America's Best Stock-Index Option Look Even Better" (ca. 1990), PHLX Archives.

109. Interview with Al Brinkman.

110. PHLX, "A Blueprint for America's Free Markets," 14.

111. PHLX, *Annual Report* (1989); William Briggs, speech at the PHLX memorial service for John J. Wallace.

112. Interview with Fred Martin.

113. Caskey, "The Evolution of the Philadelphia Stock Exchange," 35–39.

114. Interview with Nick Giordano; Caskey, "The Evolution of the Philadelphia Stock Exchange," 41.

115. Caskey, "The Evolution of the Philadelphia Stock Exchange," 39–42 (the quote is from p. 41).

116. Quoted in ibid., 34.

117. Interview with William Uchimoto; PHLX, "A Blueprint for America's Free Markets."

118. Interview with Al Brinkman; PHLX, *Annual Report* (1989); Caskey, "The Evolution of the Philadelphia Stock Exchange," 43–45.

119. Interview with Al Brinkman; Caskey, "The Evolution of the Philadelphia Stock Exchange," 46–49.

120. Interviews with Nick Giordano and John Egan; Kurt Eichenwald, "Amex and Philadelphia Markets End Talks," *New York Times*, October 10, 1989; William Power, "Big Board Reopens Preliminary Talks on Acquiring Philadelphia Exchange," *Wall Street Journal*, November 20, 1990.

121. SEC, "Special Inspection Report Regarding the Philadelphia Stock Exchange" (March 4, 1997); interviews with William Uchimoto, Nick Giordano, and Meyer "Sandy" Frucher (February 11, 2004); Leslie Eaton, "S.E.C Inquiry at the Philadelphia Stock Exchange," *New York Times*, April 19, 1997.

Chapter 8

1. http://www.nasdaq.com/newsroom/presskit/timeline.stm (visited February 25, 2008).

2. Interviews with Nick Giordano (December 11, 2003), John Egan (February 19, 2004), Meyer "Sandy" Frucher (February 11, 2004), and John F. Wallace (February 26, 2003).

3. This was reported in the *Philadelphia Inquirer* (June 10, 1998) and *Investment Dealers' Digest* (June 15, 1998); see also Andrew Osterland, "Trading Small, Treading Water," *Business Week* (June 22, 1998): 182.

4. Interview with Meyer "Sandy" Frucher.

5. Ibid.

6. Steven M. Sears, "Philadelphia Exchange Chief Planned Restructuring While Discussing Merger," *Wall Street Journal*, April 27, 1999, B30.

7. Interview with Bill Terrell (December 3, 2003).

8. Interview with Norman Steisel (April 11, 2008).

9. Interview with Meyer "Sandy" Frucher; Joseph N. DiStefano, "PhilEx Renews Bid for Growth after Collapse of Merger Talks," *Philadelphia Inquirer*, April 23, 1999, D1; Joseph N. DiStefano, "PhilEx Is Roaring Back after Several Tough Years," *Philadelphia Inquirer*, January 21, 2001, E1.

10. PHLX press release (January 2, 2004).

11. PHLX press releases (January 2, 2004 and December 28, 2006).

12. Interviews with Richard Feinberg (April 24, 2003) and Fred Martin (May 6, 2003).

13. PHLX press releases (January 2, 2004 and December 28, 2006).

14. Bill Bergstrom, "Philly Exchange Members Vote to Demutualize," *Associated Press Newswires*, November 26, 2003; Todd Mason, "Philadelphia Stock Exchange's

Vote Mostly Addresses Chairman, CEO," *Philadelphia Inquirer*, November 14, 2003; Larry Rulison, "Stock Exchange Gets Options: PHLX Demutualization Makes Room for Growth," *Philadelphia Business Journal*, January 30, 2004, 3.

15. PHLX press release (February 16, 2005).

16. Aaron Lucchetti, "Wall Street Plays the Markets: Regional Exchanges Draw Bets from Financial Firms as a Hedge Against Clout of NYSE, Nasdaq," *Wall Street Journal*, August 30, 2006; PHLX press releases (June 16 and August 16, 2005).

17. Both quoted in PHLX press release (June 16, 2005).

18. Benjamin Lowe, "Phila. Stock Exchange Aims Higher after Sale," *Philadelphia Inquirer*, September 11, 2006.

19. Quoted in PHLX press release (August 16, 2005). See also Gregory Morris, "Smaller Exchanges Survive by Specializing," *Financial History* 81 (2004); Alexa Jaworski, "The e-Philly Strategy," *Securities Industry News* 18, no. 2 (January 16, 2006): 1–18; Peter Chapman, "Philly Moves to ECN Strategy," *Traders Magazine* 19, no. 249 (February 2006): 24–28; PBS's *Nightly Business Report*, "One on One with Meyer Frucher," airing May 9, 2006.

20. "Nasdaq to Buy Philadelphia Stock Exchange," Reuters, November 7, 2007.

21. "Timeline—Recent Stock Market Mergers," Reuters, May 25, 2007.

22. NASDAQ and PHLX, press release (November 7, 2007).

23. Charles Zehren and Edgar Ortega, "NASDAQ Plans to Acquire Philadelphia Stock Exchange," Bloomberg, November 6, 2007.

24. Aaron Lucchetti and Dennis Berman, "NASDAQ Woos Philadelphia Market," *Wall Street Journal*, April 11, 2007, C3; "A Philadelphia Story for NASDAQ?" *Business Week Online*, April 12, 2007, http://businessweek.mobi/detail.jsp?key = 8028&rc = inv (visited June 29, 2009); Joseph Radigan, "NASDAQ Deal Talk Puts Spotlight on PHLX and OMX," *Securities Industry News* 19, no. 15 (April 16, 2007): 1–19; Sarah Rudolph, "NASDAQ Flirts with the Philadelphia Stock Exchange," *Traders Magazine* 20, no. 267 (May 2007): 22–26; Telis Demos, "Exchange Merger Mania, Round Two," *Fortune*, July 9, 2007, 28.

25. Ben Craig, notes on NASDAQ-PHLX acquisition (in possession of the author); Aaron Lucchetti, "Exchanges, Trading Firms Consider Bids for Phil-Ex," *Wall Street Journal*, October 20, 2007; and Aaron Lucchetti, "NASDAQ Leads Race to Buy the Phil-Ex," *Wall Street Journal*, October 31, 2007. See also "NASDAQ to Buy Philadelphia Stock Exchange," CNBC.com, November 6, 2007; Tim Paradis, "NASDAQ to Acquire Philadelphia Stock Exchange," Associated Press, November 6, 2007; Jeff Blumenthal, "NASDAQ to Buy Philadelphia Stock Exchange for $652M," *Philadelphia Business Journal*, November 7, 2007.

26. Ben Craig, Notes; NASDAQ and PHLX, press release; "NASDAQ to Buy Philadelphia Stock Exchange"; Harold Brubaker, "NASDAQ Deal for PHLX Reported," *Philadelphia Inquirer*, November 7, 2007.

27. Lucchetti, "NASDAQ Leads Race to Buy the Phil-Ex."

28. Some old PHLX members (now stockholders) chafed at the fact that the six

Wall Street firms that paid $33.75 million for a nearly 90 percent stake in the exchange, where they represented 40 percent of the options order flow, would reap the great majority of the proceeds from its sale. That said, those six firms' investment in the exchange accounted for much of the increase in value of a seat (or one hundred shares post-demutualization), which shot from $15,000 in early 2004 to almost $300,000 at the time of the NASDAQ deal. A legal settlement in 2007 also forced these firms to distribute $17 million and 14 percent of their shares to pre-sale stockholders, boosting old members' share of that sale from $69 million to $151 million. Harold Brubaker, "Stockholder Anger at Sale of Exchange," *Philadelphia Inquirer*, November 11, 2007; Mason, "Philadelphia Stock Exchange's Vote Mostly Addresses Chairman."

29. By comparison, more than 40 percent of Harvard Business School grads stay in Boston. "Plugging the Brain Drain," *Philadelphia Daily News*, April 9, 2003.

30. U.S. Census, American Community Survey, "Philadelphia Population and Housing Narrative Profile" (2005–7).

31. Its 380 employees, with 585 more at member or related firms as of 2007, made it a significant generator of mostly high-end service jobs.

32. Interview with Malcolm Pryor (March 16, 2004).

33. Harold Brubaker, "Philadelphia Stock Exchange Staff Cut 25 Percent," *Philadelphia Inquirer*, August 8, 2008.

Index